THE CALL OF THE TOKAY
ECHO IN ENGLAND

THE CALL OF THE TOKAY
ECHO IN ENGLAND

Ivan Kruys

JANUS PUBLISHING COMPANY
London, England

First Published in Great Britain 2002 by
Janus Publishing Company Ltd,
76 Great Titchfield Street,
London W1P 7AF

www.januspublishing.co.uk

British Library Cataloguing-in-Publication Data
A catalogue record for this book
is available from the British Library

ISBN 1 85756 591 6

Typeset in 10.2pt Baskerville
By Chris Cowlin

Cover Design Hamish Cooper

Printed and bound in Great Britain

*To Nadia, without whom this book would have been impossible,
and to my wife, Ulla, for her encouragement.*

CONTENTS

Prologue	Nadia's Story	1
1	The Waringi Tree	12
2	A Good-Luck Sign	24
3	Internees	32
4	An Altar Without Rites	40
5	Ambarava No. 10	50
6	Bread	68
7	Leaflets	80
8	A Man Called Harry	96
9	*SS Tabinta*	109
10	Amsterdam	119
11	Redgates	135
12	Language	147
13	School	162
14	Winter Clothing	172
15	Winter	183
16	Upheavals	193
17	Squatters	206
18	Scholarship	222
19	Dutch Roots	235
20	A Third-Former	244
21	Latin	258
22	Half an Acre of Nettles	270
23	A Place in Society	284

NADIA'S STORY - prologue

Her maiden name was Nadiejda Pavlovna Nikiferoff.

Though sagging a little, her skin is relatively unwrinkled. Her face is still rounded, not by the deposition of excessive fatty tissue, but by her jaw-line and musculature whose shape has been dictated by her Slav origins. She has the kind of appearance that is so typically Russian, neither European nor Asiatic. Her hair is still thick and arranged into a loose bun that was once dark blonde but is now partly grey. She sits with her back straight though she is eighty-seven years old.

As she tells me her story her blue eyes sparkle behind the magnifying lenses of her glasses. Sometimes she breaks off because she forgets to mention certain facts and episodes and has to go back to complete the picture. I listen with intent to a story that I have heard in parts several times before, for the storyteller is my mother.

Nadia was born on 29th April 1913 in the Siberian town of Irkutsk while her parents were on their way to Kamchatka.

Her mother, Maria Dimitrievna Belonogov, was of peasant stock but her grandfather had worked himself up to be a magistrate in the town of Omsk. When she was only sixteen Maria met and fell in love with Aleksej Rosanov, the son of the wealthy owner of a gold mine. However, being the daughter of a magistrate was not good enough for Aleksej's father who had plans for their son to marry another girl with a high social status. Despite this, Nadia's parents were so much in love that they got married against her grandfather's wishes and decided to start a new life in Kamchatka well away from the gold mine.

The long journey eastwards was a slow one because they had to earn their money to pay their way. Almost inevitably Maria became pregnant when she was only eighteen and when they came to Irkutsk Nadia was born. This altered their situation and their plans to start a new life in pioneer territory had to be changed. They therefore travelled back to the Urals and decided to settle in Yekaterinburg

1

instead. Eighteen months after Nadia's birth, when they had hardly had time to establish themselves, they produced another daughter named Alevtina.

The First World War was already raging in Europe, dragging Russia into its turmoil, which, soon after Alevtina's birth, resulted in Aleksej being called to the Russian front against the Germans. The shock came a few months later in 1915 when Maria received the news that Aleksej had been killed in action.

When Maria's parents received the news, her mother came to stay with her to help look after the girls while Maria worked and it wasn't long before they established contact with Aleksej's parents, the Rosanovs, who invited Nadia to stay with them. Nadia has memories of the palatial residence in Omsk with its shiny marble floors and green malachite columns. Though it seemed strange as a home, the warmth of her grandparents softened the cold atmosphere of their palatial marble home. They made sure that she was well looked after, even arranging for her to be vaccinated against smallpox.

In their anxiety for the welfare of Maria and the girls, the Rosanovs arranged for Maria to meet Pavel Nikiferov, Aleksej's best friend, who happened to be working in Yekaterinburg, and this meeting was so successful that it wasn't long before they decided to get married. This resulted in the two little girls having a new father. Pavel took them on as his own and the girls had been given his surname, Nikiferoff.

The Bolsheviks had begun to take control of the area and soon they were shocked to hear that Tsar Nicholas and his family, who took refuge in a mansion nearby, were murdered. Nadia recalls that for some time after the murder, that house was ringed by a high fence and she remembered seeing the tip of a moving bayonet, the only visible indication that there was a guard patrolling on the inside of the fence. She was about five at the time. The search for suspected royalists became so intense that the new family had to move. They thought about Omsk but as the Bolsheviks were especially interested in annihilating capitalists like the Rosanovs who owned a gold mine and a stately home, seeking refuge with them would be courting danger.

This made them decide to leave Russia the comparative safety of

China and when they paid the Rosanovs a final visit in Omsk they were given two ingots of gold wrapped in sacking to help them make their new start in Manchuria. They joined the refugees fleeing eastwards, collectively known as the White Russians, who felt that fighting the Bolsheviks was a lost cause.

The fact that they had to flee during the winter had mixed blessings. Though they had to walk most of the way, Pavel could utilise a sledge to carry the heavier essentials and they trudged their way eastwards, letting the girls ride on top of the sledge when they were too tired to walk. Occasionally they could utilise cattle trucks to make the journey easier, but mostly they had to walk in temperatures as much as thirty below zero. They were heading for the town of Harbin in Manchuria. When they reached Lake Baikal they had to walk across its frozen freshwater wastes and through amazingly clear patches of thick bubble-free ice, Nadia remembers seeing fish deep down below their feet. It was so cold that their thick Russian felt boots were frozen solid and were impossible to remove for some time after they had reached their destination. Even then, they were still stiff with ice and they had to peel off their socks together with large pieces of old skin sticking to them.

Unfortunately, little Alevtina, who unlike Nadia had not been vaccinated, went down with smallpox and died before they reached their destination. This was a deep shock to them, but even then Nadia had the innate awareness that permeating their loss was the underlying need to survive. They arrived in Harbin totally penniless and without the gold that the Rosanovs gave them in Omsk, for during an unguarded moment the two ingots were stolen. Despite this major setback they managed to find accommodation and it wasn't long before Pavel could use his talents in starting a business dealing in office equipment. As thousands of other Russians had fled to Northern China, they had at least the knowledge that there was very little need to learn Mandarin Chinese.

By that time it was the spring of 1920, when Nadia was already seven. There were so many Russian ex-patriots that they almost constituted a little Russia within Manchuria. As many of the White Russians were affluent and came from the aristocracy, they brought with them valuables that they could sell, and the market in Harbin soon became flooded with precious collector's items that went for prices much lower than their real value.

Pavel was not slow in realising that there were opportunities for him to pursue his interest in antique books and as soon as he had begun to earn enough money he developed a trade in antique books as a sideline, selling first editions and rare books. Thanks to his business acumen, it wasn't long before this enterprise became so successful that he also opened a small special library. At the same time, Maria began to earn an additional income by starting a millinery business, since there were plenty of upper class Russian ladies who felt that they had to keep up with the fashions in Europe.

Incredibly, the arrival of famous ballet dancers, artists, actors and authors had caused the comparatively unknown Manchurian town of Harbin suddenly to blossom into a centre for Russian culture. It was thanks to that crème of refugees that they had access to theatre, concerts and ballet. When Nadia thought about it, she couldn't have had a better background to her education if they had lived in a large Russian city like Moscow or St Petersburg.

She reflects that the Russian school in Harbin provided her with a good education, thanks partly to the easy access to the best of Russian literature. She always had books in her home and that nurtured an interest, especially when she was old enough to help her father with the running of the library. She did well enough at school to enable her to start her first year as a dental student and her parents were by that time well able to support her financially, but just as she was completing her first year, the Japanese invaded Manchuria.

In order to save face in the League of Nations, the Japanese stated that they did not confiscate property. Instead they claimed that all the property they had acquired was bought, but their payments were only nominal. All the family possessions, their books, furniture and house were taken over by the Japanese for less than a pittance and with the resulting tiny sum of money they fled to try to make yet another start in Shanghai. They had just enough means for a month's rent and a little food.

Without Pavel's resourcefulness it would have been extremely difficult for them to stand on their feet again. Nevertheless, though his opportunities were limited by his scanty knowledge of English, he succeeded in finding an administrator's post with a charity organisation set up by Queen Alexandria, called the White Flower, that helped people suffering from tuberculosis. Maria, in the meantime, managed to re-establish her milliner's business, while Nadia got a poorly paid job at a Jewish library. She worked there for some weeks until one day Maria met the manageress of a bakery that produced high quality cakes and biscuits and whose main customer was Kleineman's, the most exclusive café in town. She found out that Kleineman's were short of staff but only the most aristocratic and elegant Russian girls in town were selected to work there. Nadia took the chance, applied for, and got a job as a waitress.

She leans forward, anxious to make the point clear.

'It wasn't an ordinary waitress job,' she says, 'we worked as something of a mixture between waitress and hostess, welcoming and helping customers that had a high status. Only top people visited Kleineman's and that meant that though it was hard work, the job paid well.'

It was at Kleineman's she was able to practise her school English and make it a living language. After a few months, she was so well regarded that Kleineman made her manageress of another similar establishment in town while she was still only twenty-three. That was where she met Jan, her future husband.

As she was well aware that the employees must not socialise with the clients she turned him down twice, but when he invited her parents as well she could hardly refuse. He was charming and quite good looking, his glasses giving him the aura of wisdom and education and after they had been out together a few times, Nadia rather liked him. Her mother on the other hand was completely delighted by him while Pavel thought he would make Nadia happy.

Jan was a twenty-nine year old Dutchman sent to work in Shanghai by his employers, Nederlandsche Handelsmatschapej, where he was working as an accountant. He had a good job, a fair income and had a car and though he said little about his background they could all gather that he came from one of the old respected families in Holland.

My father told me very little about his family and early years and as he died in 1985 I could only rely on the information given to me by Nadia, most of which came in small snippets as time passed, together with the story as she now tells it.

Jan Martinus Kruys was born in 1907. His father Johan, born in 1867, was a successful tea and tobacco merchant trading in St Petersburg, which followed a family tradition that went back several generations. Inevitably this led to an element of Russian blood in his branch of the family and Johan himself was half-Russian.

The Kruys family, which could be traced back to the fourteenth century from the town of Vriezenveen, had also a well-known naval tradition, Johan's uncle Gerhardus making his name as a vice-admiral in the Royal Dutch Navy and later as a naval minister. The family even has a coat of arms.

Johan became rich and bought a seventeen-room mansion set in six hectares of land in the village of Diepenveen. During one of his many business visits to Surabaya, he met and married Martina Westmaas, who belonged to one of the numerous Dutch families that lived in Java.

Johan and Martina moved to their new house, called Klosters, and had five children, of which Jan was the middle child. As a father, Johan had Victorian attitudes and ruled the house like a tyrant. Being gifted, knowledgeable and a good businessman, he had high expectations of his children, but was disappointed to realise that only two of them were bright. Jan was not one of them, for he didn't do well at school and his only talents seemed to be football and carpentry, which did not allow for a good relationship with his father. When Jan suggested that he would like to take up a trade as a cabinetmaker, his father would have nothing of it and said that such a trade was quite unsuitable for a member of the Kruys family. Instead, through one of his many contacts, he sent him to be articled as an accountant.

Nadia pauses to say, 'Let's have a cup of tea.'

Though I am used to the way she speaks, she expresses that very English suggestion with an accent that is still decidedly Russian, which I notice again after not seeing her for some time.

Having lived in England for over fifty years Nadia's tea is as English as it could be. It is quite strong and made in a large pot. No question of samovars: she hadn't seen a samovar for over sixty years.

We drink our tea while I ask her questions about her life in China.

'I must confess that my family is now poor,' said Jan when he proposed. 'My father has lost a lot of money during the depression and now all we have left is our modest house in the country. It is called Klosters.'

Jan had explained to her that though they still had the house, his father had lost a considerable amount of money during the depression by withdrawing a large number of shares from the Dutch Shell Company and transferring them to a company that went bankrupt. He even knew Sir Henry Detterding, the founder of Shell. It was perhaps the most foolish financial move that Johan made in his life.

Jan and Nadia went about together for a short time in Shanghai before he was transferred to Sumatra to manage the finances of a large tobacco plantation. They kept up a correspondence and when he had established himself he made arrangements for Nadia to travel over so that they could get married and start their life together. Jan booked Nadia a passage on the luxury German liner *Potsdam,* which was designed to be easily converted into a battleship in the event of war.

Nadia could hardly forget the voyage from Shanghai to Sumatra. On board she remembered seeing a small wiry-haired gentleman as a frequent guest at the captain's table. His name was Mr. Einstein! He was travelling with his sister. There was also an Italian prince by the name of Umberto. During the voyage, which included a stop at Manila, she was well looked after and sat at the first officer's table. She enjoyed the social life on board and she became so well acquainted with the first officer that she invited him to the wedding.

The wedding in Medan in Sumatra was a simple register office affair, in contrast to the honeymoon, which they spent at the most beautiful places in Sumatra, including the mountain resorts of Berastagi and the enchanting volcanic lake, Lake Toba, then hardly exploited by tourism.

She remembers the time they went off on a crocodile hunting expedition up one of the river estuaries and how Jan showed his fine marksmanship by shooting a crocodile right between the eyes. She didn't turn out to be a bad shot either, showing her prowess by killing a black and yellow mangrove snake with a little .22 at thirty metres. Then there was the time they went hunting for wild boar and after they saw not a trace of a boar the whole evening, they succeeded in smashing into one while driving back home.

The young couple made their home in a fine colonial house in the outskirts of Medan and they had a full complement of servants to run it. In response to Jan writing to tell his parents that he was getting married to a Russian girl, Johan decided to take the next passage to Sumatra to meet his new, his first, daughter-in-law. Nadia was quite impressed that he should embark on a six-week voyage just to meet her.

She recalls her first meeting with Jan's father and how she was struck by the difference between father and son. He was slimmer and taller than Jan, his grey sleeked hair giving him the air of importance and respect that was clearly appropriate. They conversed in English as Nadia at that stage had still not become fluent in Dutch and Johan, despite being half-Russian on his mother's side, could not speak Russian. He was educated, could converse on most topics and was keen to tell her about the Kruys family and how for two centuries the family had business ties with St Petersburg. She thought that this may partly explain why he seemed to have a soft spot for her, for he spoke to her in a kindly way. However, it was evident that he was a dictator as far as his children were concerned, even long after they were all grown-up.

Satisfied that Jan had married a fine young woman, Johan returned home and the young couple continued their life in Sumatra, Nadia managing the home while Jan was away at work. They paid a visit to Jan's older brother Wim at a tobacco plantation within a day's ride in Sumatra. It was Wim's job to produce the highest quality tobacco leaves that make up the outer layer of a Havana cigar. Nadia found him to be pleasant, quietly spoken and modest and clearly a very skilled and knowledgeable planter.

Some months later, when Nadia told Jan that she was pregnant she did not get the expected reaction. His face did not light up. Instead, in an almost aggressive tone he told her that it meant having to travel up to Holland, to Klosters, their family home, where she could give birth to her son. Jan did not like the thought of Nadia's condition and he was obviously not enamoured by the thought of having children.

But having come to terms with the situation he took it for granted that it could only be a son and no son born to the Kruys family ought to be born in the Indies! Nadia thought this attitude seemed rather strange as Jan himself was born in Surabaya. Strangely enough he had the features and shade of skin that could belie a Southern Asiatic tinge. But he seemed to have inherited his skin colour from his mother who was also born in Surabaya and who, though of pure Dutch stock, was also dark.

But for all his faults, Jan was not boastful. Nadia recalls that it wasn't until they were on the train in Holland on their way to the family residence that he reminded her that after being millionaires and losing their fortune during the depression, they were now poor. They had only one cook, two housemaids and one gardener.

Bearing in mind the kind of privations she had experienced in China, she had no objections to Jan's kind of poverty at all! Nevertheless, it was a pity that his father, being a significant share-holder in Royal Dutch Shell, decided to sell during the depression and invest in another company. If he had hung on, things might have been different for the Johan branch of the Kruys family.

Klosters turned out to be seventeen rooms of late nineteenth' century pride. It stood like a large turreted brick cake, the hub of a six-hectare wheel of parkland, gardens and orchards, the Kruys Estate in the province of Overijsel in Holland. The word 'poverty' that Jan had intimated was hardly appropriate and must have been used in a purely comparative sense.

Unlike Jan, his father beamed to see the roundness of her pregnancy when they arrived. For her part, Nadia was glad that they had already met in Sumatra and shaken off the wrappings of formality. The next hurdle was to be her new mother-in-law.

She turned out to be the opposite of Jan's father. Her intellect was very restricted and her attitudes and habits were those that belonged to the nineteenth century. It seemed that her sole purpose in life was to keep the house in tip-top order. She must have been an ogress to the domestic staff, keeping a constant check on them and using the large bunch of keys that hung at her waist to give her access to every cupboard in the house. She was very fussy about the piles of sheets

9

in the airing cupboard being in perfect alignment!

Though Klosters represented the former status and best of that branch of the Kruys family, it was also a provincial monument to the worst of the nineteenth' century class hierarchy.

Nadia recalled that when she and her mother-in-law went to the local grocer's she was made to address the grocer's wife as 'Miss', despite her being a mature married woman.

'We who belong to the upper class of Holland never address ordinary women as "Mrs", irrespective of their marital status,' said her mother-in-law imperiously.

While she did not feel in tune with her new mother-in-law, she got on with Johan like a house on fire and it was obvious that he both liked and respected his Russian daughter-in-law. Jan told her afterwards that it was most unusual for him to receive anyone at all while he was reading in the library, with the exception of his eldest daughter who was apparently very intelligent, but had left Holland to live in South Africa.

Nadia remembers that my birth suddenly provoked a change in Jan's attitude. He rushed down the stairs to proudly announce to those waiting that Nadia had given birth to a son. He then proceeded to lead them up the stairs to show them his son with all the pride of a father.

Nadia smiles when she relates how the story of the voyage to Java with her baby son was a memorable experience. Thanks to his contacts, Johan was able to get them a cabin on a cargo vessel. He also made sure that powdered milk and baby foods were all provided.

Nadia breaks into a broader smile as she tells about the time when the captain asked her to hang out the nappy washing unusually early one morning. This she was asked to do in time for meeting a northbound P&O liner, which on sighting the unusual row of 'fluttering white flags', signalled 'congratulations'.

At that time Jan was good company, being cheerful and sociable, and the crew responded to their passengers with a warmth and friendship that Nadia had never experienced before. They established such a friendship with the captain and some of the crew that contacts were kept up after the voyage.

Nadia disembarked at Medan in Sumatra and we stayed with Wim, while Jan continued the journey to Semarang where he secured a job as an accountant at the port authorities. Nadia then took me, aged about six months, to stay at a hotel in Semarang where we all stayed before finding a home in the residential area.

Nadia has told me as much as she can manage, but this, together with what she told me over the years and the memories that I have of my childhood, allows me to write my story. Though she had explained certain events and helped me to put them into context, my story is based on the happenings as I remembered them.

All the people involved in my story were real, but I have altered their names, in case they are still alive and do not wish to be included. Members of my family, however, are portrayed with their names intact.

1. The Waringi Tree

We were like a tiny bubble on the crest of a wave of three centuries of colonialism, a wave that was soon to be engulfed in the storm of the Second World War.

Like nearly all the ex-patriots living in the Far East, we lived a life of luxury in Java without having to be rich by the normal western standards of the time. Only the usual status symbols like size of house and staff reflected comparative wealth and the position on the white social ladder, but the material comforts of even the lowest ranking European were considerably better than that of the average native Javanese. Colonial life was such that it was quite unremarkable for an ordinary Dutchman to have a staff of house servants, which may include a cook, a gardener or two and domestic servants. Of the latter, the most important for me was a babu, who apart from being a general factotum in the running of the house, would also be nanny to the young children.

Being a minute cog in the Dutch colonial machinery, my father Jan had a job as an accountant at the port authority. Though his social status was insignificant, it went without saying that our home had to be in that part of town where it was proper for Europeans to live. If we had lived anywhere else without owning, or having a managerial position in a rubber or tobacco plantation, we would have been social outcasts, such as the odd Dutchman who had 'gone native'. And with the possible exception of those in lower management in the business world, one was definitely persona non grata if married to a Javanese or half-caste.

My parents obeyed these unwritten rules of colonialism and led the kind of life that society expected of them. Our home, however, was a little unusual in that it was not a typical colonial bungalow. Instead, my parents were offered the opportunity to rent a guest pavilion belonging to a large estate owned by a Dutch industrial magnate in Semarang. They had, however, acquired their own furniture and all the trappings to make a home in the Dutch East Indies, including

native servants. The house had its own grounds and was set back
some thirty or forty yards from a wide tree-lined suburban road
called Sindoroweg. It was in an old part of town known as Old
Tjandi that was well shaded by grand old trees whose broad crowns
protected its suburban gardens and roads from the worst of the
tropical sun.

Though my parents were both European, they were, like their
house, a little out of the ordinary because my Dutch father had
married a Russian woman. Since the fashion of the day dictated that
obesity in a baby was a sign of health, I was fed to produce the
desired roundness, which in my case was mainly manifested in my
cheeks. The few photographs that survived the turbulent years of the
war portrayed me as if I were going through the motions of blowing
a trumpet.

My sister Vera was born in Semarang in June 1941, when I was not
yet three and too young to understand my mother's pregnancy and
the fuss preceding Vera's birth. Jan took me to the hospital where
Nadia, was lying looking pale and a little puffed up. Next to her lay
the new arrival, an amorphous package of pinkness with a shock of
black hair. For me the most interesting thing about my baby sister
was that during the following months her hair changed colour, from
black through a beautiful copper hue to blonde, while my own hair
was as nondescript as the dark brown soil of our garden.

Since Nadia had lost a lot of blood after Vera's birth and it was too
hot and humid at home, Jan took us up to the mountains to the
south-west of Semarang. At an altitude of over 2,000 feet the climate
was cooler and, despite occasional mists from low clouds, less humid
and less oppressive. Though the nights were cool it was hot enough
during the day for the sun to warm the streams that ran down the
mountainsides. Some of these streams were impounded at guest
houses and hotels to form bathing pools. One such pool at the guest
house where we stayed had countless numbers of small dark fish that
were impossible to grasp as I stood up to my waist at the shallow
part. A man who was a friend of Jan's also staying at the resort, took
me with him to a deeper part and got me to kick with my legs while
he held my arms. Jan, on the other hand, seemed distant and
avoided body-contact with both Vera and me.

The front of our house was shaded by an enormous waringi tree, its giant crown extending over the lawn like a mega-umbrella almost without any holes. In the early morning the umbrella would come alive with the sounds of hundreds of different invisible birds, twittering, whistling and cooing. At midday the tree was almost silent but in the late afternoon it began to chirp and whine with the sounds of cicadas. As a toddler I was left on my own in a wooden-railed playpen under the waringi tree that would shade me from the baking sun and fill my subconscious with the concert of sounds.

Like that of most two or three-year-olds, my brain was dominated by what I heard. I could not help but hear the sounds in the form of words that came from the adults around me and these were absorbed by the developing speech centre like a desiccated sponge absorbs water. These words were in turn mimicked as easily and naturally as laughing, even though the actual concept of language, if it existed at all at that stage, was rudimentary.

However, to me this natural ability to soak up words was rather complicated by the fact I that lived in an environment where four languages were spoken. It was Russian when I spoke to my mother and I exchanged a few words in Dutch when speaking to my father. But I could probably claim to have Bahasa Malayan, or Indonesian, as my first language, as most of my early childhood was spent with my Javanese babu who was employed as my nursemaid.

The fourth language was not directed at me at all. It was the language of exclusion used between my parents when they wanted a private conversation and since I was never addressed in that language, I didn't need to learn it. I later learnt that that language was called English.

Nadia would bathe me in the evenings and teach me to say my prayers in Russian while kneeling in the classic way by the side of the bed. I was taught to ask God to bless mother, father and baby sister Vera and end with Amin, which is the Russian version of 'Amen', but which I interpreted as a blessing for our babu, as she happened to be called Amin. This misconception went on unnoticed until Amin left us a short time later and I ended my prayer with Sukarni, the name of our new Babu!

One day I heard a phrase that cropped up irrespective of which language was spoken. The phrase itself sounded strange and it seemed to belong to the Language of Exclusion, but it was used in an atmosphere loaded with tension and anxiety. My brain ingested it, ready for use.

'Sukarni,' I asked in Malayan, 'what does Pearl Harbour mean?'

She said that it was a place that was part of a big country called America and that a country called Japan had attacked it. She explained that it could mean the Japanese intend to invade us too and that is why everyone was worried, but she was sure that the Dutch army could keep the Japanese away.

Sukarni's comforting words worked only for a short time, however, as I sensed that the main topic of conversation among my parents and their friends continued to be Pearl Harbour.

On most occasions such conversations were carried out in Jan's language, when the visitor could be a colleague at work, or an acquaintance that lived down the road. Sometimes friends would come at the weekends to make a foursome in mah-jong. The smooth green-backed tiles were once left scattered on the table until the following morning when I discovered them, only to become fully absorbed by their smooth feel and pictorial designs.

Sometimes Nadia invited a Russian female friend, who like her happened to be married to a Dutchman. This was usually during the daytime, while Jan was at work.

I was an unobtrusive child, my presence being noticed by guests with remarks such as, 'What a nice quiet boy he is!' or 'Aren't you lucky to have Ivan he's so quiet, you hardly notice him!'

During my passive presence I somehow managed to gather that a harbour was an important place for ships and that there was a harbour in Semarang where we lived.

A short time later, my Uncle Ben who was Jan's younger brother visited us for a day and took us for a trip down to the harbour in Semarang. From his open convertible I realised that the resonant sounds of cranes and pile-drivers and the clanging sounds made by the lifting of timber and metal were all playing their part in making a harbour sound very memorable indeed.

But despite the consternation caused by the invasion of Pearl Harbour, life continued more or less as normal for a young Dutch family in the Dutch East Indies. Our lifestyle seemed to be virtually unaffected by the German conquest of most of the continent of Europe and we seemed to live in a world apart from the ravages of Hitler.

Being virtually on the equator Java has a tropical climate with rain coming at almost any time during the year, but it rains every day in the wet season between October and the end of April. At that time the air is a little cooler but saturated with moisture as the rains gush down, making people sweat from the humidity rather than from the actual heat.

Each tiled gully on the roof of the veranda that circled the house produced its own waterfall, as if the house were ringed by a tight row of open taps pouring their own jets into a deep gutter in the cement path by the side of the house. Grey-green land crabs scuttled along the bottom of the gutter as the water flowed along it to evoke a spate of arthropod activity, but when the gutter was dry the crabs led a secret life under large stones and in moist crevices. The crabs in their hiding places aroused my curiosity when all I could see was an occasional claw, the visible part of a mystery that wouldn't emerge, despite my efforts to tease the creature out with a stick.

Sukarni let me splash around naked in the grey warm wetness of the rain, revelling in the slushiness of the water as it met the soil to make runnels of brown muddiness. Muddy mixtures fascinated me to such an extent that even when it didn't rain I would find a small puddle and stir it with a stick until a delicious gooey brown mass was produced. As I stirred round and round, producing a changing pattern of rippled circles, it seemed entirely right to say 'goggle, moggle, goggle, moggle, goggle...' until the whole process became too monotonous, even for me. The words 'goggle moggle', however, were not my invention: they are the Russian for egg-flip, which Nadia used to make as a treat for the adults but which she once let me try with just a tiny dash of rum.

But I wasn't a dirty child. My sailor suit, together with its matching kiss-me-quick sailor hat, put on ready for the arrival of guests, remained unblemished after messing about in the garden. Even after falling out of my favourite child's rocking chair in the form of a double swan, my clothes were miraculously unscathed. When sitting

16

at the coffee table together with adult visitors, I invariably evoked praise because I could eat bread and jam without leaving traces of my fare on my clothes: all Nadia needed to do was to wipe the corners of my mouth. This unbelievable cleanliness, together with my unobtrusiveness prompted praise from the visitors but it gave her good grounds to wonder whether she had produced a normal child.

For a main meal Sukarni would take me in to feed me with nasi tim, a gently seasoned rice and chicken dish mild enough for young children, or Nadia would treat me to a favourite of mashed potato and spinach. On a good day a mangosteen, a maroon-coloured tangerine-sized fruit with a delectable juicy white interior, might follow the main course. The mangosteen was perhaps my favourite, but a guava, a juicy papaya, a ripe mango, or a small mellow milk banana, pisang susu, would delight my three-year-old taste buds nearly as well, as if I were a flightless fruitbat.

Once Sukarni showed us a brown package shaped like two small saucers placed face to face and wrapped up in thin strips of dried palm leaf.

'This is gula Java. You must try it,' she said, turning to me.

After she took off the palm leaf wrapping, she carved out a piece and handed it to Nadia, who put it in her mouth and nodded with approval.

'Hmm, this is good quality gula Java. Give a piece to Ivan.'

The sweet, almost burnt toffee taste of its crystal crunchiness quickly changed to a melliferous liquid as it flowed in my mouth before disappearing into my system in one ecstatic swallow.

'Ooh, that was good, may I have another piece?'

Sukarni cut another piece, while Nadia said that I ought not to have too much as it was bad for the teeth. Gula Java was, after all, a solid form of palm sugar molasses.

The sound of a man shouting something at regular intervals reached my ears. As the shouting on the road drew nearer and became more audible, I could hear him call, 'aa-yam kip . . . Aa-yam kip!' in a pleasant tenor pitch.

'Can you hear the man?', Nadia laughed, 'He's selling chicken using the Malayan and Dutch words for chicken at the same time!'

I knew what aa-yam meant, but didn't realise that kip was also the Dutch word for chicken.

The vendor, who carried his wares suspended on each end of a yoke, faded away into the distance without having the pleasure of a sale to our household on that occasion.

Vera's bedtime was hard to define as she spent most of her first months of life like any other baby: on her back. But before dark she was bathed and fed by Sukarni and Nadia and talcum powdered all over. Sometimes she fell asleep to a Russian lullaby and at other times Nadia made her gurgle with laughter by picking her up and rocking her slowly at first to the first line of a popular song:

'Taa...raaa...raaaaa...BOOM-bee-yay, taa raa ra boombeeyay.'

Her baby eyes grew wider and wider with the anticipated first 'BOOM', which came at the same time as Nadia swung her up to face level, upon which she burst into a hearty explosion of laughter. We all laughed, my enjoyment of the spectacle being nearly as great as that of both Vera and Nadia in their performance.

At nightfall a swirling mass of nameless insects came out of the dark humidity to be drawn to the veranda light. Many settled on the wall in the immediate vicinity of the light and attracted small beige-coloured gecko lizards, or chi-chaks. Like so many creatures the chi-chak was so called by the natives because of the sound it made. I could often hear the noises the chi-chak made above the city of nocturnal sounds coming from crickets, cicadas, frogs and other night creatures of our suburban environment.

They scampered out of nowhere, using the small pads on the tips of their anthropomorphic fingers to cling to the walls and propel them forward with rapid wriggling movements. Were it not for a pair of large dark bulging eyes adapted to see small movements in dimly-lit areas, their beige colouring made them almost camouflaged. I watched them racing along the walls and ceilings of the house to disappear and wait behind a picture that was illuminated by a nearby wall lamp. The patience of the chi-chak was almost matched by mine in waiting for the high-speed ambush of a hapless insect victim from behind the picture, a spectacle that I sometimes had time to see and marvel before Nadia put me to bed.

One evening, just after saying my prayers, now modified to include

Sukarni as well as end with Amin, I heard something which sounded like 'tock...eh'.

'Listen', said Nadia, 'that's the call of the tokay, which is like a very large chi-chak.'

'If you hear it call three times in a row,' she continued, 'that means good luck.'

'What if you hear the chi-chak call three times?'

'That doesn't mean a thing - according to the Javanese, it's the tokay that matters.'

We listened again, straining our ears to hear the tokay calling three times, only to hear it call once again, this time more distant.

Just as insects were an inevitable part of the household at night, much to the joy of the chi-chaks, so were mosquitoes a ubiquitous irritation and danger after dark. This meant that each bed had its own mosquito netting, or kelamboo, suspended from the ceiling. After saying my prayers, mine was opened like the entrance to a white cave ready for me to creep in. After Nadia ensured that no mosquitoes sat on the inside of the suspended netting, she tucked it under the mattress and I was enveloped in a misty haziness predisposing me to sleep.

Daytime was spent either playing on my own on the lawn in the shade of the waringi tree, rocking quietly in my swan, or developing an acquaintance with the tools of war by playing with a toy Spitfire plane, given to me by Jan. It had a fixed clockwork key in its side and I just about had the strength to wind it and allow the plane to run forward with its propeller spinning at the same time.

When a child of my age was invited to play with me, the event inevitably led to both of us playing in the isolation of our own imaginations. Being surrounded by adults right from the start, an adult environment seemed to me to be more natural, despite my passive behaviour in their presence. The two adults who were the central figures in my life were my mother, Nadia, and my babu Sukarni. To me my father Jan was more peripheral.

Sukarni dealt with routine matters at home, while any exciting outing or unusual event was always planned and accompanied by Nadia. The trip to the local swimming pool towards the town centre was a highlight. My mother would hail a bejak, a kind of open-fronted pedal-powered rickshaw, while Sukarni looked after Vera who was only about six months old. The driver pedalled behind us and was invisible, but for a small communication opening behind our heads. Above ur heads a canopy just large enough to give us shade and keep the worst of the rain away was supported at the sides above the front wheels. Apart from a slightly upward curving footrest the whole of the front was open for me revealing the real world outside my home.

We rode along past bicycles and a host of other road users including other bejaks. We drove past the market with its bamboo and palm-leafed stalls, past creased old men squatting by the roadside, women in multi-coloured batik sarongs. Heaps of tropical fruit and chillies, chickens and muscovy ducks penned up in round hand woven palm leaf and rattan cages, stacks of small bird cages were among the wares that caught my eye.

There were even small stalls selling only bundles of gula Java. All this visual feast was merged in a background hotchpotch of odours, the dominant features of which came from rotting tropical fruit, untreated sewage, wood smoke and oriental cooking, the total effect being rather pleasant. It was the fragrance of the tropics; the tang of tropical humanity as it must have been for centuries.

The pool was a little Dutch oasis in this pot-pourri of native sights, sounds and smells. It was surrounded by a high wall and excluded both the native Javanese and half-castes, a policy that constituted the essence of the type of colonialism practised by Northern Europeans.

I floated around the shallow end of the pool, supported in the warm water by an inflatable rubber ring that gave a wonderful sensation of buoyancy while being aware that I had the added security of my mother's vigil. A thickish metal pipe, suspended about a foot above the water, served as a divider between the shallow and the deep parts of the pool. It was an adventure to paddle under the pipe to find myself suddenly floating over the deeper hue of seemingly bottomless blue depths. Perhaps Nadia's aim was for me to be at ease when in water, perhaps it was just a nice way for a mother to spend a couple of hours with her small son, but either way I was no waterbaby. For me it was just a matter of enjoying the bejak rides and splashing around in the swimming pool water while revelling in the buoyancy provided by rubber and air.

Though I was content with my home life, Nadia realised that what I really needed was to mix with other children of around my own age. As my parents didn't know many young couples with suitable children, I was taken to a local Dutch kindergarten.

There were perhaps a total of about a dozen children between the ages of three and five, but somehow I found contact with them to be very difficult. I was therefore given things to do or make, like weaving coloured straw or messing about with model clay. This had the advantage of keeping me occupied, but it had the drawback of doing nothing for my social development and I continued to be a loner until I arrived one day to find the atmosphere in the play school had changed.

Just like at home, a large waringi tree dominated the front lawn of the kindergarten. The gardener had gathered a mound of branches and twigs that he arranged round its huge furrowed trunk. I was ushered to join a line of children some distance from the tree. Whilst we were waiting for all the children to arrive, we were informed that the waringi was home to a huge python and that it was to be smoked out. As Sukarni had already schooled me about dangerous snakes it became clear why we were made to stand so far away from the tree.

With mounting excitement we watched the gardener light the bonfire and gazed up the trunk to catch sight of the snake as the smoke billowed up into the dark canopy. It happened in a flash. I never saw the snake come down, but there it was, a mass of writhing brown patterned coils on the ground, the gardener triumphant with a large pole in his hand. We were then given a long stick each and urged to beat the snake dead, not aware that its convulsions were the results of its sudden death. We stood rooted to the ground, not daring to make a move before our teacher showed us with her pole how to beat the snake. She beckoned us to do likewise but for a few seconds we didn't move until one boy ventured to step forward to follow the teacher's example. His action was the start of a frenzied beating of sticks, by which time the nerves of the long writhing creature had relented and the snake that I found myself hitting with a mixture of dread and daring was motionless.

I joined the others to receive a rewarding fruit juice in a bright orange beaker made of pioneer plastic. Each drink was drawn up through a paper straw producing sucking sounds of satisfaction with the illusion that each had made a contribution to the death of a monster.

After that experience at kindergarten our own garden no longer provided the haven of domestic security that I took for granted. As well as being a comforting combination of shade and sounds our own waringi tree could also harbour a monster hidden either in its crown or in the intricate convolutions of its massive trunk. Fear and caution had become a part of me, causing me to keep a safe distance away from the trunk, despite Sukarni's assurance that our gardener would never allow a snake to live in our tree. For me our waringi could no longer be trusted as a secure refuge from the heat of the sun.

However, the secrets of our waringi were not always unviolated. Like most European men, Jan kept a gun, his being a light 22-calibre rifle that he could use with great accuracy. He stood on the front veranda steps and pointed the gun up into what seemed to be a dark silhouetted jumble of branches and leaves. The sharp crack of the rifle was followed by something green falling and hitting the ground with a light thud.

The green object lying on the ground turned out to be a lifeless pigeon, fascinating with its beautiful leaf-green plumage, a soft sadness that was once alive and hidden up in the waringi tree. For me it was quite remarkable that Jan not only saw it, but also killed it with one shot way up in the huge crown with hundreds of nuances of green.

It was a triumph for my father that was acknowledged by the household servants not only because he was a good shot but also because the pigeon was to serve as a welcome ingredient in their nasi goreng.

A large conglomerate of small cages with two brown bare feet moved along the road, the feet walking in a series of rapid small steps followed by a pause when they disappeared with the descent of the bunch of cages onto the ground. This I knew was the bird vendor. He bore a yoke with numerous small skilfully made rattan birdcages hanging from each end. Each cage contained one or a pair of small birds caught in the area.

'Ivan,' said Nadia who happened to see the mobile stall of avian captives, 'shall we buy a little bird?'

She knew the question to be rhetorical and knowing what my response would be, we were already on our way to the mobile cagebird stall, while the feet appeared once more, this time to reveal their owner as he turned his load and came to meet us. The wild birds fluttered frantically in their rattan restrictions, making it even more difficult to choose an individual bird. There were small finches and sparrow-like birds, little bright green parrots and small grey doves.

I really wanted my mother to buy them all, but I knew that was impossible. Instead we spent some minutes looking at the array of feathered wares and finally made a choice out of the many birds on offer. Nadia bargained him down to buying a little bird fluttering about in a cage barely large enough for it to stretch its wings. When it paused briefly in its wild efforts to be rid of its imprisonment it sat tensed on its perch with its plumage pressed flat against its body. We could then see how beautifully it was clad in the cleanest pure grey, despite any damage that might have occurred during its violent efforts to escape. It had a black head with white cheeks and a short seed-eating pink bill. The one we chose was a Javanese rice sparrow.

The real excitement came when the vendor had left as it was time to set the beautiful prisoner free from the small cage that came with the bird.

'Couldn't we keep it for a while, Mamma?'

'No, we must give him his freedom. Isn't he beautiful?'

My emotions were a confusion of the desire to possess and that of empathy, but my mother's persuasive argument about how the little bird would enjoy its freedom always came through.

However, we once did keep a pair of miniature doves to enjoy their cooing sounds for a few days. Once again, it was difficult to be rid of these mixed emotions and when it was time for them to be released I was left with both regret and satisfaction for a time after the birds flew away to freedom. It was the contentment of knowing that a bird is free to fly anywhere it wants, coupled with the sadness of losing a possession of beauty.

2. A Good-Luck Sign

The Japanese arrived in Java in March 1942. From where we lived, there was no sound of bombing or gunfire or signs of violence of any kind, and there was no mention of 'harbour'. They just arrived.

At first we were still allowed to lead our normal lives, but I noticed that there were undercurrents of gloom and tension in the house. Then Jan came home one day to announce that he, together with all the non-German European men and their families, had to assemble at a certain place in town at a specified time. We travelled to some open part of town to join hundreds of other Europeans while the Japanese took stock of us. But it was only the men who had to report on the following day and to take with them the essentials for internment.

This event had made me realise that the Japanese were the ultimate controlling force over our home and town, that they had the power to take away the head of our home. I understood that the Japanese had taken the place of my father as the rulers of our home and it was this fact that struck me rather than the actual absence of the head of our house. Though for me Jan was merely in the background, he did represent a kind of security and with his departure my world felt unstable.

I lived in a world where the daytime routines were regulated by my babu. But the bedtimes were highlights and they were special because my mother conducted them. It was at one such bedtime, just when Nadia tucked me up for the night that she said, 'Listen!'

We heard it '...tockeh...tockeh', a little pause and then 'tock...eh'.

Hearing the tokay call three times was meant to be a sign of good luck, but the arrival of the Japanese and their abduction of our head of the house seemed anything but conducive to good fortune. Perhaps the situation made the need to believe in native folklore even stronger.

My environment bounded by Nadia and Sukarni began to change. Since the Japanese had removed all the Dutch men from the town not only were the Dutch households without their men, but what was left of the police was under the control of the Japanese. This meant that the native police had become the tool of the Japanese with little if any regard to the welfare of the colonial Dutch. The result was that it became dangerous to remain at home, and soon the rumour appeared that bandits began to rob houses, first in the darkness of night, then in the openness of day. The tension in our home reflected the general state of affairs in the town. Nadia, Sukarni and the other servants expressed anxieties, so that I couldn't avoid hearing in detail what it was all about. I heard that though they were aware that they could carry out their crimes with little fear of arrest, the bandits were practically naked and smeared with oil to lubricate them against capture by household servants. I imagined the terrifying scene of brown slippery naked men with knives coming out of the trees to rob and kill, then to vanish in the darkness.

The tension in the Dutch suburbs mounted with the increasing frequency of reported break-ins and it became such a dominant topic of conversation that even I began to worry about being actually attacked by sinister Javanese criminals.

Consequently Nadia's decision that it would be better to pack and store some of our belongings and move away to a safer part of Java sounded very positive to my ears.

While she and Jan were in Sumatra they met and became friends with a middle-aged couple by the name of Baginsky. He was a Latvian who held a senior post with a large German company in Sumatra at the time.

They kept in touch and after the Baginskys were transferred to Surabaya they occasionally visited each other. When Nadia told them about the consequences of the internment of the men in Semarang, they invited us to stay in the comparative safety of their home. Nadia assured me that Mr Baginsky was not interned with other European men mainly because he was not a Dutch national. He was also employed as a skilled engineer by a German company, a company allied to the Japanese. Consequently, as Mr Baginsky was indispensable to the company, he was also indispensable to the Japanese. This meant that not only was his home relatively secure from burglary but they were also less likely to be interned.

Nadia packed her valuables, consisting mainly of jewellery, silver and rolled-up pictures, into a trunk that she took together with essentials to a Chinese whose business was to safe-keep valuables.

I cried when we had to say goodbye to Sukarni. I knew that would be the last time I would see the warm and friendly smiling brown face. Her ankle-length batik sarong and her black hair tied into a bun at the back of her head made her look like so many young Javanese women at first sight. But Sukarni was different: she was part of my life and I knew that I would miss her soft voice, her comforts.

We moved to live with the Baginskys in Surabaya together with two Russian friends, Ludmilla and Olga. Olga and Nadia were in the same class at school in Harbin. Since both Nadia and Olga had married Dutchmen they both ended up in Java, and like Ludmilla, were mutual friends of the Baginskys. Olga's husband was in the Dutch merchant navy.

Mr Baginsky was a beaming benevolent gentleman, whose bald head was fringed with white hair. His wife, who was addressed by the two Russian women as Anatolia Nikolaiyevna, was a tall busty lady in her fifties. I was told that I could address her as Auntie Tolya. Everything about her was flowery: she wore flowery dresses, had flowers in the house and a whole array of flowers displayed alongside the paths in her open sunny garden.

Once again I was alone in a world consisting of adults and a baby. As there was little to keep me occupied I began to take an interest in what was growing in the garden, the different colours of the flowers being the prime attraction. Alongside the path I happened to touch a plant with fine feathery leaves and was startled to see the leaves rapidly close up, the stalks droop down and the whole plant becoming a shadow of itself in a matter of seconds. It was as if the plant was frightened of me. When I ran into the house to tell Nadia about my discovery, she laughed and said that I had touched a sensitive mimosa and it was quite harmless.

The sensitive mimosa was a great source of wonder but I hadn't the patience to wait for the plant to recover its normal shape. Instead, I was curious to see what the rest of the garden had to offer. It was in the Baginsky garden that I discovered that flowers were scented. I began to sample their subtle differences of fragrance by inhaling deeply with my nose from one flower to the next, enjoying both the sensation and the excitement of discovering that as well as looking different, they also varied in their scent.

At the sound of a woman's laughter, I looked up to see Mrs Baginsky rocking with amusement. Nadia was standing by her side, her face without much expression.

'Just like Ferdinand the Bull,' guffawed Mrs Baginsky.

But as far as I was concerned being compared to Ferdinand could only be regarded as a compliment. Nadia read me the story on several occasions from the book version of the Walt Disney film so that I knew that as the story went, Ferdinand turned out to be the strongest bull of the herd. Though I sensed that Mrs Baginsky's laughter was derisory, I was not at all insulted to be compared to the hero of my favourite story. Nadia, on the other hand, seemed a trifle annoyed by her hostess' outburst.

'You'd better come in before the sun gets too hot,' said my mother.

Not far from the Baginskys there was another opportunity to experience the wonders of Walt Disney in the form a bamboo and palm cinema house. A week or two after our arrival at the Baginskys, Nadia took me to see Snow White and the Seven Dwarfs dubbed in Dutch. It was the most enthralling phenomenon in my nearly four years of life, marred only by the horror of watching the 'Mirror, Mirror on the Wall' changing the evil beauty of the witch into evil itself.

Nadia's motherly comfort muffled my cries of fright to allow me to enjoy the end and the triumph of Snow White and the dwarfs.

We soon settled down to a kind of routine in the Baginsky home so that both Nadia and Ludmilla began to contribute to the running of the household, which also meant that there were plenty of adults, including the Baginskys' babu, to keep an eye on small children. With this in mind, my mother took it upon herself go to the market to buy provisions. She waved down a bejak and, as was the custom, came to an agreement about the price, paid the man and climbed in, casually placing her handbag and shopping bag by her side on the seat. On reaching the local market she took her shopping bag and hopped out.

Her handbag! The seconds that it took for her to realise that she had not taken her handbag were enough to allow the driver to melt away in the profusion of people, cycles, cars and other bejaks. He had simply vanished and there was no way of catching him. He must have taken the handbag through the little window behind her on the way to the market.

She was desolate. Not only was she forced to walk back without having bought provisions for the household, but had lost all her money. Unfortunately, she was wise after the event. She realised how foolish it was to have carried all her assets in cash in order to make her contributions to the household as the need arose. She knew then that she ought to have taken enough just for the shopping and left the rest in a safe place at the Baginskys'.

Back at the Baginskys', she described what had happened and how upset she was and that she no longer had any means of contributing towards the household. Mrs Baginsky listened to her story and looked at her thoughtfully.

'We'll discuss your situation this evening and see what we can do,' she said.

That evening, after his wife told him about Nadia's problem Mr. Baginsky came to her and said kindly, 'Never mind. I think I might be able to help you. If you leave the children to us, perhaps I can get you a job.'

When Mr Baginsky returned from work on the following day he brought Nadia some good news:

'Look, I talked to a friend of mine today. He runs a Chinese noodle factory not far from where I work. He said that he could fix you up with a job. If you travel in with me tomorrow morning, I can drop you off at the factory and you can decide if you want to take on what he has to offer.'

Nadia returned the next day having spent her first day working as a cook for the Japanese who took over the factory. The job itself was arduous but it paid quite well, well enough for her to pay her and her children's way at the Baginsky household.

Vera and I were mostly looked after by Mrs. Baginsky and her babu, who was rather distant and with whom I could never form the same attachment as I did with Sukarni. Occasionally Mrs Baginsky took Vera and me to a friend, who had three teenage daughters who took charge of us, but those visits were brief and we were mostly at the Baginskys'. Having no children of her own, Mrs Baginsky took on the role of mother during Nadia's absence. Once she took me into her sunny garden to a plant growing by the side of the house. It had long tapering dark green leaves lined with thorns and must have been related to the aloe family of succulents. Using a sharp knife, she cut off one of the foot-long blades at the base and said that she would show me something new.

I followed her into the house wondering what sort of thrill I was about to experience and watched her wash the mystery blade under the tap, shake off the drops of water and then scrape its hollow side with a teaspoon. The result was a bubbly mass of greenish slime on the saucer, which she then proceeded to season with salt by lavish sprinklings from a salt cellar.

'Take this,' she said putting a teaspoonful of her work into my mouth, 'it will help to make you grow.'

All I could taste was the salt. The cool slimy feel of it hardly made the best gastronomic experience for a boy nearly aged four, but since Mrs Baginsky said it would make me grow I took it as a sort of medicine, convinced that I would become as strong as Ferdinand the Bull.

On another occasion, Mrs Baginsky took Nadia and me to Surabaya Zoo while her babu looked after Vera at home. The usual zoo animals like tigers and lions didn't seem to make much impression on me, but the most memorable experience was when Mrs Baginsky lifted me up on to a wall surrounding a crocodile pit. The sight of an enormous tooth-armoured gape was enough to strike terror in my infant imagination and I thought that perhaps she was trying to frighten me. I said nothing, stiff with fear and hoping that she would not let go. Fortunately, seeing the expression on my face and the stiffness of my body, Nadia took hold of me and when I felt the security of her grip, I relaxed.

For me, the most pleasant creatures in the zoo were the New Guinea giant crowned pigeons, up to my waist in height, looking beautiful and impressive in their slate-blue plumage and their delicate crowns of feathers. I wanted to stare at them for a long time to try to make contact with their beady red eyes, but Mrs Baginsky dragged me away.

The weekdays went by uneventfully, making evenings and weekends more interesting because Nadia could then devote some of her time to us.

We took a bejak to a swimming pool not far from the Baginskys'. As we entered, I was shocked to see a group of naked men standing under a shower. They were more like the Javanese but lighter skinned. It was clear to me that they were definitely not European. It wasn't just their nakedness that stunned me: it was the change in the atmosphere of the whole pool. A public swimming pool that was once a lido exclusively for the Dutch and other Europeans had become dominated by people that didn't look at all European and as if to emphasise the difference, there they were, standing around in their startling nudity.

I stood gaping at them.

Noticing my stunned reaction, Nadia stopped and looked at me.

'They are Japanese,' she said in a matter-of-fact manner. 'Don't stare at them.'

The statement was more of a confirmation than an explanation. Once again I was reminded that the people that ruled Java were no longer the Dutch but the Japanese, though my first real encounter of our new rulers was not through experiencing the ravages of war but by witnessing their naked dominance at a public swimming pool.

As I didn't have my usual rubber buoyancy I wallowed around in the children's paddling pool, rolling around in the shallow lukewarm water like a little seal in the tropical heat. I was mesmerised by the changing scene from sky to the close view of the bottom through ten inches of water as my body tumbled round. Suddenly there was a new ingredient in the changing images, which caused me to halt. It was the sight of several grinning naked Japanese men staring at me with obvious amusement. Though they weren't European they seemed like normal human beings and I found it difficult to associate them and their smiling faces as the cause of so much fuss involving the key words 'Pearl Harbour'.

A moment later the sound of Nadia calling made me understand that entertaining the Japanese was an unsuitable form of behaviour and this was confirmed by the way that she hastily took me by the arm away from the scene.

But it was impossible to avoid them. When we first arrived at the Baginskys', I hardly noticed the presence of the Japanese, but as time passed they were to be seen more and more frequently.

Not long after the swimming pool experience I was surprised to see a uniformed Japanese soldier opening the door, entering the house without being met, and going into the bathroom. It turned out that, despite their relative security from native criminals, the Japanese regarded the Baginskys as a part of their property. Though they were less likely to be burgled, they were not immune from Japanese soldiers who considered it their right to come into the house uninvited to take a shower or use the toilet. They became a common sight both indoors and outdoors. The privilege that the Baginskys thought they enjoyed had faded to almost nothing and the atmosphere in our new home became nearly as tense as that of our home in Semarang.

There were no more trips to the swimming pool or the cinema, for soon after our lives took another course.

3. Internees

The Japanese ordered all Dutch women and women married to Dutch men to leave their homes and assemble at certain points by a given time. We were made to leave the Baginskys' and to take only those items that we could carry, but we were also allowed to have one double mattress that was large enough for a mother and two small children and which they would transport for us. The Baginskys themselves were exempted, their home presumably continuing to be an amenity for the Japanese.

All males over fifteen were already interned, while women and children were initially placed in private houses that once belonged to the Dutch and these were used as assembly stations prior to distribution to concentration camps. By coincidence the house where we found ourselves belonged to Jan's cousin and I don't know whether it was by further coincidence or design, but Mrs Kruys and her son Rudi, who was my age, also happened to be in the house that was once theirs. Soon after we met, however, Rudi became ill and died within two days of an illness that Nadia later told me was meningitis.

A few days later we were marched off to the Surabaya railway station. We were told that our mattresses would be given to us when we reached our destination. Nadia staggered like an overburdened mule, loaded with two large well-packed suitcases. Apart from items that took up minimal space, such as small pieces of precious jewellery and some photographs, they were filled with the essentials that she considered necessary for survival, including a bottle of cod liver oil. My baby sister Vera, at the age of barely eighteen months, carried a potty, while my burden was a five-pound golden-coloured tin of butter. Nadia had also made a small cloth bag which she filled with her most precious jewels and strapped onto the inside of her leg.

When we reached the station we were made to climb into cattle trucks into which we were herded like the originally intended occupants. It was hot and humid and rather dark in our railed confinement, the only sources of light and fresh air being the gaps

between the timber sides of the truck. Murmurs of worried speculation as to our destination and our fate floated about as if we were
farm animals making meaningless noises.

About two hours later, after a stiflingly slow rumbling ride, we
came to a halt. Somebody looked through the gaps where the light
shone in and cried, 'Semarang!' We were back in Semarang.

When we were ordered out of the darkness of the cattle truck the
blinding heat of the sun was almost a relief compared with the
stifling heat inside the truck. White walls that I recognised as
belonging to the railway station where we boarded the train bound
for Surabaya several weeks previously blinded me. But being at that
station reminded me of when it was much more pleasant to travel by
train, even though at that time we were saddened to be forced to
leave our home and Sukarni. The sight of a young Javanese woman
in a sarong on the platform made me think of Sukarni and how I still
missed her. I wondered if she felt the same about us and whether she
liked being ruled by the Japanese, for I was aware that only
Europeans were being rounded up by them.

Once again the Japanese organised us into a column and we began
our march by walking along the railway track, which we left after
perhaps ten minutes. The column of women and children moved
slowly towards an unknown destination, many were overburdened,
perhaps some, even at that early stage, regretting the packing of the
household silver and other portable family heirlooms.

The Japanese soldiers that I saw were no longer like the friendly
naked strangers that I remembered from the swimming pool. Now
they were uniformed in khaki and wore peaked caps. Now they
treated us with a distant contempt, for we were merely the chattels
of the men vanquished by the Emperor of Japan, thereby making us
nearly the lowest of the low. Nadia explained to me that it was clear
to the Japanese that people with such a low standing must be taught
at an early stage to obey every order without question. This also
meant that knowledge of the relevant Japanese language must be
acquired as quickly as possible. Only the native Javanese were considered by the Japanese to be a little inferior to us but at least they
were able to live in their homes, even if they were very badly treated
and taken for granted as Japanese property like the Baginskys'. The

Japanese utilised the indigenous people like slaves, making them work without pay or any kind of reward, except the verbal promise that they would liberate them from the Dutch colonialists. Instead, they set about being their own kind of ruthless colonialists, which instilled a deep hatred for them among the Javanese.

After more than two hours of slow progress in the intolerable heat, we arrived at our destination, a collection of large tall white buildings that might have been a factory before the Japanese arrived. Too weary to take in the hallmarks of internment, such as barbed wire and guards, the column shuffled its way to an outside tap to relieve the dehydration caused by the heat and strain of the day.

We were then made to wait in groups and shown our quarters by a large expressionless Dutch woman who must have been assigned by the Japanese. We came to what looked like a railway station platform without the rails, perhaps a kind of loading bay with a corrugated iron roof.

On the loading bay a construction made of bamboo and rattan that was erected between the roof supports was to be our abode together with other women and children. The absence of walls instantly generated a sense of open vulnerability. Vera and I were told to wait while Nadia went to join a few women to fetch their mattresses that were dumped somewhere else in the compound.

We waited motionless, too tired and hungry to talk or cry. Finally our mother, helped by another woman, staggered back with our mattress and dumped it on the platform. She was about to leave to help other women with their mattresses when Vera said in Malayan, 'Mamma, I want some nasi tim.'

'Wait here, darlings,' she said in Russian, 'and we'll soon get something to eat.'

We waited for what seemed eternity while the women organised their living quarters and we tried to rest away our hunger and lassitude on our new bed and home.

Our open environment, with only a corrugated iron roof for shelter, emphasised the need for mosquito netting, which Nadia had the good sense to pack. The women had managed to find strips of wood and bamboo, which they tied to the posts supporting the roof, so that the netting could be suspended. String and scissors turned out to be more useful items that her common sense had told her were necessary when she packed. She also had the foresight to take a spare sheet, cod liver oil, medicines and vitamins, as well as the tin of butter that was my burden. Nadia was prepared for the possibility that the war and our internment could last more than a few months.

All the larger precious things that she had packed into a trunk in Semarang were left in charge of a Chinese and any jewellery she took was limited to a few items weighing very little. Many women chose to be burdened by heavy household silver, precious ornaments as well as heavy necklaces and bracelets. Not only did they do this at the expense of the more necessary items for survival in a concentration camp, but those precious items that they took had also lost their original value, thereby losing their purpose for the future.

Nadia did, however, take just four items of cutlery: two table knives and three large dessert spoons, the handles of which were engraved 'C.K. 1832' in copperplate style. They were part of a silver service presented to my great great-grandfather Claas Kruys, on the occasion of his marriage in 1832. She also took a small Russian silver goblet given to me by my grandfather on my birth. But one of the heaviest items of her luggage was a large well-cured piece of ham, which she had carefully wrapped in greaseproof paper.

When Nadia returned, she said, 'They are dishing out the food now, so if you wait a little longer, I'll bring it to you.'

We waited, invigorated by the anticipation of food. Soon Nadia returned with three halves of coconut shells balanced in her hands.

I was confronted by a brown coconut shell containing what must have been about one small ladle of boiled white rice, the whiteness of which was only relieved by small dark pebbles. The effect was to make the rice appear polka-dotted. We speculated that our rice was scooped up from the bottom of the pile heaped on the ground before it was cooked. There was neither meat nor seasoning, there were no vegetables, and nothing to remind me of nasi tim except that it was rice. Nadia took out the ham, unwrapped it and using one of the C.K. knives, gave us a small slice each.

As we were tired, weakened by the walk and hungry, the little half-coconut shell of boiled rice and a slice of ham were quickly eaten with one of the silver dessert spoons. Nadia helped Vera to eat hers, making sure that every spoonful was free of stones. The effect of the hunger was to make it difficult not to swallow the polka-dot pebbles and I scraped the coconut so thoroughly that some of its veined inner structure began to peel away resulting in small fibrous bits enmeshing themselves in the last grains of rice.

Nadia gave us some water from a tin can in an effort to make up for the lack of food, and we drank it while she went to the tap to wash our coconut shell dishes. We were still hungry but there was no more.

By nightfall we were securely and cosily entombed by our kelamboo. Nadia lay with her head nearest the outside edge, while we lay on either side of her feet, which as she was only five-feet-two tall, were about level with our hips. After the babble of women and children's voices died down we heard only the usual sounds of the tropical night, including chi-chaks, frogs and cicadas. Despite the openness of our platform we did not hear any disturbing sounds, except those that came from somewhere on the platform itself, such as children crying, women talking and the occasional shout or reprimand.

But the lack of walls did expose us to tropical rainstorms, despite the roof. The platform was divided along the middle, giving enough room for two bedlengths that were separated by a space of about two or three feet. When there was a rainstorm the wind blew water onto our beds at the foot end, Nadia's head end. However, the centre area of the platform was mainly dry, except where there were holes in the roof: fortunately there were no such leaks above our part of the platform.

After only a few weeks these primitive living conditions began to make their mark. The ham did not last much more than a week and as even it would degenerate in the tropical heat it could not be rationed out to last longer. The totally inadequate diet, lacking both variation and substance, first gave way to a general feeling of lassitude and weakness. Later this was combined with a low resistance to infections. This, coupled with our partial exposure to wind and rain, made us easily prone to colds and ear and chest infections.

A principal source of trouble was the tap water which must have come directly from a well without much, if any, treatment. This soon led to various stomach complaints, including deadly forms of dysentery, the most devastating and exhausting being the amoebic form. People who lacked the foresight to take mosquito netting suffered from insect bites, the most common consequence being malaria. Lack of hygiene facilities, including poor sewage disposal, gave rise to cholera and typhus. Our enamelled child-sized potty was the only receptacle we had for the disposal of both liquid and solid excrement. Nadia emptied it regularly into the camp latrines which Vera and I never approached.

After only a few weeks of internment we soon heard of people dying. Though these early deaths affected people mostly at the extreme ends of the age scale, it made us aware of our vulnerability. Nadia was worried about how Vera and I would weather the storm of diseases and malnutrition but she was among the many women with children who sharpened their senses of precaution. She made us scrape our coconut shell dishes so smooth and polished that they were less likely to trap bacteria. She had a store of vitamin pills that she rationed out to us and she had opened the tin of butter that contained fat-soluble vitamins. This butter went round to be added to the rice (sometimes without stones) until the remainder went rancid in the heat, despite her efforts to keep it cool in the shade of the platform. She even made sure that Vera and me went out in the morning sun with only a pair of shorts in order to receive a daily portion of vitamin D.

Despite these precautions I became ill. One night my right ear began to ache, the pain gradually reaching such intensity that I couldn't avoid moaning and rocking my body in an effort to cope with the torture. Nadia reported my problem to the camp doctor, an elderly man who the Japanese allowed in our camp and who organised a kind of medical centre using the bare essentials. Since I was shaking with a fever he had to come to me and after examining me with his otoscope, said that I had an ear infection and that the only thing he could do was to syringe it with warm salt water. I cried out with pain from this treatment, having to be content afterwards with the doctor mumbling that I was a brave boy. But it seemed to work, for after a few days the earache disappeared.

Not long after I recovered from the ear infection I began to suffer from acute pains in the stomach, coupled with urgent needs to use the potty. Nadia urged me to drink to compensate my fluid loss, but the more I drunk the more liquid I produced at the other end, which resulted in half my time being spent in the squatting position and what was at first diarrhoea turned to squirts of watery mucus.

Nadia inspected the results on every occasion and it wasn't long before she said, 'Ivan, look at the blood in the slime that you are producing! I think you have amoebic dysentery and I'd better call the doctor and see if he can do anything.'

All the old man could do was to see to it that I must continue to drink water, but he would arrange that the water I drunk had been previously boiled, in the hope that it would be sterilised. This meant that Nadia had to collect my water in a bottle from the doctor's on the way back from emptying the potty.

The following days were filled with anxiety for Nadia. I was in a semi-conscious state, waving my arms about and moaning in a state of high fever. It seemed that I was close to death and Nadia was fraught with worry. Her fears increased when she remembered that I had a sensitive stomach long before we were interned, often having diarrhoea even after simple meals. But perhaps this enteric tendency to reject even 'normal' foods was what saved Nadia from losing her son.

My recovery began after about three days of high fever during which a drop in temperature allowed me to lapse into a deep sleep that must have lasted a long time. I continued to drink boiled water from the doctor's dispensary and began to be able to eat our daily meals of polished rice. However it was a long time before I had the strength to get up and walk and resume what was considered to be a normal life in a concentration camp.

The Japanese, being a nation of bathers, had taken the trouble to see to it that we had access to a communal shower housed in a concrete walled enclosure. Though our capture and imprisonment made us the scum of the earth they were quite keen to see to it that we were not as filthy as our status would suggest. Nevertheless, as the bathing enclosure had only two showers that had to serve a thousand women and children it was necessary to book weeks ahead.

This was the first time that I not only saw my mother naked, but noticed the difference between naked women and men when I remembered all those naked Japanese men at the swimming pool. Even Vera's attention was drawn to all those different sized breasts and triangles of hair. It was remarkable that even after months on a starvation diet that many women were still able to keep their round feminine shapes.

When we visited the bathing enclosure after my illness, Nadia was careful to make sure that I didn't drink the water from the shower, for the water supply that cleaned our exteriors was the same that contaminated our interiors.

4. An Altar Without Rites

Despite the increasing frequency of deaths, the continuing influx of internees, resulting from a continuous reshuffle by the Japanese, had overloaded the camp. This in turn caused the Japanese to decide to move some of the women and children to another area. As the Japanese regarded us as being beneath their contempt, they manipulated us as they pleased without the warrant of an explanation and we had to take things as they came.

After several months in that deplorable concentration camp Nadia, Vera and I were made to march to another camp. It was difficult to ascertain why we were to move. Perhaps we were picked out by chance, or perhaps the old doctor was consulted to select those who ought to be moved out: no one will ever be able to determine the truth, but we hoped that a move to another camp could mean an improvement in our conditions. It was hard to imagine that we would move to a camp that would be even worse.

The women organised our mattresses and Nadia packed our belongings. As the heavy tin of butter was used up, I was spared that load and carried a bottle of water instead, leaving Vera to carry the potty again. The bottle, which had a stoneware and rubber screw top, was one acquired by Nadia who filled it with boiled water from the doctor's dispensary.

Weakened by various illnesses and a totally inadequate diet as well as walking long distances in the tropical heat was enough in itself without having to be encumbered by baggage.

The walk proved to be slower and heavier than envisaged, partly because we were weaker than we realised, and partly due to the fact that we seemed to be gaining altitude. However, the knowledge that we seemed to be heading for a camp located at a higher altitude had the effect of boosting morale and somehow helped to spur us on, for Nadia said that we could be on the way to a place that enjoyed a better climate.

The few hours of stumbling along a hot dusty road seemed like an

40

eternity but we were finally allowed to rest under some large eucalyptus trees. The aromatic smell of the dry, brown, fallen eucalyptus
leaves made the lukewarm water that was my load seem cooler as we
drank our share that Nadia rationed out. There must have been over
a hundred women and children in our group, some of the children
crying from exhaustion and malaise. The Japanese guards made us
get up and continue when we felt anything but ready to do so.

Late in the afternoon, we were confronted by a tall white building
that Nadia said was a church. We saw women dressed in black and
white, their heads being decorated by large fancy white embellish-
ments. Nadia said that they were nuns and that we appeared to have
arrived at a nuns' convent.

The nuns gave us water to quench our thirst and we found
ourselves in the abbey, the church-like building that first confronted
us. Wooden platform areas for beds were erected on either side of
the aisle over the pews. The ceiling was white, high and vaulted, too
high to reach for the suspension of mosquito nets. Instead, a
framework was constructed round the platform beds so that those
who had mosquito nets could prevent the threat of malaria.

We walked in a daze trying to find a suitable space for our living
quarters. Despite the nuns' assurances that there was space the
impression was that the abbey church was full. The whole area of
platforms seemed to be totally used up, the occupants staring in a
combination of silent hostility and despair, though there were background noises that were mainly made up of the crying and whimpering of children. At the far end, on a raised area, there was a
smaller platform and in front of it a box like structure that was
covered by a sheet. Nadia said that the sheet covered what must have
been an altar. A long gothic stained glass window of a simple design
lighted the higher, smaller platform at the far end. It gave a special
light and made the far platform look different.

A woman stood in front of the altar waving and shouting to us,
pointing to a space on the platform behind the altar. It was Ludmilla,
but she didn't come to meet us because she seemed intent on
reserving a space for us while there were others coming to make a
claim.

Nadia dropped her load on the floor and rushed towards her

friend with open arms that closed in to reciprocate in a tearful embrace.

'Are you all right?' they asked each other. They looked for a moment into each other's eyes, tears and smiles combining to express joy and relief.

Vera and I stood by our baggage too weak to speak, too tired to cry.

Once again there was the search for our mattress. We sat on our space on the altar platform waiting for Nadia and Ludmilla to organise the bedding and mosquito netting.

'Mamma, I'm hungry,' said Vera when they came with the mattress.

'I feel weak,' I said, knowing that our mother knew how we felt, but unaware that the stating of the obvious was symptomatic of our condition.

'Just lie down on the bedding while we put up the net and rest until we get our food.'

We did as we were told and as I lay down I noticed that Nadia was busy hanging a kind of small picture, using a piece of string to tie it onto one of the uprights that supported the mosquito netting. When she was ready I could see that it was mostly made of a shiny grey metal cut out in the middle to portray what I guessed must have been the Virgin Mary holding baby Jesus.

'What's that?' I asked, wanting to know more about it.

'It's a special picture known as an icon, which I have had with me ever since I left China. You can see how the Virgin Mary loves Jesus by the loving way she holds him and by how she looks down at him. I think it's quite suitable to hang it here by the altar of this church.'

'But why is the picture surrounded by metal?' I asked, now recumbent.

'The pictures in Russian icons are usually surrounded either by gold or silver.'

She paused and then added, 'This one has a silver surround that can tarnish and look dark - especially if you have done something wrong.'

I stared at the icon wondering if I was going to cause it to darken but the hunger and weakness from both the long march and several months of malnutrition made me feel so helpless that all I could manage to do was to lie down. Vera was already asleep on our new altar platform and within moments I drifted into the same state.

We were woken by our mother's voice saying that it was time to eat.

'Look what the nuns have given us mixed with our rice. This will do us some good,' she said.

This time the rice in our coconut shell bowls was mixed with small green pieces of vegetable instead of small stones. Any initial doubts about the new appearance of our food were soon quashed by an overwhelming desire to eat. Our hunger was constantly a part of us and haunted us like a shadow with an endless need to be satisfied. The sight and smell of the rice activated that need like a stab. The result was that the first mouthful was heaven and swallowed far too quickly. The small pieces of vegetable not only slightly improved the nutritious value of our rations, but also made a considerable difference to the taste after months of just plain rice, which made the urge to gobble even more acute.

We wanted to eat it all at once.

Aware of the situation, Nadia reminded us to take time before swallowing, that we must savour every mouthful as if it were the last. Despite this, the last mouthful came all too quickly, my saliva working overtime in the futile anticipation of eating more and more. By now we were used to having just one small meal once a day, but because this tasted better than the polka-dot rice and since we had exhausted ourselves, it seemed as if we hadn't eaten for days.

I was desperate to eat more.

Vera reflected my thoughts by asking, 'Isn't there any more?'

Our mother's answer was predictable, 'No, darlings, I'm sorry but there isn't any more. But we are going to have a cup of tea!'

The tea came in the tin cans used for drinking. It was hot and tasted good and most of all it went some way towards satisfying our hunger.

Compared with the previous camp, the abbey offered much better accommodation. This wasn't just because we were no longer exposed to the elements, the air felt slightly cooler and fresher because the convent itself was at a higher altitude. The air inside the abbey building also felt better thanks to the high ceiling. Apart from that, it felt as if we were privileged to be domiciled on the altar platform: it was a step higher than the rest of the abbey, which made us feel at least that people could not look down on us. Whether they looked up to us because of our exalted position was a matter for speculation.

During our first two or three days at the abbey Vera and I were too weak to be active, most of our time being spent on the platform, either asleep or just lying down doing nothing. At night-time Nadia would tell us stories, either those she knew as a child or she might tell us about her childhood in Harbin in Manchuria, about how she learnt to swim in the River Sungari which was as warm as soup in the hot summers. She either whispered or spoke in a very low voice in order not to draw attention and disturb others.

Ludmilla told Nadia that Olga was also at the same camp and it wasn't long before all three were reunited. They began to meet quite often on our altar platform, not only to reminisce about Russia and things Russian but also to sing Russian songs.

Vera and I were enthralled to listen to them making use of the acoustics of the abbey as they sat together on our altar platform. They sang songs such as the song about the young man with a quiff in his hair or 'Black Eyes' or 'The Red Scarf'. Sometimes they became more melancholic and sung psalms and hymns of the Russian Orthodox Church, their voices echoing in the ecclesiastic splendour of the abbey church. Many of the Dutch women paused to listen to them, despite their Lutheran or Roman Catholic upbringing.

Thanks to the slightly better diet, better water and cooler air, as well as the tins of tea water we became stronger and I didn't have any relapses of amoebic dysentery. I began to get curious about my surroundings and started to explore the grounds of the convent that made up the concentration camp.

A long open cloister raised one step above the level of the ground, led out from one side of the abbey church. Were it not for the fineness of its smooth floor and its elegantly tiled roof the cloister could have been compared with the loading bay that housed our platform in the previous camp and one could speculate on its future utilisation by the Japanese. With this in mind it felt good to be safely established behind the abbey altar.

At the far end of the cloister, a flock of white birds stood motionless under the shade of the roof and as I approached them I was surprised that they didn't fly up. They had fine pure white feathers and long black bills, long graceful necks and long black legs. They came up to my hip in height. I was fascinated both by the birds and by the fact that I could come so close to them. Knowing that it was wrong to do so, I tried to catch hold of one, but when I attempted to do so the whole flock flapped up into a nearby tree, making it look like it was festooned with numerous white flags that hung limply on a calm day. While I continued to stare up into the tree, I thought that it seemed both curious and fitting that these graceful egrets should frequent such a holy place, but I was soon to discover the real reason for their presence.

On the other side of the cloister from the abbey there was a high wire-netting enclosure. Spurred on by a burning curiosity I approached it, aware that it might be something belonging to the Japanese and thereby out of bounds. Instead, I discovered that it was a kind of pen with several chickens scratching around in the bare ground. As I looked about me I noticed a nun digging with a spade some distance from the chicken pen and some of the egrets were walking quite close to her in the hope of finding titbits as she dug the soil. As I continued to watch both the nun and the chickens, some other children joined me to stare at the nun. When she stood up to straighten her back she saw us and beckoned to us. She stooped down to pick up an enormous white grub with a brown head. It was quite as large as her finger, but appeared limp and motionless as she showed it to us.

'What are you going to do with that?' Asked a boy, asking the question in Dutch.

'Come with me and you'll see,' she said.

We followed her to the chicken pen and she threw the grub over the fence onto the bare ground. Two chickens immediately rushed for it, the lucky winner swallowing the large grub at a stroke, closing its eyes as it squeezed the lump down into its gizzard.

'Now,' said the nun, 'the Japanese want us to keep these chickens to provide them with eggs, but if you can find grubs like the one I showed you, perhaps you might be rewarded.'

When I rushed back to the altar to tell my mother about our new prospect of getting a reward for digging grubs, she said that perhaps I wasn't strong enough to dig for grubs, but that she could try instead.

This she did. She and Olga talked to one of the nuns, offering their services as grub suppliers for the chickens, asking for no payment but they would be grateful if an egg or two came their way without the nuns getting into trouble with the Japanese. They worked so hard that they not only improved the lot of the chickens, but in the process also helped the nuns to prepare more ground for growing vegetables.

A few days later one of the nuns quietly produced a cold hard-boiled egg from the depths of her habit. 'For your children,' she whispered to Nadia.

This resulted in our next rice meal being mixed with small pieces of egg. For obvious reasons the nuns were actually quite reluctant to openly show that they had access to chicken eggs. Officially, as far as the internees were concerned, any eggs that were not handed over to the Japanese were strictly for frail children in need. Officially, as far as the Japanese were concerned, no eggs were available for either nuns or internees, whatever their medical condition.

With or without eggs, our health improved at the nunnery. As the weeks went by I felt stronger and was able to explore the grounds of the camp a little more extensively. It appeared that all the buildings of the convent were fully occupied by the internees, the nuns themselves having been forced by the Japanese to restrict their living quarters.

They had also organised a kind of small hospital for children who were seriously ill. Most of these were babies and very young children up to Vera's age. For some reason unknown to me, Nadia, Vera and I visited this miniature hospital crowded with metal-railed cots to see a two-year-old boy who had died. I was struck by the sight of a little dark-haired boy lying motionless on his back with his blue eyes open, glazed by death. It was my first sight of a dead person and I found it hard to understand that anyone could die with his eyes open. The mother stood by, her head bowed in silent sorrow to the continuous sound of crying small children. Afterwards, I asked Nadia whether people normally die with their eyes open.

'Sometimes they do,' she said. 'Maybe his mother wanted to say goodbye to him while he had his eyes open. She would then shut them before burying him.'

Even at the age of five, I was still very much a solitary individual, preferring either my own company or that of my mother. However, there were plenty of opportunities to meet other children, especially as Nadia sent us out for an hour or so in the morning sun to have our daily ration of vitamin D. For this purpose, both Vera and I were bare-backed and Nadia kept an eye on Vera while I was left to wander on my own. After that we were to wear a shirt to prevent sunburn. Though there were no waringi trees, or at least no large ones, the grounds of the convent were well interspersed with trees of various types and sizes. When I noticed flocks of small green birds flying round the tops of palm trees I longed to be able to take a closer look at them. Knowing that was impossible, I began to take an interest in the large grasshoppers that hopped and flew about in the straw-coloured vegetation, many of them being so well camouflaged that I was startled by their sudden explosion of activity. I saw large yellow butterflies and curious insects that Nadia told me were praying mantises. Looking at the wildlife was a fascinating pastime that did not demand much energy, but it wasn't long before the hot sun made it both unpleasant and tiring to be out and I had to return to rest in the relative coolness of the abbey.

One day I saw a boy of about twelve carrying a small cage similar to the ones I remembered the bird vendor had back in Semarang. At a distance the small captive that he was carrying looked similar to the green birds around the palm trees. The boy had already assembled a small crowd of children who wanted to take a closer look at it, at the same time asking him questions about what kind of bird it was and where and how he caught it. When he pointed up at the palm trees, I realised that it must have been one of those mysterious small green birds. How he caught it and what he fed it on, I never found out, but when I came close to it to see its fine khaki-green plumage and its small beady dark eyes, I wished that it could be free again with its friends among the palm trees. Presumably he made the cage himself, which made it harder to tell the boy to set it free, as I could only wish him to do.

47

The older boys in the camp often spent their time finding pieces of wood to make models and sculptures and the creations of those who might be fourteen or fifteen were to my eyes amazingly lifelike. One boy had made a model biplane that looked so realistic and impressive that I was determined to try to emulate his skill. It was complete with a rotating propeller and fine wooden struts connecting the two wings. It reminded me of the time Jan took us to an air display where we could actually touch one of these planes when they were lined up on display. I remembered feeling the soft texture of the tail-plane belonging to an orange biplane and being impressed by their life-size appearance when I had only seen them previously looking like toys in the sky.

The fact that the model plane must have had a wingspan of about a foot made the object even more wonderful, especially when one thought about the practicalities of timber and glue. Where he acquired the wood was a mystery, but the source of glue could be ascertained by watching boys making holes in a certain tree to use the resin that oozed out. The first problem of finding a piece of wood was solved by Nadia who managed to come by a four-or five-inch piece of light-coloured wood and she let me use one of the C.K. silver knives to allow me to express my skills as a wood carver. Unfortunately, not only was the knife blunt, but I felt distinctly inadequate both in strength and skill to produce the model spitfire that I had in mind. However, with more help from Nadia than I would admit and a considerable amount of perseverance, I succeeded in shaping something that might look like a fuselage with a nose and a suggestion of a fin.

Our search for suitable wood for the wings and tail-plane was not successful, however, for by that time any odd pieces of wood, including dead branches of trees, were snapped up to be used by the boys of the camp for their wood-carving activities. We could not help being astounded at some of the work that the boy-carvers produced. Not only did the camp abound with model planes of various types and sizes, but we also saw ships, yachts, battleships and perhaps most suitable to our camp location, numerous crucifixes. Some of them were so beautifully executed in detail with Christ hanging on the cross that I wished that I could find a piece of wood to make one.

Some time after all the available wood seemed to have been used up I saw one boy aged about eight busily carving a round shape. When I asked him what he was doing, he replied that he was carving a fort out of stone. He showed me a round stone about four inches in diameter, into which he was carving a series of fine steps leading onto small walkways and round entrances, the whole looking like a miniature sand castle. The stone he was carving was light grey, fine, quite soft and must have been a kind of limestone or chalk, lumps of which were quite easy to find about the convent. That boy was one of the pioneers to launch a flurry of stone-carving pursuits, keeping many children of both sexes occupied.

It wasn't long before I found a suitable stone that Nadia allowed me to carve with one of the C.K. knives. As the tip of the knife was rounded my steps were unavoidably curved, but to me that didn't matter because my main aim was to be able to execute the step-like carvings in the soft stone. That achievement in itself made me feel almost equal in status to the eight-year-old and other children who engaged themselves in stone carving.

Nadia must have realised that as I was capable of using a knife, blunt as it may have been: at the age of five I was also old enough to begin to learn how to read and write. The nuns had enough to do in tending to our physical needs and to the sick, without having time and energy to see to it that the children received some kind of schooling. Some parents began to organise small classes for the older children, but as five-year-olds had the lowest priority in this respect, Nadia began to teach me the alphabet and numbers by scratching out their shapes on the bare, dry soil.

It wasn't long before I was getting the knack of drawing out the shape of an 'S', then the more advanced 'B' and the figure eight at the same time as my mother taught me what they meant.

But the beginnings of my schooling came to an abrupt end when we were told by the abbess that we had to pack our bags again.

5. Ambarava No. 10

Our ten-month stay at the convent was a blessing. Though the diet was almost totally inadequate, it was better than the camp near Semarang and thanks to the nuns who helped to improve the general living conditions, the death rate was not as high as it might have been. This meant that many women and children had enough strength to cope with yet another move.

A row of army lorries was parked in front of the abbey and women began to load our mattresses onto them, but were instructed to load them in such a way as to allow space for both the mattresses and their owners. We were to be driven to our next destination and we didn't have to carry our belongings on a long hot walk! Perhaps it was because the Japanese regarded the nuns as having a little higher status than the rest of us that they could use a little persuasion. Whatever the reason, at least the journey to wherever we were bound for was to be easier, however bad the next camp may be.

The journey proved to be relatively short and easy, not only because we didn't have to walk, but also because the trip itself lasted not more than about half an hour. It was half an hour of jolting about amongst mattresses and people, with very little else to see.

We arrived at an entrance to a large compound surrounded by a high, white ten-foot wall. The lorries drove in through an opening in the wall that was guarded by two solid wooden gates with a Japanese soldier posted on each side.

As our lorry came through the entrance, groups of apathetic women and children stared up at us, wondering perhaps about how our arrival would affect their situations. We drove on through a wide yard bounded on the right by a long iron railing set on a low wall behind which there were several compounds, each lined on three sides by numerous doors. On the left the yard was flanked by a row of tall trees behind which I could make out a large building with many small windows. We had certainly not arrived at a convent, nor did it appear to have been a factory. In fact the only impression that

50

made sense was that of a prison and it soon became apparent that our new concentration camp was a jail built by the Dutch. Hardened native criminals were the previous occupants.

The lorry drew to a halt at the gate of the furthest compound or block and we were motioned by a Japanese soldier to get off, the children being helped down by the women.

We found ourselves standing in the yard of the furthest of four compounds, or blocks as they were known, ours being block D. A woman directed us to a half-open door situated in the middle of the row of doors to the left of the gate. As we approached it, we could see that the door was the entrance to the tiniest of rooms, barely wider than the door itself. Normally it could be described as a cell, but because it was divided horizontally by a platform constructed to hold a mattress about three feet above its floor, the whole effect was to make it look like a large cupboard. In the bottom half of the 'cupboard', under the platform, there was enough space for another occupant. While we were inspecting our cell I noticed a pair of bare feet under our platform, which also caught Vera's attention.

'Mamma, there's someone here,' said Vera.

'I know, you mustn't disturb her.'

To me, it felt strange to have to share our cell with just one hitherto unknown person, a different feeling from having to be on a large platform shared with a host of other people as in our previous camps. Our little private platform was to be both our bed and our home, supporting not only our mattress but also all our belongings.

As no sound came from the owner of the motionless feet underneath us, Nadia put her finger vertically across her mouth to indicate that we must not disturb our neighbour by making a noise.

A small iron grid covering a ventilation hole was situated high up on the wall opposite the door, which meant that mosquitoes had free access to the cell. Perhaps the rusty nails that stuck out of the wall higher up had previously served as attachments for a mosquito net or to hang up decorations or photographs but Nadia used them to hang up our net. She also hung up the icon on a lower nail near the door.

A raised concrete walkway, two steps high, ran round the three sides of the block in front of the cells. The tiled roof of the cells sloped inwards and extended over the walkway to provide shelter and shade. While Nadia was making our cell into some kind of a home Vera and I sat quietly on the edge of the concrete double step in the comparative coolness of the shade. In the centre of the yard I noticed a circular stone wall about three feet high and a diameter of perhaps eight feet. Despite the usual feeling of weakness and lassitude in the heat of the day, my curiosity got the better of me and made me investigate the wall. When I reached it, I could just about see over the top, to discover a wooden cover set in to conceal whatever the round wall surrounded. But as I neither dared nor felt I had the strength to lift the cover I had to return to the step determined to satisfy my curiosity as soon as the opportunity presented itself.

A small grey-haired woman, considerably older than most of the others, stood by the gate of our block and shouted: 'All new arrivals must collect their identity numbers. I have them here.'

Nadia emerged from our cell and walked towards the small group that had already assembled around the grey-haired woman.

We sat on the step outside our cell watching the women being handed small items, the nature of which we could not discern. It was a pity that it wasn't something more important, like food, or something to drink, I thought. There was a tap a couple of doors away, a single pipe sticking out of the step on the edge of the walkway, but I knew by now that it could be dangerous to drink water directly from the tap.

As we watched from our steps, we sank back into our usual anaesthetised gloom, only to be jolted by the voice of our mother who spoke with a sense of urgency.

'Now listen, our block representative,' she said, meaning the grey-haired woman, 'has given us something here that you must wear every day. If the Japanese catch you without this on you, you will be beaten.'

She showed us a small rectangular token made of a white piece of cloth sewn round a strip of cardboard with a small safety pin attached to the back. Neatly written on it in indelible pencil was a combination of numbers that I could already read. Mine showed number 2300 and Vera's 2301. Nadia was already wearing hers on her blouse and while she proceeded to pin Vera's onto her dress I could see that 2299 was written on it. She pinned mine onto the breast pocket of my short-sleeved shirt.

'Don't forget to have these on every day: you must remind me if I forget,' she added. 'Now I think it's time for a rest in our new cell.'

Nadia helped us onto our platform, now lined by our mattress and sheet, while our mystery cellmate still lay silent underneath us.

We slept through the heat of the day.

I woke to the sound of voices and sat up to see my mother talking to a scrawny, mousy-looking girl who might have been in her late teens. I caught only a smattering of the short conversation but enough to understand that the mousy girl was our cellmate. She was the owner of the motionless pair of feet that greeted our arrival at our cell.

It was late in the afternoon and the sound and sight of the girl was soon overshadowed by signals coming from within me. I felt the familiar empty feeling that made my whole being want to eat: it didn't matter what, just to eat. It was a strange combination of the drive of hunger coupled with the lethargy of weakness. All it could achieve was to draw my mother's attention.

'Mamma, hungry.'

'I feel weak,' said Vera, now awake, using the Russian word 'slabinka' that seemed to express weakness in precisely the right ono-matopoeic way. 'Can't we have something to eat?'

The mousy girl was nowhere to be seen, which could mean that she had disappeared to fetch her food. A short time later Nadia had gathered from our representative that as we were new arrivals we could have a bowl of rice which we had missed when we arrived.

It was no surprise to see that our well-worn coconut shell bowls were half - filled with white boiled rice. It was only rice, no stones, no vegetables, no additions of any kind, except that there were traces of what appeared to be small insects and many of the grains were not whole, as if they were partly eaten. Once again we had to discipline ourselves to eat slowly, so that every morsel in our bowls counted. Nadia was better at eating slowly than we were, so that when Vera and I finished we looked covetously at her while she finished her last morsels.

'Don't look at me like that,' she said. 'You know that if I give you my share, I will die of starvation and you will soon have no mother and then you would have no one to look after you, which means that you will also die. Now, if you wait a little, you will have some tea.'

At least our new camp had a kitchen that provided with us water that had been boiled and served in the form of a weak tea. Each of us had our own tin that we took with us from the convent. The tea and the rice were not much, but together they staved off the worst pangs of hunger.

Nightfall came as suddenly as the end of our meal. As mosquitoes made it too risky to be out after dark we had to wash ourselves under the outside tap and make ourselves ready for bed before the mosquitoes began to make their presence felt. Nadia helped us onto the platform and we waited under the kelamboo for her to get herself ready.

We spent the first night at Ambarava No. 10 without our mousy cellmate. Nor did she return to take her place under our platform: in fact we never saw her again. When we discussed her absence Nadia presumed that rather than put up with a woman and two small children above her head, she had a friend to go to somewhere among the 5,000 internees of our camp. Wherever she might have vanished, the outcome was that we had our cell to ourselves, and when we later realised this, her space under our platform served as our luggage compartment.

In the morning our grey-haired block representative informed us that we were actually to have breakfast! When it came in a large metal bucket from the kitchen, women and children were already lining up with their coconut bowls waiting to have their share ladled out. A look at the activity around the bucket ahead of us soon revealed a colourless semi-transparent glutinous mass being transferred to each waiting bowl. On the receipt of my portion, a closer look had the momentary effect of dispelling the usual pangs of hunger. It was neither solid nor liquid, neither jelly nor glue and it was colourless. It was also piping hot.

Noticing how Vera and I just stared at our breakfast, spoons hovering indecisively at the edge of our bowls, Nadia said, 'Eat it. It's called tapioca blubber. It's better than nothing and it will give you some energy.'

I tried a little of the hot glue on the tip of my tongue. It had no taste. At least plain boiled rice tasted of rice, but this was . . . completely tasteless. It may have been a source of energy, but its chief purpose as far as I was concerned was to mitigate the worst of the hunger. It was much easier to eat tapioca blubber slowly and I did not scrape the bowl as thoroughly as when we had rice.

The blubber diminished our hunger but made us thirsty.

'Why can't we have some tea? I'm thirsty,' I said.

'You can have water from the tap' I found out that it's quite all right to drink because the water is treated here. The Dutch had made the water drinkable for the prisoners when it was a jail.

Vera and I took our drinking tins to be filled with water and Nadia washed our bowls and laid them out in the sun to be both dried and sterilised. She was about to tell me to take my shirt off to soak up a little vitamin D-producing morning sun, when our block leader shouted that we must all stand out in rows outside our block to be inspected by the Japanese.

'Don't forget your identity numbers,' she added.

Soon the whole block of about a hundred women and children were standing in about four rows in front of the block gates. As we stood, I noticed that there were as many people standing in front of the next block down and about as many in front of the block beyond and the block beyond that.

We waited in the heat of the morning. Finally two Japanese soldiers came to us. I looked down once again to make sure that my number was securely fastened to my shirt then gazed at the soldiers as they arrived. One shouted 'kyotsu', meaning 'attention', while the other proceeded to walk round our lines, presumably to see that we had worn our numbers. Our grey-haired block leader bowed and said something loudly in Japanese to the leader of the two, which Nadia found out later meant something like 'all present and correct'.

I stood stiff with fear in case the inspecting soldier found something wrong and dared not look at him. Instead, I concentrated my gaze on the other Japanese, the one that seemed to be higher ranking. I looked at his peaked cap and expressionless, small dark eyes. The inspection appeared to proceed without incident, but our block leader shouted to us to remain standing to attention.

Some minutes later the reason for the drawn-out stand to attention became apparent. Further down the main yard, near to the main gate, we could see women carrying long wooden boxes that served as coffins. Several women bore each coffin about waist high on bamboo poles. Though I knew that deaths were a daily occurrence in the other camps we were not made to stand and watch a procession of coffins before. This was a new experience and as we stood there in the morning sun I wondered whether they were children or women and why they died. Was it disease? Did the Japanese beat them to death? Or did they starve to death? Did they die of old age? Did they suffer a lot before they died? I wanted to ask my mother these questions but I knew it was the wrong time to do so.

Six or seven coffins passed through the main entrance, which we were later told was fewer than usual. We had to stand still until the coffins and women on burial duty disappeared, which took rather a long time and made the wait uncomfortable in the growing heat. Vera began to jerk about and finally expressed her need to use the potty.

'Shh', said Nadia, 'it will soon be over. Don't make a noise or the Japanese will be angry.'

Strangely enough I felt the same need as Vera, and was about to say so when our representative said that we could return to our block.

'The Japanese care more about the dead than the living,' said Nadia to another woman as we returned to our cells. She nodded silently in agreement.

Vera used the potty first and after I emptied my bladder, Nadia took it nearly full to be emptied in the latrines, which were somewhere near block A.

'I need to go as well,' said Nadia. 'I think it must be the tapioca blubber: it makes you thirsty as well as want to pee.'

She went off to the latrines with the potty, having slipped on her wooden flip-flops in order to avoid her feet being contaminated by the latrine floor. Otherwise we all walked on bare feet.

The sun burned in the mid-morning sky. The lower step of our walkway was already too hot for our fingers to touch, but not too hot for the callused soles of our feet. Nadia said that it would be possible to fry an egg on it. If only we had an egg! It was unwise to take off my shirt, but Nadia encouraged me to be outside for a time while she had to report to our block leader. Perhaps I could find some friends to play with, she suggested, but I decided to do a little exploring and to take stock of our surroundings.

I walked past the other blocks towards the main gate as close as I dared, which meant that my fear of the Japanese allowed me to approach to no less than about twenty yards from the guards posted by the gates. To me, a rather timid five-year-old, venturing any closer was asking for trouble. This caused me to have a rather vague perception of the geography of the area around the main gate, and it took some days and a little explanation from Nadia before I could understand how the camp was organised.

Nadia gathered that we were in Banjungbiru Jail, renamed by the Japanese as Ambarava No. 10, which implied that there were at least ten concentration camps round the small town of Ambarava, which was about forty miles from Semarang. It was difficult for us to know how far we actually were from the town itself, but we were at a lower altitude than the convent. That meant that once again the climate would be hotter and more humid than it was at the nunnery, which also meant that it would be harder for people weak from malnutrition and disease to survive.

Inside the wall on the right-hand side of the main entrance gates there was a building that was both a guardhouse and the Japanese living quarters, as well as the nerve centre for the administration of the camp. An adjacent building behind housed the camp kitchen and I guessed that somewhere between the kitchen and block A was where the latrines were located, but I never found out exactly, as I always used the potty that Nadia emptied when necessary.

The wide yard extended along the whole length of the camp enclosure. Beyond the kitchen and extending along the length of most of the wall on the right of the yard was a row of four inner compounds or blocks, each bounded on the yard side by railings supported by a low wall. Ours was block D, the furthest block from the main gate. Though it felt like an inner prison within the main prison compound, there was free access from the four blocks to the main yard and the rest of the camp, as the iron gates to each were not locked.

On the other side of the main yard, opposite the four blocks there was a row of tall trees which partly shaded a large three-storey building that housed hundreds of cells of similar dimensions to ours. Presumably this was the main prison building before the Japanese occupation while the four blocks contained prisoners of another kind when Banjungbiru was under Dutch colonial administration.

I returned to find that Nadia was not at our cell. Vera said that we were to wait until she came back, which should be quite soon. As she spoke, her blonde hair, which was gathered on the top of her head and tied with a small ribbon, waved a little like the fronds of a short little palm tree on a desert island. We sat dutifully on the step outside our cell and waited for her return.

I walked over to the round wall in the middle of our yard and succeeded in lifting up the wooden top a little, but I was neither strong nor tall enough to lift it high and see what was underneath. As I lowered the cover I heard something that sounded like a small stone dropping into water. There must have been water somewhere inside that round wall enclosure.

The wait was long and hot in the heat of midday despite the shade of the cell compound roof overhang. At last we saw our mother coming back together with some other women. They walked slowly, almost shuffling their way with their backs hunched and heads down. Their bodies were wet with sweat.

'I'm very tired,' said Nadia. 'I'm going to have a little lie-down, in our cell and I'll tell you what happened afterwards.'

She barely had the energy to heave herself up onto to the platform and when she was up it was all I could do to lift Vera in order that she could be pulled up. I could nearly climb up myself but Nadia needed to give me a final pull up onto the platform.

She lay sighing on our bed, beads of sweat from both the heat and exhaustion formed small wet lines on her pale forehead. Vera and I sat facing each other, each back leaning on the facing wall.

'Are you ill, Mamma?' asked Vera.

'No, I'm just very tired.'

'What happened?' I asked, knowing that she was going to tell us when she had rested but having no patience to wait.

'Well,' she said, drawing a deep breath, 'several women and I were called to unload sacks of rice from a lorry to the kitchen. The sacks were large and very heavy and when two of us started to get hold of each end of a sack a Japanese guard got very angry and started shouting. He pointed at a sack and raised a single finger to show that only one woman was to lift one sack. As I said, the sacks were very large and heavy, but when one woman tried to lift a sack on her own, she got it on her back and then collapsed on to the ground. So I did the same, trying to lift the sack without any success at all, so that I pretended to collapse to show the Japanese that we could not lift the sacks on our own. All the ten women did the same thing, all sitting or lying on the ground muttering that it was impossible. The Japanese in charge, realising that the situation was hopeless, then raised two fingers signifying that two were allowed to carry the sacks. Even though two of us were allowed to carry each sack they still felt very heavy and there were many sacks, which is why I'm so tired and have an aching back.'

With that she closed her eyes, which meant that we might as well follow suit and sleep.

Not long after, we were woken by the now familiar voice of our block representative saying that it was time to eat. From then on we were to have our rice in the middle of the day and our tin of tea was to be served at about an hour before dark. This meant that we had to be content with tap water after our midday rice.

Our bedclothes were simple, consisting of a singlet and underpants and since we had worn them for over a year, they were beginning to be both tatty and tight. But it was an indication that somehow Vera and I must have managed to grow a little despite the starvation. After a year of internment we still had a good reserve of soap, having several bars in stock but since we didn't know how long they had to last, we rationed ourselves carefully and Nadia washed Vera in order to minimise the waste.

My pre-internment routine of saying my prayers before being tucked up for the night had now changed to a bedtime routine involving the three of us. It was a mutual early bedtime forced by the conditions of internment. But the physical restriction of life on a platform in a cell resulted in a special intimacy between a mother and her two small children. It was the best time of the day.

Nadia told us about her childhood in China. She told us how her family was forced to move to Harbin in Manchuria together with many other Russians that fled from the Russian Revolution. She told us about her schooldays, about naughty children and their pranks, as well as about the goody-two-shoes and how they sucked up to the teacher. She told us about her home, her parents, our grandparents that we never met and about and their intelligent fox terrier called Lulka. Sometimes she told us the Russian versions of 'Little Red Riding Hood', or the 'Three Little Pigs' or stories from Hans Andersen, like the starving matchgirl or the 'Ugly Duckling'. She also told us stories from the Bible and how Jesus walked on the water and performed other miracles. I often asked for a favourite to be told and re-told many times as the evenings passed, 'Ferdinand the Bull' still featuring as one of the leading stories. Vera was not ignored for even at the age of two she had her say in the choice of story. As she didn't take any books to camp, all that Nadia had to tell us came directly from her, which had the advantage of coming out with certain degrees of variation and which allowed interruptions for questions. Our bedtime was the nearest thing to being at school and our mother was the best teacher we knew.

She sometimes ended storytime in a religious mood with a little word of prayer while we looked up at the icon. Vera was usually asleep by that time.

One morning, just as Nadia had given us our portions of blubber, we were startled by the piercing scream of a child. A little girl of about four was writhing in agony on the ground in obvious pain. Two coconut shell portions of blubber were spattered both on her and on the ground. A large blonde fleshy woman called Marijka ran towards the little girl, who must have been her daughter and who was clearly badly hurt. She picked her up still screaming and started walking back to her cell on the side opposite to us.

'You lazy cow,' shouted someone, 'get your blubber yourself instead of getting your children to do it for you!

'Take her to the hospital! She seems to be badly scalded!' said my mother.

The building that served as the camp hospital was small, built of brick, and was situated across the yard directly opposite our block. Marijka disappeared in the direction of the camp hospital with her whimpering daughter.

We heard afterwards that she was badly scalded on the chest, stomach and one arm and Nadia explained that she would not be able join the play-group for some time until she had recovered. Her recovery would be retarded both by the lack of medical facilities and poor resistance to bacteria. Her burns would have to be carefully tended every day and she wondered whether Marijka was able to cope with it. Marijka was shaken enough by the incident not to send her younger daughter to fetch the blubber breakfast, but not enough to alter her slovenly ways.

After our blubber breakfast, the blubber scalding accident and the inspection with the wait for the passage of the dead, our representative assembled all the women in the block. They were being organised to either volunteer for, or delegated to, different duties. Nadia told us after the meeting more or less what it was all about. Those women were on burial and coffin-bearing duty had just that job, which varied from day to day according to the number of deaths in the camp. Then there was the latrine cleaning duty, which though not the heaviest, was rather unpleasant and dirty. Another was to dig defence bunkers outside the camp. But the best job was to work in the kitchens, which although it was hard work lifting heavy cauldrons and keeping the fires going, gave the privilege of access to nutritious titbits.

'I'm sorry I didn't get the kitchen duty,' said Nadia. 'I'm to help to dig and build bunkers outside the camp.'

'What shall we do while you're away?' I wondered.

'Both you and Vera are to be with other children at a play centre organised by the block. You will have other children to play with.'

I was not at all excited by the idea, as I had not noticed any other children of about my age in the block, but Vera seemed to accept it better than I did.

A short red-faced woman about the same age as Nadia approached us, followed by a fair-haired boy who was a little younger than I was.

'Ah, this is Myrna and her son Rudi,' Nadia said in Dutch. 'Myrna and I will join those working outside the camp, while you can play with Rudi at the playgroup, Ivan.'

Myrna greeted us in a Dutch that did not sound as if she were Dutch, her sunburned rather wrinkled face creasing up into a broad, kindly smile. Her round head was topped by medium-length, medium-blonde hair vaguely parted in the middle to reveal a high wrinkled forehead above two widely separated small round blue eyes. She was short and stocky, even shorter than my mother. I compared the two women while they were talking. While my mother's hair was about the same colour, it was long and plaited, the thick plait being wound up into a bun at the back of her head, rather like that of Sukarni. Myrna was not as beautiful as Nadia but she seemed a very amiable and warm kind of person. Nadia told us later that Myrna was in fact a Hungarian woman married to a Dutchman.

We all walked together towards the gate where our representative was waiting to direct the women to their respective work sites. We children were told to stay behind within the confines of the yard, where we would be supervised by one of the women not on duty.

I was reminded of being left at the play school two years previously in Semarang, but this time there were no toys or any amusements. An elderly woman, who was presumably unfit for strenuous physical duties, was left in charge of us and set about minding the very young while children of my age and above were more or less left to ourselves, provided we stayed within the confines of our block. Vera seemed to be in her element and soon made friends with another two-year-old called Sergei. I watched her taking complete charge of him, getting him to do exactly as she said without Sergei making the slightest protest, the little palm tree on her head shaking as if to enforce her commands. She was completely absorbed in her new toy boy and he seemed to adore his newly found queen. His mother was also called Vera and as chance would have it, also Russian, which allowed communication through the medium of the language that their mothers had in common.

Vera had a strange habit of peering closely at whatever captured her interest, whether it was Sergei or the steps on which they played. It soon became apparent that my little sister was short-sighted - even at the age of two and a half. Nadia speculated that her myopia might have been inherited from Jan's side of the family but had been exacerbated by the effects of the concentration camp diet.

Sergei had a brother called Otto who was a year or two older than me but we seemed to have very little in common, apart from the language. He lived in his world and I in mine.

The other children were Dutch, except for a boy and his twin sister who, despite their dark hair, were Swedish. Like so many non-Dutch nationals the Japanese had interned them because they happened to have a Dutch father. It wasn't as if they had inherited their dark brown hair from their father: they were small copies of their tall dark-haired Swedish mother, both in colour and build. They spoke a strange language amongst themselves that I took to be Swedish and they seemed to prefer their own company and hardly spoke to anyone else, but we happened to notice them in particular because they were in the cell next to us.

It was a playgroup that hardly deserved the name, not only because there was nothing to keep children occupied, but also because over a year of malnutrition and disease had incapacitated the childish drive to play. Only Vera and Sergei seemed to keep each other occupied as they pulled each other about on the steps. As there was no paper to draw on or practise writing the alphabet, Rudi and I tried to scratch out outlines in the dusty soil, but we soon lost interest as there was no one to give us inspiration to develop our skills. Apart from that, it soon became too hot to be out in the sun that beat down on the exposed patches of soil and we were really both too weak to achieve much else.

A boy of about six or seven appeared on his own by the gate. He did nothing but stand on a pair of matchstick legs, his equally thin arms hanging phlegmatically down from his narrow shoulders. It was not unusual to see an emaciated child, for we were all thin in various ways. The remarkable thing about him was that his head was enormous. His jaws, mouth and nose were normal sized, but higher up his head became disproportionally wide, separating his small eyes to bulge out into a huge melon-sized skull topped by thin wisps of hair. I couldn't help staring at him, though I knew that it was unkind to do so. Perhaps it was the collective stares of some of the children that soon caused him to walk into the shade of his cell across the yard.

At about midday the women returned worn out after their duties. Whatever activity there was in the playgroup broke up as the children went to meet their mothers and follow them to their respective cells. Nadia told us that it was hard work digging trenches and moving stones for the Japanese and that she felt tired, needed a wash and was hungry. I said that there was nothing much to do at the playgroup, while Vera said that she played with Sergei. When I wondered how it was that a boy could have such a huge head, Nadia said that she had seen the boy and both he and his sister had an illness caused by fluid round the brain not being able to escape. She said that they had it from birth, the affliction caused the head to swell up and that there was nothing that could be done to help them, even if they had access to a normal hospital.

Nadia went to the tap to freshen herself up after Myrna had used it and then slumped onto the platform to recover from the exertions of the morning. Vera, who was also tired after her exertions with Sergei, whined to be pulled up to join her while I chose to sit on the steps to idle my time away as I was neither too tired nor had the drive to do anything.

After a few minutes I became aware of a scraping sound on the gravel outside our block. The sound increased in volume, causing me to look up to see someone running with a long bamboo pole. He was holding one end with both hands as he ran while allowing the other end to scrape on the gravel at the same time as he was making sounds like an agitated chimpanzee. He was big, about the size of a ten-year-old but his head was small and his fair hair close-cropped. His red-ringed blue eyes were strange and expressionless as he ran and roared and howled, giving me the impression that we had a dangerous monster in the camp. I was determined to bolt into our cell if he or it came into our block. An equally strange part of his appearance was that he was dressed in a pair bright pink shorts, held up by two bright pink straps crossed at the back over a shortsleeved white shirt. Several other children were watching the spectacle as the pink ogre turned outside our gate and roared his way back down to the other blocks with his bamboo pole dragging behind him. I remained seated on the steps waiting for the return of the apparition, but all was quiet in the heat of the afternoon sun and I gradually returned to my state of lethargy.

After a short rest it was time for rice and my mother was once again badgered by questions, this time about the person in pink. From her chatting with the other women when out on duty, she gathered that the pink apparition was in fact a girl, her short-cropped hair making her look like a boy and that she was born with a genetic defect known at the time as mongolism. She said that she belonged to block C and that despite her behaviour, she was completely harmless and that in actual fact such people were very loving, especially to their family. Once again my mother was an unending source of information and comfort but notwithstanding that, her explanation did little to reassure me and I dreaded the thought of the mongolistic girl entering our block.

After our rice and water we had our siesta. We found ourselves getting accustomed to a kind of routine consisting of blubber-breakfast with water, followed by the daily inspection and the stand to attention in respect for a passage of the coffins. We then had to relieve our bursting bladders and idled our time away in the block to wait for the return of a tired mother at midday, rice and water for lunch, rest and a tin of tea, followed by bed at dusk. As time passed I accepted that strang-looking individuals were neither special nor to be dreaded. The only real cause of the fear was the Japanese, especially the fear of being beaten for forgetting to have my identity number pinned on my shirt.

The older children in our block were kept occupied by helping the women in their duties, the type of task depending on age and physical condition. Usually children over the age of nine were considered possible assistants if they were physically fit enough. Among these was a Dutch boy of about fourteen who was as tall as an adult and had the voice of a man. He and his eleven-year-old brother were always cheerful and smiling and looked like fair-haired Wagnerian heroes as they went off with the women to help them with their duties. A couple of months later the older of the brothers had to take his leave of our block because he had turned fifteen and had to be moved to a men's camp. His younger brother, who was called Kees, no longer had his cheerful smile and confident swagger when he went on duty with the women. As his mother had already died he was now alone in his cell and though he was clearly able to look after himself, I felt deeply sorry for him.

Each day seemed the same as the next, which would have been extremely boring if we were properly nourished and active. However, as we were too weak to do much anyway, time seemed to pass in a haze of lassitude with midday rice and siesta as the highlights. But life was not entirely uneventful.

One morning, after inspection, our representative asked for a volunteer to give blood to a child who was so ill that he would soon die if he did not have a blood transfusion. Her appeal for a blood donor was met by a silent lack of response, which was eventually broken by Nadia saying that she knew what her blood group was and would volunteer. This meant that instead of going on duty she would spend the morning at the camp medical centre to give blood.

We stayed behind as we would on a normal day, Vera with her toy boy Sergei and I with Rudi. When our mother came back, which wasn't long before midday, she had a broad smile on her face.

'How did you get on?' asked our representative.

'Oh it was no bother giving blood. The problem was that it was very risky for the child as there was no way of knowing what his blood group was but as I have a common blood group, the chance was worth taking. Fortunately, when I left the child did not appear to react against my blood, so there is hope. But the best thing was that I got a bowl of warm rice with sugar, not to mention a rest and a sweet cup of tea!'

It seemed that the camp hospital had a little reserve of energy-giving sugar for medicinal purposes. The news that sweet tea and rice with sugar were the rewards given to blood donors spread like wildfire and it wasn't long before people were queuing to give blood. Unfortunately Nadia's blood went to no avail: the child died a few days later.

Apart from Sergei, Vera had acquired an additional companion in the form of a beautifully made cloth doll, which she called Tasha. Tasha was the work of a woman who had a soft spot for Vera. She came up to her one morning after blubber and said that she would like her to have something that she thought she might like. In the next moment she produced a cloth doll with finely embroidered facial features and beautifully stitched limbs to form a figure that represented a miniature little girl of Vera's age. It was the first doll that Vera accepted and loved.

6. Bread

Even the Japanese allowed a day of rest, which meant that Sundays were the exception to the routine of daily work and fatigue. Since the women were able to organise and carry out their duties more effectively, all except those on kitchen and funeral duty were allowed to have Sundays free. This allowed us to socialise with those that were not in our own block, and for Nadia it meant the opportunity to meet her Russian friends. It was a chance to catch up with the latest camp news and gossip and to keep posted on any acquaintance that might have passed away.

She knew that both her friends Ludmilla and Olga were interned at Ambarava No. 10 and that their cells were located in the large building behind the trees on the other side of the main yard. Nadia took us up a dark staircase to Ludmilla's cell that she shared with Olga Nederloff. Once in the cell, Ludmilla showed us a large collection of buttons of all sizes and colours that she had for some reason taken with her to camp. Though the colours and variety of the buttons impressed me, it was Vera who was completely fascinated by them. She was so absorbed by their shapes and different colours that Ludmilla said that she could remain in the cell and play with them while we went off for a walk in the main yard. As I walked along with the three women while they talked, I pretended not to take notice of what they were saying.

But Ludmilla became increasingly irritated by my presence and finally said, 'Ivan, you're a nice looking boy, but did you know that you'd look even nicer if you stood over there?'

Eager to look even nicer, I ran to where she pointed, a few yards ahead.

'Here?' I asked.

'Yes, you look very nice there but you would look even more handsome over there,' said Ludmilla pointing some twenty yards ahead.

'Here?' I shouted.

'Now you look fantastic!' She shouted back.

The three women burst into laughter and it took a while for me to realise what Ludmilla was up to: I then knew that my place was some distance away from the women when they wanted to chat among themselves.

Another woman joined them. She was short and thin and had wispy dark hair and a sallow complexion. Behind her there was a boy who was a little taller than I was.

'Ivan! Come here and meet Galina and Leonitjka!'

Leonitjka was rather quiet; a little reticent, a bit like me. We seemed to be on the same wavelength and soon got on like a house on fire, talking about everything we knew, from the Japanese to blubber. He had already turned seven, which made him a year and a half older than I was.

We talked about the boredom of having to be with the other children while the women worked, but he always looked forward to his mother Galina coming back because she usually had some titbit for him from the kitchen where she worked. I hoped that my mother would get kitchen duty soon.

When we returned to Ludmilla's cell Vera was still busy with the buttons. She had nearly sorted them all out according to size, a feat that impressed all the women, especially with the knowledge that Vera was barely two and a half.

'You're very clever with buttons!' exclaimed Ludmilla to Vera. 'You can have some buttons to keep if I could borrow Tasha for a while,' continued Ludmilla while gazing at Vera's doll that lay beside her on the bunk.

Vera hesitated and was about to say something but Ludmilla read her doubts and said, 'You can have Tasha back soon. I would like to borrow her for just a short time.'

'All right,' said Vera and in a business-like manner proceeded to choose the buttons that she would like.

For weeks afterwards Vera went to Ludmilla's cell on Sundays to try to reclaim Tasha but she was always persuaded to have a button in exchange for allowing Tasha to remain a little longer on Ludmilla's bed. I couldn't help but wonder why Ludmilla wanted to borrow Vera's doll for so long. Finally my curiosity got the better of me and caused me to ask Nadia.

'Don't tell Vera, but Ludmilla has stuffed Tasha with her jewellery to hide it from the Japanese. If the Japanese saw Tasha they would assume that she belonged to a daughter who had passed away and for that reason they would never pick her up to examine her. I should never have allowed Ludmilla to take Tasha from Vera. It was very stupid of me and wrong of Ludmilla to do this to Vera.'

After a pause Nadia added, 'I'm quite sure that Ludmilla will not let Vera have Tasha back. I hope Vera will get over it.'

My mother did not have much hope of being allocated kitchen duty, as it was a much sought-after position. Instead, she continued to help the Japanese build their air-raid shelters and trenches outside the camp.

In addition, as the morning checks were not enough, she was on a rota for reporting to the Japanese the numbers of people in our block. I found out what that involved when it came to her turn. She had to check for deaths and illnesses in every of the fifty or so cells in our block and then to report the results to headquarters near the gates. The other women and the block representative who were in the camp before we arrived taught her how to report it in Japanese. This enabled the Japanese camp commandant to keep a check on the situation in every part of the camp at the end of the day. Sometimes she returned soaking wet after having to go when it was raining.

Not content with keeping check on us, the Japanese also wanted to be sure that we were not hiding undesirable possessions. I could not understand what these possessions might be, but one morning, just before blubber, we were told that we were to clear our cells and display all we had in front of our cell door, as we were to have such an inspection that morning. An hour later two Japanese went round accompanied by our representative. They seemed to be more interested in the empty cells, giving the mattresses a few pokes to detect possible objects rather than closely inspecting the items on view in front of the cell doorways. I knew that whatever they were looking for, we had nothing to hide but the whole procedure was quite nerve- racking. In the end, as there were no sudden tantrums from the Japanese it seemed that no one in our block had anything to be reproached for.

It was November 1943. The short spells of rain that came nearly every day changed to the continuous downpour of the monsoon season, but unlike at home in Semarang, the water fell in streams directly onto the ground, as there was no gutter. That explained why the walkway outside the cells was two steps above ground level. Soon the whole yard was covered by a sheet of milk chocolate-brown water, the rising level of which was checked by an outflow into the main camp yard. As working outside was impossible, Nadia and Myrna had a well-deserved rest, while we children had very little else to do but stare at the continuous downpour. We were not allowed out to take a shower direct from the sky, as our emaciated bodies would be very susceptible to a chill. Occasionally, however, when there was a pause in the seemingly endless precipitation, we were allowed to paddle about in the yard. One of the women took the wooden cover off the mystery walled enclosure in the middle of the yard, which revealed for me what a well was. Its water, which was quite clear, was up to the same level as the yard and some women began to use it as an alternative place to wash. Nadia said that this was not very sensible as the water in the well may contain infectious bacteria. Not only that, if the cover was left off for any length of time it would be a source of even more mosquitoes.

The Japanese, realising that there were four potential sources of mosquitoes, each of the blocks having its own well, ordered the block representatives to see to it that they were filled in. Apart from the Japanese being as prone to malaria as the internees, their reliance on the piped water supply to the camp gave them grounds to consider the wells superfluous.

When the monsoon was over and the water level in the well had sunk, the women were set to work dumping soil and the stones from the well walls to fill them in and what was for me a source of mystery gradually disappeared.

While the work was progressing, we were all struck by the prolif- eration of snails. They weren't only hiding in the well masonry; they were everywhere. It wasn't long before someone persuaded a woman on kitchen duty to drop a few into boiling water to see if they were edible enough to add some protein to a diet that otherwise lacked everything except carbohydrates.

The pronounced edibility of the snails caused both women and the older children to feverishly search for them under stones and at the base of walls. This resulted in the eradication of the entire snail population of the camp within a matter of days. However, before that happened we were among those privileged to try a snail each at rice time when Nadia used a bamboo splinter to extract the greyish contents of the shell and put it in her mouth. As she was chewing hers she extricated mine and nodded for me to try it. It was rubbery and had a kind of earthy taste that might have been improved by salt, but the little salt that was available to the kitchen was used for the rice and then mainly for the Japanese.

Towards the end of the monsoon the grass in the yard shot up green and lush to make the ground look like it had a new coat of paint. Even the bare soil that covered the former well was putting up green shoots. In a matter of days, the vigour of its growth overcame the usual effect of the tramping of feet, so that along the edge of the block wall, where the new grass was virtually untouched, some started to pick a fistful and stuff it into their mouths. I watched Kees doing the same, energetically picking a handful and popping it into his mouth, not looking anywhere but at the ground as his jaws worked overtime. When I asked Nadia whether it might be a good idea to do the same, she shook her head and said that there still was a chance that we may get some dreadful stomach upset if we ate grass directly from the yard.

'Think of all the people walking on the grass after they had been to the latrines,' she said. 'When the yard was covered with water the bacteria might end up anywhere, so it's not safe to eat the grass.'

The sudden spurt of lushness brought with it a flourish of life. Through the mosquito net I could see large moths fluttering among the clouds of insects drawn to the outside lamp and chi-chaks of all sizes scampered to reap the harvest, all to a more intense background noise of crickets, cicadas and the high-pitched screeching of bats.

During the day there were more insects and other lower forms of life, which affected life higher up in the food chain, from praying mantises to birds. House sparrows had raised young under the tiles of the main buildings and these fledglings kept us occupied trying to catch them during their attempts to fly from one clothes line to another. I succeeded in catching one and wanted to keep it, but remembering the bird vendor and the importance of freedom, I replaced it carefully on the clothes line where it wobbled for a second or two before trembling away with its undersized wings.

When we took our usual Sunday walk Leonitjka showed me a green praying mantis that he had caught. He tied one of its legs to a piece of cotton to prevent it from flying away. Fascinated by its triangular head, its huge translucent green eyes and the vicious spiked front legs, I wanted a mantis pet of my own. I ran to ask Nadia if I could have a piece of cotton, but when I told her the reason she said that it was cruel to keep a mantis for a pet and that she was sure that Galina would tell Leonitjka to release his.

On the following Sunday Leonitjka told me that after temporarily leaving his mantis tied up to a railing, he returned to find only the piece of cotton. He said that he didn't know why it had disappeared but it might been taken by a bird.

When I got up one morning to wash my face and take a tin of water, I was certain I saw a creature that looked like a cat darting into a cell in the far corner of the block. When I told Nadia what I saw, she said that she knew that one woman had smuggled a cat in with her to camp and managed to keep it hidden, even when the Japanese carried out cell inspections. She explained that though she couldn't feed it, it survived by keeping down the mouse and rat population of the camp. Not only that, its mistress herself somehow caught rodents to feed her pet. Had the Japanese known that she had a cat she would have been severely punished. It was also probable that it fed itself on the young sparrows that were plentiful at the time, which was probably why I caught a glimpse of it during the daytime.

Inspections or not, it was the Japanese policy to keep us on our toes and aware of their supremacy at all times, which meant that a camp guard would occasionally and without warning come into the block and look around. Once, when we had just finished our rice, I heard the harsh sound of Japanese coming out in screams. When I looked up I saw a guard in our block addressing himself to a boy, aged about four, called Pieter. Then, when his mother appeared to see what all the fuss was about, he gave Pieter a hard slap on the head that knocked him down to the ground while shouting at her. Poor Pieter was too frightened and stunned to cry and when the guard left, his tearful mother picked him up to comfort him, sitting on the step and cradling the boy in her arms. We were given a vivid demonstration of how a child was to be treated if he forgot to pin his identity number on his shirt.

But apart from the Japanese themselves, we all knew that malnutrition was the greatest scourge in the camp and was the main cause of the regular processions of coffins every morning. With that in mind, Nadia, like so many other women with children, was determined to do something to alleviate the catastrophic lack of nutritious food.

It was rumoured that a woman of mixed blood, a so-called half-caste, who had a cell in the far corner from us in our block, had a secret smuggling trade with the Javanese on the other side of the camp wall. Apparently at a given time she would throw a basket tied to a strong cord over the ten-foot camp wall. As she was half Javanese herself she was not only able to communicate easily, but she also had a good grasp of the etiquette involved in the kind of business where no face-to-face contact is made. Secured in the basket was a message requesting what items she needed together with the prices she was prepared to pay. My mother knew that such an affair was extremely dangerous for all concerned, especially for the smuggler who was aware she would be executed if caught. Furthermore, she was also aware that the half-caste woman would not confide in anyone without being certain that the person she dealt with could be trusted. This made Nadia doubt whether she could successfully carry out a deal with her. However, one evening she decided to push aside her misgivings and went over to see her.

Ten minutes later, when we were ready for bed on the platform Nadia returned to say that she thought that she had made a deal, but she wouldn't tell us about it in case it did not go through.

One night we were woken up by a low moaning which became louder and louder, making it difficult for us to sleep as the noise continued on into the night.

'It sounds like the Swedish woman,' said Nadia. 'She must be in pain.'

'I wish she would stop moaning,' said Vera. 'I can't get to sleep.'

'I'll tell you what,' said Nadia, 'I'll tell you a story.'

With that, we calmed down and Vera was allowed to choose her favourite, 'Little Red Riding Hood'. The Swedish woman seemed to cease moaning just at the point in the story when the Big Bad Wolf was lying in bed dressed as the grandmother and waiting for the heroine. The happy ending of the story, together with the longed-for silence, allowed the rest of the night to be normal. The following nights, however, were just as full of moans.

Then one morning, before blubber, we watched the old camp doctor emerge from the cell of our Swedish neighbours and walk over to the block representative to talk to her. Later Nadia told us that the Swedish woman was in pain because a part of her intestines was inflamed. He thought that she most probably had appendicitis, for which she must be operated on if she were to recover. She went on to explain that though she was married to a Dutchman, she was still Swedish and thereby neutral, which meant that she had the right to be repatriated to Sweden together with her children. It seemed that the doctor and our representative between them would try to persuade the Japanese to release them and arrange for them to be transported to Sweden.

A few days later, after a succession of moany nights, we were relieved to see the Swedes packing to leave the camp. Nadia wished them luck and hoped that they would soon reach Sweden. Afterwards she told us that she wasn't sure that they would bother to arrange for them to be sent to Sweden, but they were certainly to be taken somewhere. I was glad for the Swedes and at the same time looked forward to a peaceful night's sleep.

Not only did we sleep better but also on the following day, just after we got up, Nadia came with a cloth bundle. When she opened it in the cell, she revealed four brown solid rectangular objects about three inches by two in cross-section and about six or seven inches long. They were vaguely familiar and resembled smaller versions of loaves of bread that occasionally appeared in our household before internment. Not only that, she also showed us two large pale greenish eggs.

'Isn't it wonderful!' said Nadia. 'You can have some bread together with one of these duck eggs instead of blubber. The eggs are pre-cooked.'

Nadia produced one of the silver C.K. knives. She pressed the knife into the bread and began to use it like a bread saw, but instead of making a slice, all she could do was to create a deep indentation that slowly filled to give the loaf its original shape when she released the pressure. When she tried again using harder pressure, the knife slipped and the loaf fell on the floor to bounce up like a ball.

'The knife must be blunt,' she muttered as she picked up the loaf.

A third attempt at cutting a slice succeeded, but only after the loaf was nearly totally squashed and the slice itself was torn out rather than cut. She tore it into a piece each for Vera and me and then continued to extract another slice from what was left of the loaf that had to a certain extent regained its original shape in cross-section.

The juices in my mouth flowed copiously in anticipation of the treat to come but when I sank my teeth into it I felt a rubbery resistance that had no taste at all. Even the snail tasted better. Continued efforts to bite into it led to the removal of a loose lower front deciduous tooth. I extracted the tooth from the rubbery goo in my mouth and showed it to Nadia.

'Oh look, you've lost your first baby tooth. Don't worry, you will soon get a grown-up tooth to take its place.'

Vera managed to swallow a piece without it being properly chewed.

'To think that I gave a ring with a one-carat diamond set in platinum for this useless rubber,' moaned Nadia. 'We'll save the eggs for when we have rice. Let's hope they will be better than this bread. It's not fit to be called bread.'

The eggs were indeed edible and relieved the monotony of the plain rice, apart from being a source of much needed protein. But once opened, we had to eat the whole egg between us, which meant that our two eggs lasted two days.

On the next day Nadia found out that apart from the bread being so rubbery and difficult to eat, its nutritional value was no better than that of our breakfast as it turned out to be made of the same tapioca flour as our blubber. Apart from the loaf that we mauled in our attempts to consume it, she still had three fully intact loaves.

The rumour soon spread that we had acquired bread. These three small bread facsimiles turned out to be a status symbol because there were people who envied us. They were the people who were convinced that bread was bread and could surely be eaten, despite Nadia's conclusion that they must have been made especially for barter by the Javanese. The fact that Vera and I had powers of mastication that did not match up to the toughness of our newly acquired status symbols did not prevent people from making offers for the loaves. None of these offers involved food but there was one woman who offered to do a watercolour portrait of either Vera or me in return for the three loaves. The woman was clearly some sort of an artist, who had managed to take with her an assortment of brushes, paints and paper on internment. As Nadia had no pictures of Vera since she was a baby, she jumped at the chance to have a painting of her daughter at the age of nearly three.

During the sitting Vera, who normally didn't tolerate having to be inactive a long time, was surprisingly co-operative. The result was a likeness that moderately satisfied Nadia. It portrayed Vera's blonde hair bunched up to form her little palm tree tied with a small blue ribbon, her slightly almond-shaped blue eyes set in a face that was perhaps more rounded and rosy than she had in reality, but I thought that it was a good portrait.

Though we were considered by the Japanese to be low forms of life, the women were not regarded to be too low in status to be thought of as potential concubines. Our representative was told to inform the women that anyone who was willing to make herself available to the Japanese would receive certain privileges, such as more freedom, better food and clothes.

This announcement was only received by derisory comments from the women of our block and when they were told that a Japanese officer would make an inspection to look for possible candidates, Nadia, Myrna and the rest of the women refused to wash and rubbed dirt into their faces. When Nadia explained to me that they were trying to make themselves undesirable in case the Japanese wanted to use them, I fully approved, as I did not want them to make friends with our captors.

To everyone's relief the lack of hygiene and extra dirt seemed to work, as none of the women in our block were 'favoured' by the Japanese. There were rumours of others who made themselves available but must have regretted it for various reasons, including the treatment they got from their own.

Myrna, who seemed as cheerful as ever, told Nadia one day that she didn't feel well enough to accompany her to morning duty. She said that she felt weak and was sure that after day's rest she would be able to continue as normal. Instead, on the following morning Nadia received the shattering news that Myrna had died during the night, leaving Rudi alone without a mother.

I couldn't understand that such a lively and pleasant person as Myrna should die and die so suddenly. When I saw Myrna's sheet-covered body being carried away on a stretcher by two women from another part of the camp I found it even harder to comprehend that she was alive, cheerful and vivacious just a couple of days previously. That stab of emotion made me understand that Rudi must have felt devastated. Her death reminded us of the frailty of our lives in camp and gave me the unpleasant feeling of the anxiety that Vera and I could lose our mother just as unexpectedly.

Poor Rudi was left in the care of our representative. When she asked if there was any one that would be prepared to look after him, she found herself in a dilemma. She had to choose between women who already had children and could use part of his rice rations to feed their own, or those who could use his rice for their own survival. In the end she entrusted him to a woman in another block, but the rumour later came that despite precautions, poor Rudi was indeed utilised as a source of extra rice.

The following morning's inspection and respect for the dead took on another meaning, for not only had Nadia lost the best non-Russian friend she ever had, the whole block had lost a fine person. In the end after being passed from one woman to another, we heard that Rudi died as well. Nadia remarked that his death might be considered a blessing.

Our low spirits were expressed by no words. The silence of our lunchtime rice was finally broken when Nadia said, 'I told Myrna not to give Rudi her rice, even though she was worried about him. I wish now that I had insisted. I'm sure Myrna died from both exhaustion and lack of food.'

'Mamma, you can have some of my rice,' said Vera.

'No, darling, you eat yours and I'll eat mine because we must all live.'

7. Leaflets

One Sunday, when Leonitjka and I were taking a walk in the main yard we noticed that several native Javanese men were actually in the camp and were in the process of cutting down the tree nearest to our compound. The Javanese themselves were seldom seen in the camp but clearly it was a job for native workers rather than women in the camp. They used an enormous two-man saw and then chopped with mighty axes, causing a mixture of sawdust and large wood chips to be littered around. Our curiosity drew us towards the tree-fellers but as soon as we came close enough to pick up a reddish brown chip of wood we were motioned away by a Japanese guard who emerged from behind the group of workers. This drew the attention of the Russian women who shouted at us to keep clear.

The cutting and chopping went on nearly the whole day until our block representative assembled a long line of members of our block to hold a long rope that was attached to the top of the tree. There must have been over fifty women and children ready to pull at the given signal. I was among the children at the end of the rope. The tree swayed a little at the first command to pull, swayed more at the second, creaked and cracked with the third. The crown appeared to tilt a little and we paused to see if the tree would fall. But a fourth pull was necessary to make it creak like a giant unlubricated hinge. It began to lean towards the line of heaving people and accelerate into a fall with a crash and a cloud of dust and leaves. The rope was so long that the once thirty-yard tall tree fell well short of the woman pulling up front. The felling team set to work cutting off the branches while some children found fruit that looked like prunes but were said to be inedible. The other three trees were felled and cleared during the next week leaving altogether four large stumps about four or five feet wide and three feet off the ground and the main building was no longer in partial shade.

On the following Sunday I noticed a group of children who were a year or two older than me sitting on the ground next to the nearest

80

stump to our block. Their attention was focussed on a young woman who stood on the stump while she was talking to them and showing words written on a slate that she held up. Some children were scratching letters on the ground with a stick in response to what she was saying. There were three other classes with older children, each class being grouped round a newly created tree stump. As I watched the young lady teaching her class a few yards away, I couldn't help staring at her long black hair and beautiful dark brown eyes behind her black-rimmed glasses. I was so mesmerised by her that it came as a shock to see her smile at me and motion me to join the class. I walked towards the group and sat down behind them as if in a dream. She proceeded with what she was teaching but in my wistful state I could not absorb much of what she was saying and the class finished with me none the wiser, but I looked forward to being taught by her in the next session.

When I told Nadia about the new teacher she said that she was not new and had been teaching children in secret in the camp for some time. It was only because the felled trees left the large stumps that they became ideal to stand on and hold a class, which drew my attention to the existence of classes that were otherwise held in less obvious locations somewhere else in the camp. She told me that at the age of six I was old enough to join her class. She added that the teacher I described was a half-caste and she said it in a tone that implied that being half-caste meant that she was worth less respect. I said nothing because, half-caste or not, I thought that she was heavenly, perhaps just because she was half-caste. Nadia must have noted a kind of glazed expression on my face.

'Perhaps you ought to attend her class. After all, Leonitjka goes to the next class and he has practically learnt to read and write.'

I attended my new class on the following morning after inspection. But there was no class on the following day because the Japanese must have thought that the classes centred round the tree stumps looked more like public meetings and forbade them. My beautiful teacher disappeared into the nether regions of the camp, I never saw her again and I did not get the chance to start a proper education.

The beginning of the December of 1944 was marked by a period of strange behaviour by some of the women in our block. Apart from carrying out their camp duties, they appeared to be busy doing things that were unusual. Then, for reasons that I vaguely remembered from our time in Semarang, we were told to find a shoe, fill it with grass and leave it out for the night. As if by magic, some old ladies shoes suddenly appeared in odd places around the steps of the walkway so that we were able to do as instructed. When we asked Nadia whether Sinter Klaas was going to come, she merely said 'wait and see'.

That late afternoon, just before our tins of tea, a figure with black skin and black clothes, ran into the yard shouting and waving his arms in such a way, that all the younger children, including me, bolted into our cells.

'I want Gijs! Where is he?'

'That is Svarta Piet,' said Nadia with a broad grin on her face. 'He is Sinter Klaas' assistant and is looking for naughty children but is rather naughty himself. He knows that Gijs must have been a naughty boy and he wants to give him his punishment.'

Gijs was an older boy who I vaguely knew. With much reluctance he came out of his cell to be grabbed by Svarta Piet, who began to force him into the sack, while his mother pleaded,

'Please don't take my Gijs away! He'll promise to be good.'

Whereupon other women began to plead for his forgiveness and some children began to cry. The whole atmosphere reached a climax of pleading women and children when Svarta Piet opened the sack to let Gijs go back to his cell, much to my relief. I was still scared that he might take me instead when a whole string of questions arose within my mind. How would Svarta Piet get past the Japanese? How did he get there in the first place? Was he really Svarta Piet, or someone dressed up? The questions supplied their own answers and my worries changed to questions as to who organised it all. Gijs must have volunteered to play the role of a bad boy.

'He looks after Sinter Klaas' horse and it is his job to find naughty children and see to it that they are punished in some way or other, but if you have left a shoe with something to eat for the horse he will be kinder to you,' said Nadia.

'Ah, so that's why we were asked to leave a shoe-full of grass,' I said with relief. 'Now I remember that we did the same thing at home before camp.'

'That's right,' said Nadia.

'I've left mine next to Ivan's,' said Vera.

'After tea you must have a good night's sleep and see what happens in the morning.'

I looked at the icon but couldn't detect any signs to show my sins. That made it easier for me to get to sleep, despite the excitement about what might happen on the next day.

On the following morning the grass in the shoes was gone and there were no signs of Svarta Piet.

'Look! The horse has had my grass,' said Vera holding up an empty large old black shoe.

'And mine,' I said, looking at the shoe I had put out and noting that it lay on its side a little further out into the yard.

We thought that was the end of the matter until just after we had finished our blubber, a figure of an old man dressed in a long red garment came slowly into the yard bearing a sack that looked heavy and almost full. He had a long, fine white beard and wore a double pointed kind of hat. His appearance seemed totally incongruous; at the same time as it caused us all to stare in wonder.

Vera gazed in open-mouthed amazement at the figure in red and I was equally stunned into silence. Before we could say anything, Nadia said, 'Sinter Klaas has arrived. Now you will be asked whether you have been good.'

He put down his sack and sat down on a box at the end of our walkway. He then proceeded to call out the names of the children in a wavering voice that sounded neither masculine nor feminine: it just sounded old. When our names were called, Vera and I joined the other children in a queue. He talked in a quiet voice and gave each a package before returning to his cell. Vera stood in front of me in the queue and when it was her turn I heard Sinter Klaas say, 'Have you been a good girl?'

'Yes,' said Vera in a very quiet voice, which was nearly overcome by a state that was on the verge of crying.

'Then you shall have this from Svarta Piet and me,' said Sinter Klaas mildly.

Vera rushed back to Nadia at our cell, while I stood prepared to be dealt with in the same way by the kindly figure in red. As he asked me whether I had been good, I noticed that his long white beard was so fine that it was like cotton wool. He must be very, very old to have such a fine beard, I thought.

I hurried back to our cell hardly able to wait to tear off the brown paper wrapping of my packet. Vera had already revealed her present, which turned out to be a grey cloth rabbit with large floppy ears. She did not seem so enthusiastic about her present. Perhaps she was thinking about the only cloth toy that she liked, but Tasha was still with Ludmilla. Instead, she was more curious to see what mine was. The first tear of the paper revealed something made out of orange cloth and it took just a second to reveal that I received an orange cloth cat with four sturdy legs, a short orange tail and a cheerful face with black whiskers stitched onto it.

'Isn't he fantastic! I shall call him Vass!' I announced.

Vass became my faithful bedtime companion that I cuddled before falling asleep.

As if to crown the day, one of the women in the block came with large plate that was filled with a kind of beige-coloured foam.

'Come and get your kofieklopp! There is enough for everyone to try a spoon each,' said the woman with the plate of mysterious foam.

To us children it tasted heavenly. It was slightly sweet and that sweetness was mixed with the other flavour that we were told was coffee. As we had savoured it, we were desperate to have more. But as there was just enough for a taste each, we had to be content with that. The questions around the origin of the kofieklopp, however, remained. Where did it come from? Who made it and how? Could we have it again?

Later, Nadia found out that someone who worked in the kitchen managed to steal a little sugar and coffee flavour from the Japanese, mix it with blubber and whip it into the party product that we could all sample.

When the fuss had died down and Sinter Klaas had left our block, my curiosity got the better of me and I couldn't help asking my mother how it was that Sinter Klaas and Svarta Piet came into the camp. How did they get in and out past the Japanese? Were they real, or was it a big boy and the old doctor dressed up? Nadia said that the doctor was too busy tending the sick to have time for that. Then I remembered that I hadn't seen our block representative for a couple of days. Had she something to do with it, and if so, who was Svarta Piet? Finally, Nadia relented and said no one else but the women of our block were responsible for the celebration of St Nicholas Day that December 6th. I then regretted my urge to get down to the truth and instead thought about the costumes and the toys and how much time they had spent in the preparation.

At the end of 1944 and the beginning of 1945, during our second monsoon in the camp, an increasing number of people familiar to us from our block had disappeared and we lost not only Myrna but several other women and children. The two hydrocephalic children were gone and so was the mongoloid girl from the next block. Those who were still alive were showing increasing signs of malnutrition, with weakness being the main symptom both from the lack of food and intestinal ailments. Symptoms of vitamin deficiency were also becoming more common, the price we all paid for our very limited diet.

People who were ill usually confined themselves to their cells so that they were not seen, but at night the sounds caused by their disorders often dominated the background of crickets, cicadas and geckos. Suddenly, a woman's singing voice that echoed with a kind of eerie beauty drowned all the other night sounds.

'Listen,' said Nadia, sure that we were awake after the singing had been going on for some minutes. 'What you can hear is the most famous aria from the opera called 'Madame Butterfly' by Puccini. I have seen 'Madame Butterfly' when I was a girl in Harbin.'

'But who's singing it and why in the middle of the night?'

'The person who is singing is a well-known Dutch opera singer who has a cell in our block. The sad thing is that she is suffering from the later stages of beriberi, which is when you become insane.'

I thought being insane meant that a person ran about shouting and doing strange things, rather like the mongoloid girl. Who was the woman? What did she look like? What did she do during the day, especially if she was insane? I speculated in silence how someone who was insane could achieve such beautiful singing and why she should be doing it in the middle of the night.

'Isn't there a cure?' I asked, wondering if some disease that we might catch caused it.

'The only cure, if it is treated in time, is to eat brown rice. What we all eat is white rice, which is brown rice that has been stripped of its husk. It's the brown part that contains the vitamins necessary to prevent beriberi,' said my mother, a constant source of information.

'But why do they bother to take the brown part off in the first place?'

'Because white rice is much easier to cook and easier to digest and probably because normally the vitamins found in brown rice are found in other foods, which we can't have.'

'But that means that we might have beriberi as well and we'll go mad.'

'Yes, the doctor said that one of the first signs to look for is a swelling of the ankles. Now try to sleep.'

The 'Madame Butterfly' aria repetitions finally stopped and I did get to sleep, but only after a long time of worry about the state of my ankles. I resolved that they must be inspected on the following morning.

That morning Nadia scrutinised and pressed the scanty flesh around our ankles and came to the conclusion that as she couldn't feel any puffiness, neither Vera nor I showed signs of beriberi.

The nocturnal arias continued for several days until our prima donna was taken to the camp hospital and was never heard, or heard of, again.

Somehow, despite an almost complete lack of protein and vitamins, Vera and I grew taller; or rather we grew taller at the same time as becoming increasingly thinner, as if we were in the process of merely stretching. This meant that if we didn't directly wear out our clothes, we grew, or stretched out of them. As no one knew how long we would be interned, Nadia didn't pack larger clothes for us to wear when we grew. But she did bring a spare sheet which she cut up to make me a shirt and Vera a blouse. My short trousers were still wearable, the legs ending higher up my thighs with my growth, but still easy to button up round a waist that did not expand. As our shoes were no longer usable we had to go around barefoot, which we did with ease on all but the hottest or grittiest of surfaces, thanks to the development of calluses on the soles of our feet.

I was pleased with my new, clean white shirt as I put it on ready for morning inspection after blubber breakfast. Nadia took another look at me and said that she was pleased with her work. Vera had already worn her new blouse for enough days for the novelty to have worn off, but for me it was the first new garment I had had for two years so it was quite an occasion. I stood with my head up high as the Japanese came to do the usual inspection.

The Japanese! I looked quickly down to where my number badge should be. It wasn't there! I couldn't believe that we had forgotten to pin the number onto my new shirt. Nadia always did it as a routine after washing and leaving the shirt out to dry in the sun, but the excitement of the new shirt broke the routine and I glanced down again to confirm that we had actually forgotten the number for the first time. I remembered the treatment that Pieter received. A quick glance at Vera confirmed that she had hers. Perhaps the Japanese would not notice, I thought. As I stood, I tried to pretend that it was there, pinned on my shirt.

His expressionless brown face looked mechanically at us as he walked round. I stood in my usual place, third from the end of the second row with Nadia at the end, then Vera, then me. He finished the first row and continued along ours, starting at the far end from us. It seemed a very long time and I felt as if I had been fastened to the ground. As he came to me his Asian eyes narrowed to slits. Then he shouted something in Japanese at me, while he pointed at my new shirt. Nadia said something in Japanese and made a deep bow, which I understood signified an apology I then found myself on the ground as if bowled over.

I got up with just numbness on the back of my head. I felt no pain, just dazed, frightened and numbed both physically and mentally. Nadia had received her humiliation in front of the others: a Japanese warrior hit her son for not wearing his identity number, and I felt ashamed for letting her down. The rest of the inspection and the silence for the coffins went on as usual but when it finished I couldn't help but sob at my mother's side all the way back to our cell.

I resolved never to forget to double-check my shirt again.

Some days later when we were returning to our cells after inspection, we noticed that Kees and a group of other boys of about the same age had assembled in the main yard.

'What's going on?' asked Nadia.

'We're to be transferred to a men's camp,' said Kees with a grin that seemed a little forced.

'But you're only twelve!' said Nadia.

'That's right, but now they've lowered the age down to twelve and there are rumours that they might even start taking in ten-year-olds,' said Kees looking at me.

Vera, who ran ahead to play with Sergei, did not say goodbye to Kees. She was still a tiny girl who lived in her own little world just like I did in Semarang three years previously.

Though I thought of Kees as much older, it was hard to regard him as equal to a man and he still had the voice of a boy. I felt sorry for him having to work and behave like a man, but at the same time I knew that since he could cope on his own in his cell, he must be tough. I knew I would miss Kees and his cheerful smile and hoped that he would survive the men's camp. Perhaps he looked forward to joining his brother again.

Nadia wished him good luck, we said goodbye and as we walked back to our compound I embarked on a line of rather depressing thoughts. It was bad enough to hear that all boys that had reached twelve would be transferred to the men's camp but I was shocked with the possibility of being taken away as a ten-year-old. As I would be seven that year I dreaded the thought that there were only three more years before I had to leave my mother and sister. And what if they lower the age down to eight? That would mean Leonitjka would be next. I began to realise that I was beginning to approach the age group of the oldest boys that were left in the camp. If even ten-year-olds were soon to be regarded as men then I wasn't far from being a man myself. It gave life a more serious tone and I returned to our block to the usual juvenile activities of the younger children and noted that Vera was bossing Sergei about in her usual way.

Sergei's big brother Otto was busy on his own, writing or drawing with a stick, scratching the dry soil, and I thought about his age and that he was approaching nine years old. I sat on the steps at a respectful distance to see what he was doing without disturbing him, at the same time wondering if he knew about the new regulations concerning boys in the men's camps.

Nadia went off to her enforced labour, but not to the defence constructions, as they were completed. Instead she was sent to work in the camp vegetable garden.

As the vegetables were grown entirely for the benefit of the Japanese it was strictly forbidden for internees to take even the smallest bit of vegetable for their own consumption and any woman caught doing so would be severely punished. However, as there were no restrictions for the consumption of weeds, those that were deemed edible were soon identified and passed on to the kitchen to be cooked or dipped in the boiling rice water. This enabled Vera and I to occasionally receive some kind of stringy and somewhat slimy greenish weed, which was slightly bitter in taste, but which was thought to be rich in vitamin C. It was known in Dutch as porslijn.

When Nadia came back with a little of this weed to have with our rice Vera refused point blank to eat it. When Nadia tried her powers of persuasion by telling her that it was good for her, Vera simply broke out into a fit of screaming. Her little body did all it could to convulse itself into a screaming tantrum that continued for what seemed a long time, long enough to cause the whole block to stare at the source of the pandemonium. Nadia stared helplessly at her red-faced raving daughter for a few seconds. Then she lifted Vera up and took her still screaming to place her firmly under the tap which she turned on to full force. The effect was dramatic. Her screaming stopped within a second, turned into a whimper and then to silence. As Nadia turned off the tap the whole block broke into a round of applause and cheers. After being dried and given a clean vest and pants, Vera was as good as an angel and even ate her share of porslijn.

It was May 1945. We could hear a distant droning somewhere up in the heavens while we were having our blubber. Though it was unusual to see or hear aeroplanes in our part of the sky, we assumed it was some kind of military aircraft, though we couldn't see it. The droning noise faded away and we began to think nothing more of it until one woman came running along the main yard with a piece of paper in her hand, shouting:

'The war in Europe is over! The Germans have surrendered!'

We all stopped eating, Nadia dropping her coconut shell bowl with its half-consumed contents spilling on the floor.

Then someone in our block found a piece of paper that stated that the war with Germany was over and that we must keep our spirits up because it would not be long before the Japanese would be defeated. Nadia explained to us that the Allies must have dropped thousands of leaflets to give us hope that soon our internment would come to an end.

The effect on the camp was dramatic. Some shouted for joy, others hugged each other, tears streaming down their faces while some just sat down and cried. Within a few moments some Japanese soldiers came rushing into our compound in a tantrum, demanding us to hand over the leaflets as they were forbidden. But the Japanese were clutching at straws and their content had already spread like the wind.

On the next day we were told to be extra careful when inspected by the Japanese, as they must have been angry about the leaflets and the fact that we knew what they were about. I had definitely to be extra careful not to forget to check that my number was securely pinned to my shirt. The inspection turned out to be uneventful but there were more than twice as many coffins on the funeral parade.

Nadia said afterwards that the news of the end of the war in Europe was such an emotional experience for some women that they simply collapsed and died. But the effect on most people was positive. The general atmosphere was more cheerful. Peals of laughter could be heard from different directions and I felt relieved to think that I need not worry about being moved to the men's camp in the future after all. The rumour was that very likely we were to be freed in a matter of a couple of weeks or so.

A woman appeared from her cell across the block yard waving a rag, which she had just washed.

'Look, I'm back to normal for the first time in nearly three years!' she shouted.

'What does she mean and why is she waving a rag like that?'

'Oh, you will understand when you are older, but it means that the good news has made her feel like a normal woman.'

I couldn't understand what that had to do with rags, but I knew that by the way my mother answered that there was no point in pressing the matter. During the next few days I also noticed that there were several rags hanging out to dry on the washing lines in the block.

A week or so later Nadia brought us our morning blubber with a broad grin on her face.

'Our representative has just offered me kitchen duty,' she said as she distributed one of the products of that kitchen. 'The vacancy was caused by the death of someone who had been working in the kitchen for only less than a week. I'll try to get you a few titbits if I can but it won't be easy.'

She returned at midday looking tired and worn as usual. Vera and I sat on the walkway steps, the usual hunger and lassitude toned down our curiosity about how Nadia fared in the kitchen and whether she managed to get us something extra to eat. Noticing the expectation written on our faces, she said: 'I didn't manage to get you much. I'll get your rice and tell you what happened.'

With that she gathered our coconut shell bowls and went to the queue of people that had gathered to collect their share of the rice that Nadia had delivered from the kitchen in a big pot. When she handed us our rice each, I noticed that mine was decorated with an orange round object that was greenish in the middle.

'Carrot tops,' she said. 'We can have only one piece each. Eat it, it's very good for you.'

'It tastes better than the weed,' said Vera, and I agreed with her. They were cooked to be quite soft and had a special taste.

'Look at the rice,' said Nadia.

'You won't find many bits of insect in it this time. I was shocked to see that the open sack of rice had masses of small beetles crawling about in it. A woman who had been working in the kitchen for some time said that they were called weevils and that there was little one could do to get rid of them. I took a large ladle and just casually stirred the rice with it. As I stirred, I noticed that many weevils came up to the surface. All I had to do to keep the numbers of weevils down, if not get rid of them, was to stir them about and then skim them off as they came to the surface, and then crush them on the

91

floor. It seems to be a good way and if it works it means that the rice will be less damaged in the bargain.'

After my mother had started in the kitchen the rice was indeed better with fewer remains of weevils and more intact grains.

The good morale of the camp after the good news leaflets were dropped began to wane as the days turned into weeks. The Japanese were still in control and rumours began to spread that they wanted to be rid of us, which only lowered the morale in the camp. Our camp commander was hated to the core not only because he had starved thousands of women and children to death, but also for his cruelty to certain individuals who dared to question his orders. Nadia didn't give me the detailed reasons as to why he was so hated. I only saw him at a distance during some of the inspections. For me he was in command of those that I dreaded and thereby the one to be the most dreaded. Nadia told us that there were some who vowed that they would kill him as soon as the war was over.

In a way it would have been kinder for the Allies not to have given us hope of a quick end to the war with the Japanese. The hope and good morale that it first created gave way after a few weeks to despair and a feeling that one couldn't last out to the end. This led to a general gloom, an even greater hatred of the Japanese and to more coffins to respect every day.

While out to receive my daily morning sun I heard a faint buzzing in the sky and looked up to see a small plane, which as I watched suddenly took a dive with a trail of smoke developing as it accelerated towards the ground. Others were out watching it but it was too far away for us to hear dramatic sounds but someone said that it was a Japanese plane and that it would crash into the same lake that was rumoured to be our future watery grave.

Two months after the leaflets Nadia discovered that I had the first signs of beriberi. When she pressed the softer areas around my ankles, the indentations left by her finger took quite a long time to disappear, which meant that I was beginning to be oedematous. The oedema would spread up my body but the most serious sign to look out for was red blotches. Nadia said that if I had red blotches as well as oedema then there would be little hope for my survival and that as my digestive system was so affected by my dysentery I could hardly absorb the little nourishment we received. This was why she had expected me to show signs of beriberi much earlier. Vera was not yet affected.

July turned into August. I would be seven years old in the middle of the month. It seemed that despite peace in Europe, we were going to die from malnutrition and disease if the Japanese were not going to help us come to a speedier end. The general morale of the camp was very low.

It was the hottest time of the day. The whole camp was in the process of recharging its emaciated, diseased and dying bodies with the usual inadequate charge of a little boiled rice and rest. The adults were ancient and the children were old and the hope for that spark of rejuvenation had almost gone.

But it came. It was two days before my seventh birthday and over three months after the leaflets that the news came. The commandant summoned the block representatives to tell them that the Japanese had surrendered and that we were free. The effect did not cause the promised murder of our commandant. Instead it caused a flood of emotions which culminated with the miraculous appearance of the Dutch flag by the main gate. For more than three years some patriotic woman had managed to hide a flag from the Japanese and the fruit of her effort was waving triumphantly in a light breeze with its red, white and blue splendour. The Japanese themselves had disappeared and the rumour that the commandant had committed hara-kiri was confirmed a little later.

When I saw both the main gates open, instead of just the usual one gate open for the procession of coffins, it was as if a new world was beckoning me to go out and explore. I was burning to know what lay outside the ten-foot high walls that confined us for over two years. But though both the gates were open and we were theoretically free, we were still restricted to the camp. The Allies dropped leaflets to inform us that as the Javanese fighters for independence had taken over the Japanese armaments it was dangerous to travel in Java. We were advised to remain in our camps until troops arrived to transport us to safety.

We were informed that our liberation came as a result of the release of two mighty bombs, called atom bombs, that virtually wiped out two Japanese cities. Had it not been for those two bombs the Japanese would have carried on fighting to the last man and we would have all died.

Though the Allies had also dropped 'Red Cross' parcels of foodstuffs, medicines and vitamins we had never received them while the Japanese were in charge: they had simply taken them for their own use. Nevertheless, after the Japanese had left and our camp hospital had access to the medicines and vitamins, people continued to die. The puffiness of my beriberi needed more prolonged treatment than the vitamin tablets that we were able to receive from the camp hospital. However, the tablets, together with the slightly better diet that came from the kitchen after the disappearance of our captors, put most of us on a better footing after a few weeks. We were even given another taste of kofieklopp, which gave our morales another boost.

Those of us that were left in the camp had little means of acquiring extra food from the Javanese, partly because there was no money to pay for them and partly because it was dangerous for them to do business with the Dutch. As Java was in the process of being taken over by the fighters for independence, most Javanese were reluctant to help the Dutch in case they were branded as traitors by the freedom fighters. Despite this, some bananas and papayas did find their way into the camp, and Vera and I were able to taste the fruit, which for Vera was virtually a first-time experience.

The fact of the matter was that for Vera nearly all foods that were taken for granted or regarded as normal before internment, were new for her. One day when it was the turn of our block to receive the contents of the parcels dropped by the Allies we received some small brown squares that I recognised to be chocolate.

'I know what this is, I've eaten this before,' I said to Nadia, more eager to flaunt my experience in life than to express the pleasure of its exquisite taste, though the memory of having tasted it before was rather vague.

'Oh, Vera!' I said with a watery mouth as I saw the brown squares before us. 'You'll love this chocolate! It tastes better than anything you've tried before!'

The chocolate was indeed exquisite, much better than kofieklopp and Vera gasped with delight as she swallowed the first piece of chocolate in her life.

Her joy, however, was short lived. No more than a minute later poor Vera was heaving with the effort of vomiting it all up again. Her stomach was clearly unable to take it after more than three years of just starch. Though my stomach took it, the intestines did not.

The freedom represented by the open gates became so tempting that a few days after the end of the war and after an insignificant seventh birthday, I ventured out on my own to see the world on the other side of the large entrance. I wanted to see the world that for over two years was excluded by a ten-foot high wall guarded by the Japanese. The little road was empty and the whole area was flat and open with just green rice fields. There were no people, no birds, and no sign of life except a scrawny mule that stood inert in front of an empty cart. There was not a sign of activity anywhere to fuel my imagination of what the free world was like. I was on my own and understood that there was nothing to see outside the walls of Ambarava No. 10.

8. A Man Called Harry

Compared with the three-month wait for the Japanese capitulation, the equally long wait for liberation by the Allies was much easier to endure. The very absence of the Japanese allowed for a much more relaxed atmosphere and those who survived the emotional impact of the news of the end of the war were slowly beginning to regain strength. The camp enjoyed a better state of health thanks both to the better quality and quantity of the food and to the availability of the Red Cross parcels. Though there was still very little protein, there was more rice, a few cooked greens, a little fruit and we could at last be spared the ghastly tapioca blubber. Under the Japanese the daily death rates could be estimated after the morning inspections during the silent stand to attention in respect for the dead. Though this procedure had ceased with the departure of the Japanese, there was a general awareness that the daily death rates had dropped dramatically. There was an atmosphere of optimism and hope and the expressionless faces of malnutrition and despair had learned to smile again. But the feeling of relief and freedom was almost an illusion, for we continued to be internees despite the absence of the Japanese and the desire to pick up the threads of a normal life was restricted by the threat of attack from rebel forces in Java.

In November we began to hear the distant firing of artillery. Convinced that we would soon be transported to safety the sounds of distant guns caused little anxiety, but as the gunfire drew nearer the general atmosphere in the camp became tense. The shells that we heard the day before as distant explosions were now close.

One night we were woken up by a loud explosion followed by voices of alarm in our block. On the following morning we discovered that a shell had made a big hole in the camp wall behind our block. We knew that we had to leave, but how? We felt trapped and frightened and were more and more aware that we could be killed by the increasingly intense bombardment. Should we seek shelter in our cells, or stay out in the open? Would we survive another night in our camp? Would all the efforts to stay alive under the Japanese be made useless by the increasingly powerful Javanese rebel forces?

The tension that welled up in the camp had almost reached bursting point when a fleet of army lorries suddenly arrived. Fierce-looking dark soldiers in khaki turbans ran around herding the women and children into groups.

'The Gurkhas have arrived,' shouted a woman in our block. I was frightened and wanted to run away from these dark, awesome men but my mother reassured us that they were here to rescue us and take us to Semarang and safety.

Nadia quickly threw the most precious items into her case, leaving our old sheet and mattress behind in the cell. Those who were able, were quickly urged to climb onto our lorry, while the strong brown hands of the Indian soldiers lifted the children and the weak on to a mattress-covered floor. We were then partially covered by mattresses to protect us from stray bullets. Between the mattresses above me I could see our guard leaning against the back of the cab, a tall dark soldier bearing a machine gun. Though his turban and black beard made him more fearsome-looking than the Japanese, the very knowledge that he was there on our side to protect us gave us a sense of security. His weapon symbolised security instead of terror.

The convoy of lorries, with our vehicle somewhere in the middle, drew away, through the main entrance to freedom, along the little road that was so empty when I last saw it. We sped through the open countryside and into an atmosphere thick with smoke. By peering through the spaces between the planks at the side of the lorry, I could see burning palm-thatch houses as we sped along a bumpy road through the smoke and dust. We slowed down as we came to a narrow metal bridge over a kali (a muddy river) and I could see a swollen red-brown coloured corpse floating in the milky brown water. A war that we knew to be over had given way to another war; a conflict that our rescuers were trying to make sure was not ours.

The dramatic scenes that we experienced from the back of the lorry distorted our perception of time. It might have been half an hour, or it could have been an hour later when we arrived to join a long line of stationary lorries. The people ahead of us were in the process of alighting and soon we found ourselves standing on the ground in bewildered groups. It seemed to be a kind of point of assembly.

At first we just stood and waited, but as more lorries arrived people began to wander about looking for friends and relatives. I became aware that I was trembling, not with fear, but with the familiar feeling of hunger and weakness. There must have been thousands of women and children but apart from the soldiers there were no men. Women who hadn't seen each other for over three years cried on each other's shoulders with relief that it was all over, the relief of surviving, the relief of seeing people who were links with life before the Japanese. But joy was mingled with the sorrow on hearing of the death of someone close.

Nadia saw a young meagre woman whom she said I ought to recognise. When we approached her, the woman's haggard face broke into a smile. She said that she was surprised to see that I no longer was the round-faced little boy that she sometimes used to mind when Nadia was at work and Mrs Baginsky was out shopping. I vaguely remembered visiting three teenage sisters who lived in a house that had a small lawn where they used to play with me, but as I could not associate her as being one of those sisters, I simply looked blankly at her. As she and Nadia talked, it appeared that she was in another Ambarava camp where, just before capitulation, the Japanese assembled the internees and started throwing hand grenades at them. Someone was quick enough to catch a grenade and toss it back at them, which seemed to put a stop to the intended slaughter. It appeared that she was the only one left of the three sisters.

The two women were interrupted by the arrival of a group of soldiers in light-coloured uniforms. Though they were soldiers, they behaved in a relaxed manner, laughing and talking their strange language in complete contrast to the Japanese. Nadia said that they were British. They helped us into the back of another lorry, this time with seats along the sides, but as the young woman that Nadia was talking to was told to join a group of women without children, we lost contact with her and her story. We were transported to what appeared to be part of a military base where we were accommodated in a large Nissen hut, the continuation of its rounded metal roof with the walls giving it a kind of relaxed feeling, like the Allied soldiers. The only possessions we had were in the case that Nadia hastily filled on evacuation from Ambarava.

Once again we were near the town of Semarang. It was a strange sensation to be brought to an enormous 'bedroom' in the shape of the Nissen hut after having spent over two years in a cell four feet by six. It was all so clean and airy with a high, dark ceiling that curved over us. We were given our own military canvas camp bed, each placed in such a way that it was an almost shameful waste of space and there was plenty of space between our three beds and the next group, which allowed a certain amount of privacy. I flopped down on my bed, tired, weak and hungry. The bedclothes were made of a silky khaki-coloured parachute cloth and the pillows were of blow-up plastic and had a plastic smell. It took some time to get used to the feel and the new smell of the sheets and pillows. A British soldier in light, well-pressed tropical uniform looking as clean and airy as our new bedclothes came into the hut and said something that to me was incomprehensible.

'We can have food as soon as we are ready,' said Nadia acting as our interpreter.

After we had established ourselves in our new palace, we were directed to the canteen housed in another large round-roofed building. There was a large metal counter, behind which a man in a white overall and white hat was serving plates of food to a long queue of women and children. Each plate had a heap of mashed potato and what looked like two brown sausages.

The smell was overwhelmingly delicious. Dipping my fork into what was familiar, I tried the mashed potato first. It had a richer taste than anything that had come into my mouth for over three years. I then ventured to cut a piece of sausage and put it into a mouth that was flowing with saliva from the sudden impact of strong flavours. It had a rich taste, so rich that it was difficult to swallow and yet I was so hungry that the dominating urge to swallow forced the half-chewed piece of sausage down my oesophagus.

Suddenly, the urge to eat changed to a strong feeling of nausea. My fork went back to the mashed potato, but it was too late: I wanted to be sick. On noticing my behaviour and the change in my complexion, Nadia took me outside and I had barely reached the door before I convulsed with a reflex that was so unpleasantly the opposite of eating. Fortunately Vera had not started her sausage and only managed to eat a little mashed potato in time for Nadia to prevent her eating more.

Perhaps much to their dismay, most of the ex-internees, especially the children, reacted to the culinary generosity of the Allies in the same way. They soon realised that the digestive systems of people, especially those of the children that had been subject to starvation and malnutrition for a long time, were too sensitive for foods that would otherwise be considered normal. Their well-meant generosity misfired. This meant that normal European foods that were intended to restore emaciated ex-internees to fitness, could only induce nausea and vomiting after the first few mouthfuls.

Instead, they had to feed us with American corn flakes and milk for breakfast and we had real white bread that was so much more edible than our last experience of bread. I gladly ate the corn flakes, milk and bread and a kind of scrambled egg made out of USA powdered eggs that came in dark khaki tins decorated with the black pattern of the Stars and Stripes. A little corned beef and omelettes went with the bread for lunch. It turned out that our main source of protein was powdered eggs together with the occasional corned beef, which for some reason we could tolerate better than other forms of meat. We were also given plenty of fruit, especially bananas, papayas, grapefruit and oranges.

We stayed at the British base for just a few days, for enough time to begin to recover; though the swelling around my ankles was still a reminder that I was suffering from beriberi.

Then we were told to pack our things and wait to be transported to the harbour, the same harbour that uncle Ben showed us nearly four years previously. The harbour that was then busy with pre-war commerce, which taught me the meaning of the word 'harbour', was now a harbour dealing with the results of war.

A landing craft waited for us to embark, or rather to step down into it, for it looked like an oversized rowing boat without transoms. We found ourselves standing on the bottom. The sides of the craft seemed higher than any of the adults and there was a curious tailgate that was closed into an upright position when the boat was full. I was worried that water might leak through the gaps, as we were standing at what seemed below water level, but despite what I judged to be several lorry loads of people, the craft was quite seaworthy. We swayed and bumped along for what might have been twenty minutes before drawing close to an enormous grey steel wall.

The next thing we knew was that we were helped onto a steel ladder that led up the steel wall while the landing craft moved up and down with the waves. We were put aboard an American warship that was to take us up the coast to Batavia and cheerful men in sand-coloured uniforms speaking a drawling language ushered us to our quarters. On board the battleship, our environment was dominantly light grey. Everything was a light grey colour: grey pipelined corridors, grey decks and huge grey guns. The Americans were even more relaxed in manner than the British. They took us on a tour to show us a large part of our new light grey environment, including the impressive and nearly ear-bursting huge engines that we could see at work from a platform at the head of some steep steps. Along one of the maze of light grey pipelined corridors we were allocated a small cabin with a tier of three luxurious bunk-beds, each having a polished hardwood side. My mother was impressed by the high standard of living that the American sailor enjoyed.

Somehow through the maze of corridors we managed to find a canteen where we were given a real American 'hot dog'. It had a rich taste and didn't make me sick, but Vera couldn't take it and the diarrhoea that followed made us both unwell for a day or two after-wards. This was a confirmation to Nadia that our diet had to be carefully regulated for some time to come.

After a voyage of about twenty-four hours, we arrived in Batavia to be transported to a suburb that might have been the residential area for the Japanese soldiers after they had taken it over from the more affluent Javanese.

We were allocated a small bungalow that had an entrance in the form of a patio. A door opened into a light room furnished with an armchair facing two single beds along the wall. Beside the armchair there was a door that led into a small kitchen and another door at the end of the room led to a darker room with a double bed. Once again we each had our own beds, this time equipped with white linen and mosquito nets. Nadia's bed was the same size as the one she and Jan had before internment. I had last seen a double bed half my life ago.

A cardboard box containing provisions stood waiting for use on the kitchen floor. For the first time for three and a half years Nadia was left directly in charge of preparing our own food from the packets of rice, powdered milk, powdered eggs in dark khaki USA packets, concentrated fruit juices, cereals and condiments. There was also some money to buy fruit, vegetables and bread locally. We were in a refugee camp that was equipped with all the basics necessary for both a physical and mental recovery from all that time in concentration camp.

Soon after we were established in our new quarters, almost a new home. Nadia was informed that all efforts were being made to reunite spouses with each other and that the surviving men were soon to be directed to their surviving wives and families. Jan was not among the first men to come to our refugee camp but Nadia had met someone who was with him in the same camp. He said that Jan was fit and well.

When Jan arrived two days later, it was not a moment for tears of joy and warm embraces. Jan and Nadia greeted each other with a familiarity that reflected the negative aspects of their marriage. He was dressed in a navy blue pair of football shorts that came almost down to the knees and his short-sleeved off-white shirt was creased in the wrong places. He looked well without even appearing to have lost weight, let alone having the slightest tendency towards malnutrition. He greeted us with a forced smile, his grey eyes looking small and expressionless behind the round myopic lenses that dominated his tanned face. He was more or less as I remembered him.

'You look well, Jan,' Nadia said in Dutch.

'You look fat,' said Jan blowing up his cheeks to make the point.

'But you like fat women!'

'You have the wrong kind of fat,' he said referring to her puffiness caused by malnutrition.

What interested me more than that conversation was whether he had made any presents for us as we had seen children playing with wooden toys made by their fathers while spending their time in camp. We waited patiently for the conversation between our parents to cease so that he could turn his attention to us. But no, he hardly even talked to us, let alone gave us a present.

Then much of their conversation took place in English, which they still used as the language of exclusion as far as Vera and I were concerned, the tone of the conversation did not suggest the kind of reunion that would lead to happy family life.

Nevertheless, we settled into a new routine in our temporary home and thanks to a diet regime that avoided anything to upset our stomachs we began to feel stronger under Nadia's care. Despite this, however, my ankles still showed signs of beriberi and I still spent long periods on the potty with a kind of diarrhoea that made me feel I should remain on it for ever as there was always more to come.

It was Christmas 1945. The Allies did their utmost to ensure that all ex-prisoners of war could celebrate Christmas in their way. Women with young children were invited to a nearby airbase. A military bus took us to a hangar where an old man dressed in a red cloak fringed with white stood, nodded and smiled amiably. Several enormous sacks surrounded him like a fortification.

We stood amongst other women and children and gaped at the figure.

'That is Santa Claus, the American Sinter Klaas,' said Nadia.

'Is he real?'

'Of course he isn't,' said Vera, uttering a pearl of her four-year-old wisdom. 'The one in camp was real. This one can't speak our language. He's just an American dressed up.'

I couldn't decide on his genuineness, but our mother explained that this one was Santa Claus and the one in camp was Saint Nicholas, accompanied by his black assistant, Svarta Piet. Besides, that was on December 6th last year when we were still in camp. The Americans and the British celebrate Christmas on Christmas Day, December 25th.

All the children crowded round the beaming red-cloaked and white-bearded Santa Claus to receive presents. He waved us to come nearer and we understood that one of the large sacks was for girls and another for boys. He beamed, chuckled and rocked, shouting

'Haw, haw haw!' while children picked their bright coloured packages from one or the other of the large sacks.

Vera was the first of us to receive a parcel that she soon undid to reveal a rather expressionless rag doll. It was not a bit as good as Tasha, which Ludmilla still had, and Vera was clearly disappointed with her gift. I got a kind of comic strip picture book in English, which didn't impress me very much, when I quickly flipped through it. Nadia said that it was written in English and might be worth keeping, but I preferred Vass given to me in person by Sinter Klaas. Vass was still my best companion, especially when going to sleep.

The whole procedure took place rather quickly and resulted in what seemed to be more disappointments than smiling faces. When all the children received their gifts, Santa Claus picked up the empty sacks and rushed out to a waiting aeroplane fifty yards outside the hangar. He waved as he ran behind the wing to the passenger door. Suddenly the draught of the propeller blew off his fine white beard, but he managed to catch it in mid-flight and held it to his face with one hand while clutching the empty sacks with the other. As he ran I caught a glimpse of his uniform-coloured trouser legs below his cloak.

My little sister was right: he was an American soldier!

When we were back in our quarters in the refugee area I flipped through the cartoon strip pages of my new book, all of which had an English text which I could not begin to understand as I hadn't even begun to learn to read in any language. Nadia said that she would try to translate it for me later, or she could suggest that Jan spent a little time with his son. Vera's new doll was completely ignored.

Though Jan lived in with us, he was often away leading a social life of his own without making an effort either to establish a relationship with us or to pick up the threads of his marriage. On the contrary, he began to be absent for longer periods of time which could not be accounted for by bridge parties. In the end Nadia explained to us that he had told her that he had fallen in love with another woman. In her bitterness she began to tell us that she had heard that Jan did not enjoy the best reputation in the camp, never being the first to help anyone in need and always being the first in the food queue. She paused and then added, 'It is typical of him to know how to look after number one.'

There was a moment of silence as if Nadia was deep in thought, then she said, 'I've asked Pappie to give me a divorce. You know that though he will still be your father, it will mean that he will no longer live with us.'

We listened in silence, not knowing how to react. After a pause, she continued, 'He was quite pleased with the idea. Presumably because he is going out with this other woman.'

The British army had given us access to a hangar that they helped to organise into a kind of community centre for the ex-internees. They organised dances for the adults and in the evenings I could hear strains of Glen Miller tunes like 'In the Mood'. On the local radio, which the Dutch had begun to run, I could hear a Dutch popular melody with the glissando sound of a Hawaiian guitar called 'Ajoen, ajoen in de hooge klapper boom ajoen, ajoen', about being in a south sea paradise among the palm trees. They organised games and competitions for the children and I took part but was disappointed not to win more than a rosette in a potato race. While all this went on Jan played bridge, often with British soldiers.

One day Jan left the bridge table to announce that he would like to introduce Nadia to a very charming English soldier who supplied him with cigarettes. He even offered to baby-sit while she went out with him.

She accepted this offer, perhaps more to spite Jan than to enjoy the prospect of socialising with the soldiers. However, Jan was only too pleased that Nadia accepted the date, as for him it meant that he was given carte blanche to see his woman more often before the divorce went through. He was in such a good mood that he even started to translate my new comic book only to give up after ten minutes as he thought it was quite boring. Instead Vera and I were sent to bed where we could sleep while he read a newspaper.

On the next day we fired Nadia with a host of questions about where she had been, whom she was with and what they did. She said that she had met a very nice Englishman and that they danced and that his friends were also nice.

One morning soon after, a British soldier arrived at our refugee bungalow on an army motorbike. He was dressed in light khaki shorts and shirt. As he dismounted he took off his peaked khaki hat to reveal a tanned face and thinning fair hair bleached by the tropical sun.

The sound of the motorbike brought Nadia out to meet him. 'Hello Harry', I heard her shout.

Everything about him was sunny, including his smile, his twinkling blue eyes shining with enthusiasm.

Nadia introduced us.

'Hello, call me Uncle Harry,' he said in a gentle baritone voice.

'Say hello to Uncle Harry,' said Nadia speaking to us in the usual Russian.

We said something like 'hello Uncle Harry', both of us being completely absorbed by his amiability.

Uncle Harry brought a large tin of peaches that Nadia opened and gave us to try. We revelled in their soft, syrupy, fruity taste, which seemed even better when afterwards neither Vera nor I felt sick. The peach experience was followed by a kind of conversation when Uncle Harry asked us about our ages, what we had for Christmas and so on, while Nadia did the interpreting. When he told us that back home in England he had two sons of about our ages, I thought how lucky they were to have a father like that. The time seemed to fly before he had to take his leave to get back to his regiment.

After that, he visited us several times and every occasion was associated with pleasantness, not only in the form of peaches and sweets but words and gestures that could only give the impression of amiability, even without the help of Nadia as the interpreter. Often when he came he would find me immobilised on the potty as I was still suffering from my interminable diarrhoea.

The weeks followed quickly while we became increasingly acquainted with Uncle Harry, while Jan was increasingly absent. We sat on his knee and he talked to us while Nadia interpreted. We had never experienced such warmth from a man before. Why couldn't Jan be like him, I thought? Despite Jan's appearance of wellbeing, as though he hadn't suffered the deprivations of concentration camp, his attitude towards us did not radiate the same kind of warmth that Harry's did. On the other hand, until I met Uncle Harry, I assumed that a father was someone who was a background figure who had more to do with other adults than with his own children, while it was the mother who was the active parent. Nadia was our feeder, our teacher, our mother confessor and adviser who listened to both our sorrows and our joys, giving praise or consolation as the occasion demanded, while since it was the father who was the one who earned the money, he hadn't time for the children

As the days followed Nadia told us more about Uncle Harry. It turned out that he was a widower, his wife having died of pneumonia during the war. She left two boys, one of whom was about the same age as Vera while the other was about a year younger than me. They were being looked after by Harry's parents. His father was an engineer at a steelworks in a nearby town. Uncle Harry had his own building firm and was now serving as a warrant officer in the Royal Engineers who were there to organise the docks in order to facilitate the evacuation of ex-POWs.

He often came on an army motorbike, sometimes with sidecar, sometimes accompanied by his friends from the sergeants' mess. To Vera and I he represented only happiness and fun and we were glad that Nadia had found a new friend in him. On one occasion he showed us a Japanese Samurai sword that he had acquired. Though I had seen them worn by the more important soldiers during our time in camp, it was the first time I had seen the weapon close to. He drew out the sword from its diamond patterned black leather scabbard to reveal a shiny, slightly curved blade. The black hilt was oval and the handle of black leather with light brown leather diamond decorations. He drew his thumb across the blade to show us its sharpness and explained its use and significance for Nadia to interpret.

'This sword,' said Nadia after Uncle Harry had finished his description, 'represents the fighting spirit of the Japanese. It is one of the finest swords in the world, and has been one of the main reasons for their military successes in the past. Though mostly used for ceremonial occasions, it has also been used to execute prisoners in this war and when they surrendered the officers handed these swords in to the Allies as their symbol for the acceptance of defeat.'

After that information, I was even more astounded that Uncle Harry actually had one of these weapons in his possession. This made him seem very important indeed in my eyes and gave me the impression that a warrant officer must be quite a high rank in the army.

My parents' divorce was granted without any fuss at all because the authorities were anxious that all ex-POWs should have an easy start to life after all that they had been through. All that they had to do was to sign some papers together in the presence of a representative of the Dutch court of law.

In February we were informed that we were to be transported to Holland. The Dutch government had decided that all civilians were to be repatriated, partly to facilitate recovery from internment and partly because it wasn't safe for civilians to stay in the Dutch East Indies because of the conflict with the fighters for independence. The Dutch authorities gave all the expatriates enough money to cover all the necessities for the move back to Holland.

A kind of grapevine of post-internment news developed. When Nadia made enquiries she found out that the Baginskys had finally been interned and that though Mrs Baginsky had survived, her husband had died. She had also found out that just before the Japanese surrender, they had indeed intended to drive us from Ambarava into the nearby lake in order to be rid of us. She assumed that the Japanese had taken the valuables that she left in the care of the Chinese and it would be hopeless to try to check, as Semarang was already in the hands of Sukarno and his freedom fighters. The only relics of our colonial past in Java were a few pieces of C.K. silver and my silver cup that she took with her to camp together with a few second-rate photographs. The best family pictures had disappeared with the valuables left with the Chinese.

As if to send us off, Jan painted the rounded lid of his old wooden chest with Nadia's name, 'N.P. KRUYS' in readiness for the voyage to Holland. He also helped us to pack and organise our suitcases and was there when Harry came to take us in an army jeep to our ship.

As Harry drove off, Nadia sat in the front seat while Vera and I were in the back. I looked back to see Jan running behind. The sight of this frantically waving bespectacled man dressed in cotton shorts tied at the waist gave me a lump in my throat. In a way he looked pathetic but that waving figure was, after all, my father. At the same time I felt that any parental bond that might have developed was nipped in the bud and gone forever.

9. SS *Tabinta*

The *Tabinta* was a converted troop carrier. She must have been launched some time during the thirties and served as a Dutch cargo ship displacing about 15,000 tons. Her crown of glory was a single broad black and yellow funnel that dominated the superstructure in about the middle of the hull. To me she looked as modern as any ship could be and as we walked up the wooden gangway it felt as if we were walking into the future. We were on our way to a future in Holland and the thought that perhaps there might be a link with England gave my steps vigour of purpose on the gangway.

A member of the crew directed us to the way down to our sleeping quarters. It was steep and dark down to the deck below. The former cargo holds were converted to take troops using an intricate iron framework designed to hold numerous canvas bunks. My bunk was the highest of a tier of three; Vera had the middle and Nadia the lowest. Below our quarters there was yet another floor constructed to take yet as many bunks, but presumably for adults without children. At least we had a porthole near our bunks. Nadia told us that from now on mosquito netting was unnecessary and I thought that it would feel strange to sleep without that white, soft security that always enveloped us before going to sleep.

Later that day, we stood at the railings to watch the ship begin to set sail. Greasy men heaved the thick hawsers from the bollards and I stared, fascinated by the thought that ropes could be made that thick and that they must be heavy because men had to throw thin ropes that were attached to stouter ropes that were attached to the hawsers. The engines began to make the deck vibrate and the water churned to a seething milky green broth between the hull and the quay.

The *Tabinta* began to move slowly away from the quay. Bound for Rotterdam, which for us meant Amsterdam.

Suddenly, Nadia said, 'Look, there's Harry!'

He sat on his motorbike with a broad smile beneath his peaked army hat, his waving signifying au revoir rather than adieu. He was visible for a time as the water widened between us and the quay, but his disappearance as the ship left did not seem so sad. On the contrary, his presence on the quayside instead of Jan's, confirmed that we would see him again.

Jakarta began to dwindle away while the late afternoon gave way to evening, as the coastline of Java became a dark strip on the horizon. Soon we were sailing into the overwhelming redness of an equatorial sunset at sea.

When, on the following day, several passengers were looking out and pointing to the horizon, we found out that their interest was focussed on the islands of Krakatoa. We could just make out a vague blip on the horizon. Nadia explained they were formed after the great eruption of a large volcano. She said that they were especially interesting because Jan's father, my grandfather, experienced the shock wave on his ship. That was in 1883 when he was en route to Java with his parents as a sixteen-year-old. Since then a new volcano, Anak Krakatoa (The Child of Krakatoa), gradually formed to become visible in the 1920s.

We saw Anak Krakatoa, a small, grey irregularity on the horizon of a sea that was so calm that the island looked like a blemish on the edge of a huge silver mirror. I thought about my grandfather who met me as a new born baby and whom I never remembered meeting and dwelled on the thought of him sailing the same sea over sixty years previously when he was there at the time of the eruption.

As the voyage progressed northwards, we gradually accustomed ourselves to the roll of the ship and to what the galley had to offer. Compared to what we ate in camp it was a heaven of culinary delights. Breakfast was warm, milky, sticky and sweetened and might have been porridge. Lunch consisted mainly of real white bread and butter served with slices of corned beef and cheese. The evening meals were hot meat and potato or rice-based dishes, all the menus being carefully selected to be nutritious without being too rich for stomachs still suffering from the after-effects of concentration camp. Nadia brought our food down to our bunks on white enamelled plates and each meal was washed down with an enamel mug of either tea or milk. For dessert we had oranges or bananas, both of which were familiar to me from the time before camp. In addition, she gave us a fruit that looked a little like a large mangosteen and when Nadia urged us to take a bite through its thin but somewhat hard waxy skin and into its pithy white centre, it seemed almost tasteless. Nadia told us that what we were eating were apples, probably grown in Holland and that they usually tasted better, but the variety that we were offered had the advantage of keeping for long periods, thereby making it suitable as a fruit for long voyages. As I failed to understand the point of keeping fruit that was not a bit tasty, I preferred to keep to bananas and oranges when the choice was given, especially after Nadia said that they had the most vitamins.

The main disadvantage of having confined dark quarters with limited access to a porthole to look through was that one was prone to suffer from sea-sickness, which Vera and I went through during the first days of the voyage. Not only was this unpleasant for us and our immediate neighbours, but it also meant that we were not receiving the full benefit of the food we received. We soon found that the best remedy was to be out on deck as much as possible.

It felt good to be out on deck with the speed of the ship producing just the right amount of breeze to prevent the heat of the sun from being unbearable. The sea air was mixed with the smell of the ship, a not unpleasant mixture of fresh paint combined with oil and tar. Looking down on the deck I saw a shiny, small gold object lying on the black caulk of the deck. When I picked it up I saw that it was a small, Dutch, gold-coloured, metal air-force badge. I ran to show it to Nadia who took it to a member of the crew who, to my relief, said that some soldier must have lost it and that we might as well keep it. When I pinned it on my shirt just where the camp number used to be, the golden winged badge gave me a feeling of pride instead of the fear that my number badge evoked in camp.

Much of my time on board I found myself by the railings staring down at the sea. Fascinated by the effect of the ship driving through the water, I was mesmerised by the changing formations of foam circles floating by as the ship vibrated through the salty water, the engine drumming on and on. Each day seemed to produce different patterns of white foam with a whole range of shades of blue, green, and grey as the background.

Vera didn't go out onto the deck as often as I. She spent most of her daytime at a play group organised by crew and parents for the younger children. For my part, mixing with other children, whatever the age, was not that appealing, so I would wander about those parts of the deck where passengers were allowed, either on my own or sometimes accompanied by Nadia.

I soon found that a sea voyage didn't only involve seeing the seawater in all its moods and colours. I took it for granted that the sea was full of fish that could not be seen, but there were other forms of life to be discovered during my hours spent staring from the railings. Strange round semi-transparent masses floated by reminding me a little of the blubber breakfasts in camp, some bluish white while others had a reddish tinge. Nadia told me that they were kinds of jellyfish. Occasionally a banded snake-like creature coiled its way to the surface, only to return to the depths. Once again my inexhaustible source of information told me that they were sea snakes and were exceedingly poisonous. That statement increased my dread and fascination of the tropical seas. Were they really snakes, or were they fish? Why were they so poisonous? Did they kill many bathers? Were they worse than sharks? Even Nadia couldn't answer all the questions that her seven-year-old son was burning to have answered.

A little later I saw a couple of triangular fins racing along the surface of the water, then to disappear. I tore myself away from the railings to find Nadia, convinced that I had seen two sharks. This inspired Nadia to join me for a period of sea watching in the look out for sharks. She then exclaimed, 'Look, dolphins!'

Looking in the direction she pointed I saw the same type of triangular fin that I had seen before followed by a leap of a large fish-like creature. My disappointment on hearing the fact that my 'sharks' must have been dolphins at first diminished my ability to appreciate the spectacle of the dolphins themselves. But it wasn't long before we were captivated by the sight of several dolphins jumping near the ship and we made our way to the bows to see them leaping up ahead of us as if they were trying to compete with our vessel. Nadia told me that, like us, they were warm-blooded and were very intelligent.

Dolphins often entertained us in their antics when they followed the ship, which helped to subdue my hope of seeing a shark. Sharks never materialised, but one day we saw what looked like a small flock of birds rising out of the water, gliding some distance between the waves, only to disappear. Nadia pointed them out as flying fish and said that she had seen many on the voyage from Holland to Java when I was only six months old. Later, a passenger caught one that had landed on the deck, an event that attracted a group of curious children including myself to the man who held it up for all to see. It would have passed for any ordinary fish, had it not been for two huge pectoral fins, each almost as long as the body.

The crew rigged up ropes to confine passengers to certain areas during rough weather, but surprisingly, one such rope-bounded walkway led all the way to the bows. Once when it was blowing a gale and the seas were high we ventured all the way up to the bows, to watch the ship breaking into the waves. It was like being on a gigantic seesaw, one moment dipping down and down to thunder into the foaming brine, only to be lifted up, up into the sky and to see the waves far below. I was very proud of having 'weathered the storm' in that way. Apart from the adventure of being outdoors in rough weather, it proved to be an excellent way of preventing sea-sickness.

One morning about a week after departure, there was a lot of commotion as if the crew was up to something. It turned out to be the preparation for a ceremony that involved those persons who were to be the first to cross the equator. The crossing of the line was the traditional ceremonial occasion that all first-timers had to endure. At the appropriate moment a list of names of those to be called to the ceremony was called out. This really meant that the vast majority of 'victims' were children who were born in Java and who were over five. Since I had already crossed the equator at the age of six months on our way to Java before the war, I was exempt from the ordeal of being smothered in soapy lather and thrown into a makeshift pool lined by canvas. Vera had also escaped the 'crossing of the line' since her fifth birthday wasn't until June. Though the crew had fun, most of the younger children didn't.

We felt stronger as the days passed. Nadia occasionally checked my ankles for oedema and though I was still quite scrawny, she was soon convinced that I had finally recovered from my beriberi.

After about three weeks Nadia announced that we had reached the Red Sea and this, she said, meant that we were about halfway to Holland. After concentrating my gaze for a moment at a calm dark grey-blue sea I asked my mother the obvious question,

'Why is it called 'the Red Sea' when it doesn't look at all red?'

'I don't really know. Perhaps it's because it looks reddish at certain times of the year, or that the sunsets are especially red here.'

The Red Sea seemed quite as large as the ocean we had already crossed and after a day or two it was easy to forget that our ship was still sailing on the sea of that name. The sea was still a very dark aquamarine and there were no dramatic sunsets to speak of. In fact, the only sources of interest on the Red Sea were schools of flying fish and dolphins and as these were nearly a daily occurrence, there seemed to be nothing to distinguish this new sea from the seas that we had experienced since leaving Java. I found out that it's only significance was that we were halfway to Holland.

In fact just as I felt that life began to be rather monotonous I saw a group of passengers staring out to sea with an extra enthusiasm.

'Look! I can see land,' shouted an older boy who stared towards the bow of the ship. I found it difficult to see anything but the usual stretch of sea, but after staring for some time, I could indeed make out a thin line on the horizon that grew larger after a while. Soon there were many passengers of all ages crowding along the railings as we came to what looked like a large port or harbour. In the distance there were several large cargo ships with masts sprouting jibs set at various angles, making them look like they were giant dead spiders lying on their backs with their legs pointing up in the air. Beyond them was a golden yellowish line on the horizon suggesting land.

Nadia said that we must have been approaching the port of Suez, in the country of Egypt. A short time later we were surprised that our ship had slowed down and was closing in towards a quay to tie up. After only a minute or two it seemed that all the passengers had emerged to investigate the cause of the slowing down of our ship and it was difficult to find standing space by the railings. By squeezing myself forward, I could see that as we drew closer to the quay, there was a marching group of odd-looking soldiers blowing metal musical instruments on the quayside. They seemed strange because they wore neither British nor American uniforms, but they were playing familiar marches like 'Stars and Stripes'. Then, above the sound of the music I heard a member of the crew laughing.

'Have you seen anything like it?' he laughed, 'Not only do they greet us with a brass band, they get a band of German ex-POWs to play American marches!'

His remark caused several titters of amusement among the passengers that heard him.

After coming to a standstill, we were informed that we had the opportunity to disembark and have a look at Suez for a few hours. Apart from the warehouses and other harbour buildings along a concrete quayside, terra firma was nothing but sand. This landscape was a totally new experience for someone who had spent nearly all his life in the tropics and half of that time in confinement, let alone four weeks of nothing but sea. As there was sand everywhere I looked I wondered if the whole of Egypt was just sand.

I left the crowd and found Nadia, who told us about Egypt, its pyramids, dates and the Sahara Desert.

When we disembarked it felt as if my legs wanted to take unnecessary steps and were slightly out of control. We soon realised that this is how one felt after spending four weeks on a pitching and rolling ship. But it wasn't long before the feeling disappeared.

We were led round a warehouse to be confronted by a railway and a line of cattle trucks. To my horror we were urged to climb into one of these trucks. Surely we weren't being sent to another camp! Vera and I, together with several other children, felt frightened and some began to cry, despite assurances by the adults that this was for pleasure and had nothing to do with having to go back to a concentration camp. Waiting for the next step in the heat of the Egyptian sun didn't do much to ease the tension.

But the trepidation of war was soon dispelled as we were helped into the cattle truck to be surprised by the feeling of freshness caused by the thick layer of straw that gave off a pleasant aroma in a hot atmosphere that was so dry that we didn't feel uncomfortable. The truck began to pull forward and continued quite slowly through a desert landscape, which we could see through the open doorway in the side of the truck. It was not at all the same feeling of hot confinement that we experienced three years before and a pleasant warm breeze streamed in through the opening. There was sand everywhere, sometimes level ground, sometimes in the form of small hills. Not a single plant of any colour was to be seen. Just sand.

We arrived about ten minutes later at the edge of what must have been the town of Suez. A member of the crew was delegated to look after the children while the adults were given the opportunity to do some shopping.

We children were ushered into a hangar-like building where there were fold-up tables with toy cars, toy bricks and spades, while the adults were escorted away to shop.

I felt little interest in the toys: instead I took one of the toy spades and started to dig in an open area of sand that was not floored over in the building. For a few minutes just digging and making heaps of sand was a sensation that made me feel involved in this landscape of sand, the sands of the Sahara Desert.

But when I got over the need to dig up the Sahara Desert, I dropped my spade and walked out to take another look at this sandy ocean. The sunlight was blindingly bright and while I stood screwing up my eyes, trying to get accustomed to it, the member of the crew who was in charge came towards me, presumably to prevent me straying away into the desert. Then he shouted and pointed in my direction. Thinking he was accusing me of running away, I began to walk towards him, but he continued to motion with his pointing finger. I turned round to find that about fifty yards away there was a man dressed in a long white robe who was leading two strange, large animals with humped backs.

'Did you see the camels?' He then added, 'You'd better come in and join the others, or you'll miss the presents.'

Inside the building the children were crowding round a table. A brown man not at all like the brown Javanese, but similar to the one that led the camels was in the process of giving each child a small brown paper bag, while another was handing out what looked like oranges. Before I received my handouts, I saw a boy picking out something brown and put it in his mouth. By the way he licked his fingers it seemed like the object was sticky.

Gula Java, I thought. But no, the contents of my paper bag contained sticky oval brown things and I followed the boy's example by trying one. The sweet slightly musty taste dispelled all thoughts of gula Java and made me come to the conclusion that I wasn't very keen on what I tasted, though the others, including Vera seemed to like them.

When the adults arrived, we climbed back onto our cattle truck together with Nadia who was carrying a new leather bag. Vera offered her what was left in her brown paper bag.

'You've been given some dates! How wonderful!'

'And we've got an orange each,' said Vera.'

'If those are what they call dates, I don't like them,' I said. 'You can have mine.'

'Eat them, they're good for you,' came the maternal reply. 'Look what I've bought,' continued Nadia who proceeded to show us a light brown, soft leather holdall, embossed with pictures of the pyramids and camels. 'I bargained the man down to a low price to buy this handbag,' she said, extracting a shiny black handbag from the holdall. It was also beautifully embossed with a pyramid design.

I told Nadia that I had experienced digging a little of the Sahara Desert and that I had actually seen a camel.

On board we were issued with clothing suitable for the Dutch climate and gathered by charitable organisations in Holland. Nadia got a smart, brown teddy bear coat, Vera a navy blue overcoat and I had a brown one, matching my dark brown hair. I removed the gold airforce badge from my shirt and pinned onto the lapel of my new coat.

The ship remained at the Port of Suez that evening. We awoke the following morning to the sensation that we were already under way and a look through the porthole gave me the unbelievable impression that the ship appeared to be sailing through the desert! I ran up to the deck and to the railings already lined by passengers to see that our ship was slowly sailing along a stretch of water that was not wide enough for two ships abreast.

I ran below to announce that we were actually on the Suez Canal.

'Now I understand why we stayed in Suez. We were waiting for our turn to go on the canal,' said Nadia.

My time at the railings was rewarded by several sightings of camels and palm trees that reminded me of my uneaten dates.

In the afternoon we came to a section where the canal widened into a kind of lake where several ships were waiting at anchor. We continued into a slightly wider section of the canal at which point my interest in sand, camels and date palms faded.

On the next day we had reached open sea, which Nadia informed us was the Mediterranean, and a week later we had to put our coats on when we ventured out on deck as we had reached the coolness of the Bay of Biscay. Nadia warned us that it was always stormy in the Bay of Biscay, but apart from some choppiness, which our sea legs took in their stride, there was little hint of storm. There was also a scary rumour that mines that had not been gathered after the war were still a danger to shipping, but as we knew that there was nothing we could do about it, we hoped that the crew were alert to them.

A day or two before we were to arrive in Rotterdam we were informed that we were to present ourselves at the purser's office where our immigration papers would be organised. Nadia timed our visit to avoid a long wait in a queue, which was fairly successful, as we didn't have to wait too long. The official at the purser's office looked through Nadia's passport without saying anything and then said that we were to be sent to some small village out in the Dutch countryside. It became apparent that in trying to prevent Amsterdam from being swamped by a sudden influx of people from the Far East, the authorities were anxious to distribute those without homes to different parts of the country.

'But I want to go to Amsterdam. We have friends and relatives in Amsterdam,' said my mother to the immigration official. 'Besides, my son is still suffering from beriberi, has nearly died from amoebic dysentery and needs the kind of medical supervision that could only be available in Amsterdam.'

The official took a hard look at me, smiled a little and nodding his head in consent, said something to indicate that he would mark our papers with Amsterdam, thereby making us one of the exceptions to their policy.

10. Amsterdam

April 1946. We arrived in the greyness of Rotterdam. Packing our belongings proved to be easy now that Nadia had the new Egyptian bag which was the smallest and most interesting of our pieces of luggage. The crew helped us to assemble our baggage on deck ready for disembarkation.

The cold wind that met us at the quayside made me shiver when we walked down that gangway towards the immigration centre, making me long for the warmth of Java for the first time in my life.

We came into a large open building already thronging with passengers that made loose queues leading to uniformed officials. Somehow the wait for our turn seemed to pass quickly, owing perhaps to the efficiency of the Dutch immigration officials or owing to the more pleasant temperature indoors compared to the rawness outside.

Finally, we were directed to the station and the train to Amsterdam. The train journey from Rotterdam to Amsterdam began with my relief to see that for the first time in four years we were to travel in a normal passenger train instead of a cattle truck and that we had proper seats. But that was where the sense of normality ended. It felt abnormally cold and people walked about the station wearing heavy coats and hats but once inside the train we could relax in a temperature that was more pleasant and did not demand the heaviness of our new winter clothing.

Though we did not sit close to the window the open plan seating arrangement allowed us to see the passing scenery quite easily. The greyness of city buildings gradually gave way to flat open countryside with expanses of bright green broken by parallels of long straight ditches of water the surfaces of which were blotched with patches of green duckweed.

Of course we had peppered Nadia with questions about what Holland was like as soon as we were told to pack our scanty belongings in Java. As the train passed through the long green rectangles

divided by lines of water, I was reminded about what Nadia told me:
that Holland was flat. Windmills were the first objects to look out for
and it wasn't long before they were commonplace, matching up to
our expectations both in appearance and number. Nadia explained
their purpose to us and some of them could be seen at work with
their sails turning round to pump water into and out of the dykes.
Suddenly the view through the window was taken up by a large rectangular shape of an intense yellow, then one of bright red, then
bright blue and then whites and a whole variety of colours and
shades. The impact of the show of colours was so violent that it took
me a few moments to realise that we were passing through fields of
flowers.

Nadia, who was not as surprised as us, explained that Holland was
famous for its spring flowers and it was the second time she had seen
these stunning displays, since she last came to Holland in the spring
of 1938 when she was expecting me.

It was as if there had never been a war in Holland, certainly not a
war less than a year ago. As if in that April of 1946 Holland had put
the devastation of war into history by flaunting a floral flourish of
colour.

The show of colours gave way to normal fields, which in turn disappeared with the appearance of buildings that were part of the
enormity of the city and our final destination. We were too tired to
take in the station and the taxi journey to our new address that
Nadia was given on the *Tabinta*.

But although there was little visible physical evidence of the recent
Second World War, we knew that Holland was very much affected.
As the war had disrupted and ended the lives of people, rather than
left its mark on buildings, it had left a number of empty houses.
These were taken over by the authorities to accommodate people
like us and our home in Amsterdam turned out to be a drab bedsitter
on the third floor of a four-storey town house somewhere not far
from the centre.

We were provided with one double bed which Vera and Nadia
shared and I was given a single bed, which folded up under a shelf,
fringed by a curtain when the bed was not in use. Though our
voyage on the *Tabinta* had allowed us to become used to sleeping

without mosquito netting in bunks, seeing our new ordinary beds confirmed that mosquito netting belonged to the past. The room was cold and dark, quite the opposite of what we had at the refugee camp, but compared with our cell at Ambarava it was still sheer luxury. The floor was partly covered by a dull, worn carpet with an oriental pattern that might have been attractive in its heyday and the walls displayed an equally nondescript beige patterned wallpaper. A worn grey functional armchair stood in a corner by the window. Our own kitchen in the form of a small sink and a two-ringed gas stove, was inside a cupboard with cream-coloured doors that must have been painted long before the war. The bathroom and toilet, which was shared by neighbours in several adjoining rooms, was on the landing one flight down the stairs. Strictly speaking, our floor was uppermost, but a little along our landing there was a door that led to a narrower, steeper staircase that opened out into a loft lit by a skylight. The loft space was criss-crossed by washing lines, which allowed us to dry the washing that was done in the bathtub. There was also a door in the loft, the purpose of which was made known to us a little later. But we were physically and mentally unable to absorb our immediate surroundings and collapsed into our beds as soon as Nadia had made them.

We were invigorated by a good night's sleep and I surveyed the view in the bright morning light. From the large sash window in our room I could see that the view was dominated by the roofs of old Dutch, brick town houses on the opposite side of the cobbled street. Nearly every roof gable that faced the street had a kind of projection with a pulley wheel. A few days after our move we were able to observe one of these structures being used as a crane to haul up furniture, which would then be taken in through an open window on the appropriate floor of the building.

Our breakfast that Nadia managed to buy near the station as soon as we arrived in Amsterdam, consisted of a couple of slices of bread and butter sprinkled with small grains of various pastel shades that tasted sugary and smelled of aniseed. Nadia told us that the Dutch name for them was muisjes, which meant 'little mice'.

We were washing this down with a glass of milk when there was a knock on the door. The visitor was a dark-haired girl of about ten or eleven who spoke to Nadia in Dutch. Though she spoke quickly, I could follow the conversation with ease, thanks to my time in camp. It turned out that the girl's name was Emilie, and that she lived with her mother up in the loft, the door to their home being what we saw beyond the washing lines. Emilie said that she would like to take us to show us round and Nadia responded by asking her to call again in half an hour when we were ready. Vera and I were thrilled with the idea and I couldn't wait to take stock of our new surroundings, a totally new environment, in Europe instead of Tropical Asia.

Emilie was the kind of person that made one feel relaxed at first sight. She met us with a smile that extended over the greater part of her finely freckled face and her brown eyes twinkled with warmth that made her almost motherly. We ran down the stairs while she heaved the heavy front door open and took us by the hand to start the tour of our part of town. She pointed out the baker's to Nadia and as we walked past, the delicious smell of fresh-baked bread and pastries permeated our deprived senses. The aniseed taste that lingered in my mouth a few minutes after breakfast had vanished. No sooner had we absorbed the bakery than we were greeted by the mixed smells of cheese and yoghurt at the nearby white-tiled dairy shop.

The morning sun dispelled the dampness of the pavement and the cobbled streets, the moisture rising to mingle with the smells of the different shops that combined to give Amsterdam its own morning scent.

After winding our way along a few streets Emilie took us into a nearby park, its neatly cut lawns broken by patterns of vivid tints of yellows, reds and blues that were small samples of the floral lavishness that we saw from the train. She told us the name of the park was Vondelpark and since it was the largest park in Amsterdam we would only walk round a bit of it before proceeding to a well-known square called Leidseplein.

The trees were not at all like those that I remembered from Java. There were no dense leafy crowns, no resemblance to the trees that shaded Sindoroweg. Instead, the trees of Holland were merely skeletons, but some, like the weeping willows, showed signs of yellow-green on their hanging branches that told me that new leaves were to come.

'Look how the trees are beginning to burst out in leaf again after being bare during the winter,' said Nadia as if she could read my questioning mind.

The scent of flowers in the park gave way to the fresh algal smell of a canal as we walked over a bridge and that in turn gave way to the distant sound of a kind of music, of drums and cymbals and piping. It sounded like a band at first, but as we drew closer turned out to be a brightly painted construction that stood on the pavement. We watched a man in shirtsleeves and cap turning a large wheel at one end, the source of power that projected melodious piping whistles, bells, accompanied by oompahs, drums and cymbals. It sounded like a full-scale orchestra but it all came from the single contraption, the Dutch barrel organ.

Despite the tangle of sounds I found the whole effect was very tuneful and the melody easy to ascertain. I stood mesmerised both by the music and the puppets that were animated to move to the tune. Before I knew it, Nadia had to take me by the hand and half drag me away after dropping a coin into the man's hat that lay on the pavement.

Emilie said that we had now reached Leidseplein, the best place to catch a tram. She pointed to a curious two-carriage train running on rails set in the road that she explained was a tram and was a good way to travel in the city.

The last city I had experienced was Semarang over half my life ago. The main streets of Amsterdam and their pavements were wider than any streets I had seen before. Though there were plenty of people there was not the sense of crowding, no chaotic intensity, not the same smells and sounds that I associated as belonging to a town before our internment. Unlike those of Semarang, the smells of Amsterdam seemed to be less blended and thereby more easy to identify and this made it seem as though Amsterdam had a greater variety of treats for the nose. The sweet scent of a smoking cigar would present itself, or it might be the scent of a flower stall on the pavement, or the exhaust of the occasional motor vehicle. Then there might be the heavy scent of occasional heaps of fresh horse manure, or it might be the electric ozone smell of a passing tram.

The colours of Amsterdam were fresh and inviting, from the floral displays of the park and vendors on the pavement, the striking colours of a barrel organ, to all imaginable colours of the shop windows. No post-war drabness affected this city. Not just because of the colours, everywhere was clean and without litter, as if the citizens of Amsterdam were determined to sweep away the effects of the horrors that ended a year previously. I liked Amsterdam.

Our guided round tour with Emilie lasted little more than an hour. It not only gave us an impression of the layout of our part of the city but also made us realise that our rather basic living accommodation had a prime location. We were close to both the greenery of Vondelpark as well as to the city centre and all the essential shops were within a few minutes' walk.

Nadia left us in the flat while she went to the bakers, butchers, greengrocers and the dairy shop to set about combating the effects of malnutrition and put us on the delicious road to recovery.

Emilie had disappeared up to her home in the loft only to knock on our door a few minutes later. She came down to show me her stamp collection and as she did so a whole new field of interest opened itself. These coloured toothed squares of paper fascinated me. So many different pictures and colours, or series with the same design but different colours were eminently collectable. I was hooked, bursting with curiosity about their countries of origin, the heads of state they often portrayed or what they commemorated. I wanted to know what was written on them and what currencies each country used.

'Why don't you collect postage stamps, Ivan?' said Nadia after returning from the shopping.

'I'd love to,' I said, wondering why I didn't know about stamp collecting before.

'You can have some of my spares as a start,' said Emilie with her infectious smile.

From then on the morning post had a new appeal and yielded mainly Dutch stamps on letters from the immigration authorities and from Russian friends in other parts of Holland. Best of all were the letters from Harry that came at least once a week, mostly from Java and finally from England. The news that they bore and that

Nadia told us was spiced by the arrival of new stamps. I learned to soak the clippings from the envelopes in water, to be able to remove the stamps without damaging them and it wasn't long before there were enough to stick into a notebook that Nadia bought for me together with a packet of stamp hinges.

Collecting stamps encouraged me to learn the alphabet and it wasn't long before I began to read in Dutch as well as speak it more fluently.

As Emilie went to school and had friends of her own she did not spend much time with us. Consequently Vera and I began to explore our immediate neighbourhood on our own. In the late afternoons we watched other children playing in the alley behind the houses lined by outhouses and small walled enclosures. They were running and shouting while playing what to me was an incomprehensible game, and yet I wanted to join in. I stood in the alley as a bystander and for some reason with Vass in my hand. A boy ran towards me and before I could react, snatched Vass from my clutches and threw him high into the air. Vass landed on the slate roof of an outhouse long out of reach. I felt a mixture of devastation and shame. Devastated because I lost Vass, ashamed because I knew I was too old to display my fondness of a cuddly toy. I pretended that it didn't matter and leant against the wall as if I was more interested in watching them. When I felt it was the right moment I ran in to tell Nadia, who said that she would try to contact a neighbour with a ladder to get him down. In the meantime she said that I would just have to learn to sleep without him.

'After all, Vera sleeps without a cuddly toy,' she said.

About two weeks later, when I had already become used to being without Vass at night, Nadia called me and said that a man was getting a ladder to fetch him off the roof and if I waited by the outhouse I would have him back. When he handed a damp dark orange item to me I did not have the same Vass in my hands. Large patches of mould and soot were ingrained into his orange cloth surface. He felt heavy and damp. Even if he were dried out he would never be the same. It was as if he had died. I cried silently not so much because I lost Vass, but more because it felt as if a stage of my childhood had also died. I had grown a little.

On the next day when Nadia came back from her routine shopping she handed us two cylinder-like objects, one for Vera and one for me.

'You can spend hours looking through these. They're called kaleidoscopes. If you put this end to your eye and point it to the light, what do you see?'

At first the kaleidoscopes were exciting, the variety of coloured patterns being unending, but soon the novelty wore off and in the end they became symbols of boredom. We picked them up when there was really nothing else to do.

We had just finished eating our evening meal when we heard a commotion of people shouting and the sound of running footsteps on the cobbled street outside. Nadia opened the window to see what was going on.

'Good God! There's a fire four or five doors away from us!'

We rushed to put our heads out of the half-open window and saw dark smoke billowing out from the house on the next storey down from ours. There were people leaning out of the window on the same level as we were. They were shouting in panic while people on the street were shouting up to them. Then they had organised themselves into a ring holding what looked like a blanket stretched between them. The volume of smoke increased as the orange tongues of flames began to appear while the occupants of the floor above the fire were being induced to leap down three storeys! I saw the half-silhouetted figure of a woman falling down to the stretched blanket below, then a man. We were unable to see if they were injured because of the smoke and the crowds. What if the fire spread to us! Would we have to jump from such a height? The sound of bells and loud engines announced the arrival of the fire brigade and soon there were ladders and spurting hoses that soon dispelled the worries of the fire spreading as far as our house.

On the next morning we were able to see that the top two storeys of the house were completely gutted and daylight was visible between the burnt fallen beams. Since then we referred to it as 'The Burnt House' in Dutch.

The weeks passed while Vera and I gradually became accepted by the kids in the street, sometimes joining them in games like hide and seek and hopscotch. Our knowledge of Dutch had reached such a standard that we even began to use it instead of Russian when speaking to Nadia, which she seemed to both accept and even encourage by replying in the same language.

Though the effects of the beriberi seemed to have disappeared and I was beginning to spend less time on the potty, not all was well with me. I had developed what seemed to be a constant cold, consisting of a persistent sore throat and runny nose. At first Nadia thought it was due to the change in climate, but she soon realised that it would be wise to visit the doctor and have Vera checked at the same time. As I had always thought of doctors as being wise old men that muttered while they spoke, I found it difficult to accept that the relatively young white-coated woman examining me was a doctor. She said that considering what we had been through both Vera and I were well on the way to recovery and there should soon be no traces of malnutrition, but that as my tonsils and adenoids were very enlarged she would send me to the hospital for a tonsillectomy.

A few days later I woke up in a sitting position in an operating stool convinced that I had recovered consciousness before they had finished the operation. I felt the thick eggy taste of blood in my mouth and saw a bloody mess on the rubber apron spread in front of me. 'Here are your tonsils', said a nurse showing me some blood-covered round fleshy pieces in a kidney bowl.

A few days of discomfort rather than pain followed. But the discomfort of not being able to swallow without the feeling that there was something sticking to the back of my throat was compensated by a daily treat of ice-cream handed out by efficient smiling Dutch nurses. When I was considered fit enough, I was almost sorry to leave.

It was early May. We ate our breakfast with the window open to let the late spring air dispel the stuffiness of our little flat.

Suddenly Nadia said, 'Be quiet! Listen! I think I can hear a nightingale!'

Vera and I stopped chatting to listen. Then we heard it. The flute-like whistles, the varied bubbling and clucking sounds floated towards us above the distant sounds of the city. Nadia said that she used to hear the nightingale singing in the large garden of the country house where I was born, Klosters, but she never expected to hear it so close to the centre of Amsterdam. She thought that the bird was singing in Vondelpark, a mere hundred yards away as the crow flies. Her memories of it reminded her that she must contact Jan's mother, our grandmother, who was still alive and living in a house somewhere in Diepenveen. She was sure to want to see her grandchildren.

She told us that the Germans took over Klosters soon after they invaded Holland but luckily Jan's parents had already sold it and bought a nice, much smaller house nearby. My grandfather did not live long after that, for he died in December 1940 at the age of seventy-three.

Nadia's telephone conversation with my grandmother, however, turned out to be negative. Since the divorce, she did not want to have anything to do with us and refused to see her only grandchildren in Holland with the excuse that the meeting would be far too traumatic for her. She had, however, good contact with my two cousins in South Africa, the children of Jan's older sister, and was satisfied to leave it at that.

Instead Nadia took us sightseeing in the city. We saw the old Queen, Queen Wilhelmina, appearing at the royal palace to commemorate one year after the end of the war.

We visited the Rijksmuseum to absorb a little of the impact of the enormous collection of Dutch paintings. Nadia's favourite artist was Vermeer, especially the portrait of the lady with the turban. She said that he had a wonderful way of painting light and shadows, which was much appreciated at a time long before the invention of the camera. She told us that our grandfather knew so many important people that he contacted the then director of the Rijksmuseum to show her round personally. She said that he taught her a lot about Dutch painting.

Among the portraits of seventeenth-century ladies, men with lace collars and broad-brimmed hats, floral still lifes and various Bible scenes, I was most impressed by a painting of St Sebastian. When I saw him with his body full of arrows I wondered how he could remain standing with his head held up to the sky. I thought that at least his head should be bent down, as he was surely nearly dead, if not already dead with all those arrows buried into him. It was a point that Nadia found difficult to explain.

We received an invitation to spend a couple of days with the Nederlofs. Olga had recently arrived from Java to join her husband where they had their home in a small village that lay in the polder country to the south-west of Amsterdam. Nadia had given our address to Olga while she was still in Java. We took the train into flat, ditch-patterned landscape to arrive at Olga and Jan's terraced house at the edge of a village and ten minutes walk from the station.

Olga had recovered from the concentration camp to regain the rosy roundness of her Russian face, her beady blue eyes twinkling with the smile that welcomed us into their home. Jan was considerably older, certainly over fifty, but he had a thick crop of short steel grey hair and his light blue eyes were framed by metal-framed spectacles that did not make his eyes look small like those that my father, Jan, wore. He was a retired merchant navy captain and kept photographic mementoes of ships and their crews that were a part of his naval past hanging on the walls of the dark, narrow hall.

The hall led to a small sitting room with French windows that opened out onto a lawn which was bordered by a canal typical of the polder country. Jan was truly an aquatic man: not only had he spent his working life on water, but his retirement home was close to water and his sitting room was embellished along one wall by an enormous tropical aquarium.

When Nadia and Olga had ensconced themselves in the sitting room to catch up on the months since liberation from camp, Jan offered to show me round and take me fishing while Vera chose to sit quietly with the ladies. His passion was fish. He showed me an aquarium with sticklebacks and tadpoles that he kept in an outhouse, where he also kept a large selection of different kinds of fishing tackle. He took a small rod that was already tackled up with a small spoon with a triple hook.

'Now I'll show you how to fish for pike, Ivanka.'

He spoke his native language, but his marriage to Olga had familiarised him with Russian diminutives. We walked across the small country road in front of the house and through a gate into a field that was recently grazed though the cattle were no longer there.

Apart from the fence along the road the border to the field consisted of a ditch with water that was about ten feet wide and no more than three deep. Where the water was not covered by patches of duckweed it shone blue or silver from the reflected sky and when approached more closely, its clarity revealed shoals of perch and roach or occasionally a solitary pike suspended motionless like a miniature submarine waiting for a passing shoal.

Jan pointed out the different kinds of fish and gave me their Dutch names. The network of ditches with their clear waters made up a natural aquarium of roach occasionally flashing their silver flanks and passing shoals of perch looking like the striped tropical fish that Jan kept at home. He chose to cast his spoon into a stretch that was covered with duckweed so that the fish would not be able to see him while I could watch sufficiently far away so as not to hamper his casting. A heron flew up some fifty yards away, making me startled by the sight of the large grey bird flapping its dark towel-like wings to rise above us.

Watching the fish together with the spectacle of Jan catching three pike made the time pass like a dream. He kept the largest of the three and carefully put back the two smaller ones so that, as he explained with a grin, they could be caught and eaten at a later stage in their lives.

When we returned to our flat I couldn't help thinking about that visit to Olga and Jan. I was completely enraptured by that small taste of the Dutch countryside, the encounter with that vibrant balance of land and water teeming with life. For me it was better than Vondelpark, the Rijksmuseum and all the other attractions of Amsterdam put together. I began to identify myself with my country of birth and thought that it would be fine to go to school in Holland and live there for the rest of my life.

The correspondence between Uncle Harry and Nadia continued to flourish and it gave me the occasional benefit of a new postage stamp. One morning Nadia was more engrossed than usual in a letter from Uncle Harry. On noticing this we asked her for the latest news.

'How would you like to live in England?' It came suddenly but was not entirely unexpected.

'With Uncle Harry? Yes! Yes!' said Vera before I could express my reply.

'The point is,' said Nadia, 'he's asked me to marry him and you know what that means!' She continued before we had a chance to say what it meant, 'It means that Uncle Harry will be your stepfather and his two sons will be your stepbrothers and that I will be their stepmother. Now think carefully: you will have to learn English and go to an English school instead of the alternative of staying in Holland and being Dutch.'

I was silent for a while. I had to dispel my thoughts about living in Holland and had to think again. I knew I liked Harry and if he was typical of his country then I was sure that I would like living in England. Vera had expressed her opinion spontaneously. Nadia was obviously keen on the idea. Why not? Being in England meant that we would have Uncle Harry as good as a father and that was as good a reason as any to move to England.

'Say that you will marry Uncle Harry!', pleaded Vera.

'I definitely want to live in England,' I said with as much determination as possible in my voice.

'Well, that's settled then. I'll write to him today and we'll begin to prepare for the move.'

Her face was red and smiled broadly. 'I want to buy some things for our new home and presents for the boys. We shall be moving in about a month's time, about the end of July.'

'You did say before what our future brothers are called but which one is Michael?' I asked, just wanting to hear more about our future family.

'Michael is the eldest and Philip is his younger brother and their surname is Neale.'

She told us that Harold must have been young when he married his first wife, as Michael was born in 1939 when he was not yet twenty-three.

'Does this mean that when we live in England our surname will also be Neale?', asked Vera.

'When you grow up you will most probably get married and change your surname anyway, but until then you should keep your father's surname. It is after all the name of one of the old families of

Holland and the Kruys family has its own coat of arms.'

Any thoughts that we might live in Holland for the rest of our lives were gone. Amsterdam took on a new meaning in our lives. My enthusiasm for Amsterdam and Holland had blossomed with the fresh colours and smells of the city in spring. Now they had given way to the warm dustiness of summer. Amsterdam became a transit city and I became content with letting Holland be the country where I was born but not the country of my home.

When we sat on our beds in the flat discussing our future Nadia told us that Lincolnshire was a kind of rural province and that we were going to live in a house in the country near a place called Kirton Lindsey where Harry had his own building firm.

Since he told her that his father was an engineer at a steelworks in a nearby town, it was clear that Harold grew up in a comfortable middle class environment. From his letters she knew that his younger brother, Cedric, was still in the navy, and had been since he was only twenty, he would probably continue some sort of further education after being de-mobbed.

'It would be good for us to live in the country.' Nadia remembered my grandfather's parting words when they left Klosters in Holland before leaving for Java: 'Encourage my grandson to be interested in the countryside and nature,' he had said.

There was a new sense of purpose in our lives. Our biological father became a distant background figure. We never saw him in Holland, though Nadia did receive a bitter letter from him accusing her of being in too much of a hurry to seek a divorce and he regretted that their marriage was so speedily dissolved because his new relationship came to nothing. Nadia told us that she wrote to him to tell him that she was engaged to Uncle Harry.

She had saved enough refugee money to take us on a shopping tour. We watched her buy two modest gilt-framed oil paintings depicting traditional Dutch scenes from one of the many art dealers to be found in Amsterdam. One showed a horse-drawn cart standing on the beach and the other was a painting of a single-masted fishing boat. The skies depicted on both paintings were cloudy and dark blue-grey, typical of the North Sea. She also bought a fine solid glass statue of the Madonna that had simple flowing lines and its fine

132

frosted glass surface gave it a silvery glow in the light. We could find only one toyshop where we chose two small cast-metal toy cars, one pale blue and the other red. Anything else was either unsuitable or too expensive.

As we made our way back to the flat we came to a shop window that displayed military items. We paused to look. Among the things on display were some model jeeps about four inches long. They were exact miniatures of the jeeps that were used when we were in Java, perfect in every detail and made of thin sheets of khaki-coloured steel.

'I wish we could buy those,' I said, thinking that we might buy three.

'Let's go in,' said Nadia.

'Good morning! How much do those model jeeps cost?'

The lady sat behind a desk and the whole room was not at all like an ordinary shop. It was more like an office, perhaps for recruiting soldiers, I thought.

'Really they are not for sale,' said the young lady who was dressed in army uniform. 'They're part of our display but we can let you have one at cost price, as we have a few extra.'

'Would it be too much to ask for three? We would so much have liked to have them as presents and my son here would like one too.'

She looked at the three of us standing in front of her. Whatever it was she saw in us made her give in to Nadia's request. After a moment's pause, she said, 'Well, I suppose we could part with three. They are rather fine, aren't they?'

'Yes they are: they're beautifully made. Thank you very much. That's very kind of you.'

The army lady took out three model jeeps from a cupboard, wrapped them up in fine tissue paper and handed them to Nadia in a brown paper bag. Nadia paid her the price that they must have agreed on but I didn't take in the exact sum because I was preoccupied with the display of model jeeps and tanks in the office.

We left the office with the usual pleasantries while the young army lady wished us good luck with the presents. Now I was in a hurry to get home and play with my jeep, but I knew that I must treat it gently as, instead of it being a toy to be played with, it was a model and made of easily bendable thin steel.

After her experience with Ludmilla and the loss of Tasha, Vera's attitude towards dolls was almost negative, if her reaction to them at the toyshop was anything to go by. This resulted in the choice of a new pair of shoes and a new dress for her fifth birthday at the end of June.

Our preparations included lessons in English when Nadia taught us some basic words and phrases, like, 'please', 'thank you', 'yes', 'no' and 'how do you do?'.

When she booked a flight to leave Schiphol for London at the end of July we were totally occupied in preparing ourselves for England, not only packing but talking about it, mulling over what England and Lincolnshire would be like. Holland was no longer attractive and as we were definitely not going to be Dutch, Amsterdam, its amenities and its inhabitants had lost their appeal. We had become anglophiles.

11. Redgates

The DC3 taxied to the end of the runway, the twin propeller engines roaring to a climax as we accelerated to take-off. The greyness of Schiphol fell away below us, giving way to the flat rectangles of polder country that looked increasingly like a map with the ascent of the plane.

Vera began to cry with pain from the earache that ensued and the pain in my ears reminded me of the torture I had endured in camp. But I did not cry, partly because the thrill of being up in the air for the first time in my life helped me to overcome the pain. The plane was ill-equipped to combat the changes in pressure and all the smiling air stewardess could do was to comfort passengers with ear-popping sweets, as well as make sure that they were well secured in their seats. These seats were the khaki canvass-covered iron frames, the canvas showing a soiled smoothness over the frames where hundreds of men and women had sat to make journeys that were caused by the aftermath of war.

I pushed my face against the window.

'Is that London?', I asked knowing full well that the enormous distorted pattern of brick houses, grey roofs and streets could not be anywhere else.

Nadia gave me the obvious answer, at the same time giving both of us a squeeze that communicated both reassurance and excitement. The descent of the DC3 was marked by a repeat of the ear popping and pain, despite the sweets given to us. The ache in my right ear reminded me once again of the excruciating pain I had in camp, but fortunately it was only a two-minute reminder, not a recurrence.

The process of luggage collecting and customs went without a hitch and it wasn't long before we were waiting for Uncle Harry. The boredom of the wait was accentuated by the drabness of the Croydon Airport buildings, their appearance reflecting their recent wartime past, which made their new role of civil aviation seem makeshift.

We sat surrounded by our luggage, including the trunk with the

135

rounded lid that had 'N.P. KRUYS' painted on it by Jan. Still no Uncle Harry. What had gone wrong?

Nadia told us to wait and then walked over to a man who appeared to be an official. She then disappeared for what might have been twenty minutes.

She returned with the news that she was advised to try Heathrow, which unlike Croydon, was regarded as the main London airport, which was why it was natural for Harry to meet her there. As it happened, he was still waiting at Heathrow and it was lucky that the Croydon official managed to contact him. Nadia and Harry arranged to meet at Victoria Station.

The hours that followed were a confusion of railway stations, together with the soot, smoke, dust, whistles, shouts and the babble of different voices that spoke the language that I knew to be English but could not understand.

I remembered that even before concentration camp, English had a special status in our home. At that time it was a language that meant that I was excluded from a serious conversation between my parents. But now this was to be my language as well and its attraction and importance began to usurp my mind, making me long to learn what the signs and posters meant.

I admired the ease with which my mother could communicate in English. She displayed this facility when she met Harry and now she had no trouble buying railway tickets or asking the way to our train. We were ushered to our train by a porter in a worn peaked cap and a uniform that might once have been navy blue: the only bright object about him was a silver chain hanging across his waistcoat. The heavy-wheeled handcart loaded with our luggage rumbled along with the porter hunched over the handles. He came to a halt and motioned us to the train in front of us while Nadia rummaged in her purse to pay him.

Despite the sleep on the plane, Vera and I were both tired and hungry and sat in a kind of numbed silence while our mother was chatting to a middle-aged woman who sat opposite. The conversation seemed to take on a variation of tone and volume that might have implied that it was about something important. But I was too dazed to ask her what she was talking about, and she was too preoccupied to tell us on her own volition.

Though the train stopped several times in its jerky progress it wasn't long before we entered the dimly-lit enormity of Victoria Station with its crowds of people, echoing sounds, smoke and steam. We made our way along the platform and out towards the main entrance.

There he was! He was easy to pick out among all the uniformed men that milled about, this time wearing long khaki trousers instead of shorts, a thick army tunic instead of a short-sleeved shirt, but the same W/O peaked hat, set at a slight angle.

We all embraced him, happy to find him and have his company.

We waited outside the station for a cab, quite different from the taxis in Amsterdam, which were like ordinary black cars. Uncle Harry waved one down, we climbed into what felt like a small British train compartment with seats opposite to each other while the driver loaded our luggage in the back and onto the platform between the opposing seats.

The taxi took us to a drab boarding house in Bayswater, which it turned out was recommended by the woman that Nadia was talking to in the train. Though the building did not seem as tall as the house where we lived in Amsterdam, it seemed more forbidding and had a dark dingy hall that somehow led to our room.

'Mammy, Uncle Harry doesn't live here, does he?' asked Vera.

'No, darling. We're just staying here for the night on the way to his house; our new home is in Lincolnshire. That's where we are going tomorrow.'

Uncle Harry said something to Nadia that included the name 'Uncle Harry' and Nadia then said, 'Uncle Harry does not want you to call him 'Uncle Harry' any more. He wants you to call him Daddy.'

'Call me Daddy,' he smiled, looking at us.

Nadia then explained that 'daddy' meant father. Now we had a 'daddy' as well as a 'mammy'.

After a couple of soft white bread cheese sandwiches and a strong cup of English tea with milk, a day full of travel and perplexity faded into sleep.

The next stage in our journey to our new life was waiting for us in the form of a long brown carriage with steam spurting out between it and the platform at Euston Station. Harry, no longer in uniform, looked like an ordinary Englishman dressed in a sports jacket, grey flannels and dark brown trilby hat. The thought of a new home, two entirely new brothers and that Harry was to be as good as a new father, drew us eagerly onto the train that was actually bound for Lincolnshire and our new home.

The train jolted and chugged its smoky way past rows of terraced houses, past bombed ruins and green parks, past the semi-detached suburbia that was the pre-war pride of northern London and into the golden greenness of the English countryside in high summer. The grimy window of the coach compartment had a kind of sooty smell as I pressed my face against it. I was surprised to sometimes see my view blocked by rows of bushes and trees that I later learnt were hedges. The scenery was full of surprises, shifting from the restricted views caused by hedges and cuttings to a sudden show of a mosaic of fields and woodland that spread out below the train. This was quite different from the flatness of Holland where the entire countryside could be seen during the first ten minutes of the journey, the horizon only being broken by windmills and occasional farm buildings. Holland seemed flat, organised and clean: England hilly, chaotic and tatty but attractive.

The flood of new images began to lose its impact and the rhythmic motion of the train predisposed us to a drowsiness, which soon gave way to sleep. Vera had already been asleep for some time.

I felt a jolt in my side and woke up to see my mother's face. She spoke in the language that was so familiar from our time in the camps: Russian.

'Ivan! Wake up! We're nearly there!'

The rhythm of the train was beginning to slow down. Vera was already awake, squirming on the seat with anticipation. Through the train window I could see a canal shining like a long silver sheet in a flat landscape. It reminded me of Holland, but the presence of hedges bordering the irregular fields made the scenery strange, English. When the train had slowed down almost to walking pace we came over another canal which was slightly curved and old brick houses stood in terraced rows that made up the body of a town. Harold was already up collecting the luggage. We drew up with a long drawn-out squeak.

Our heads jerked with the sudden halt. Steam hissed out from the brakes under the carriage and billowed up by the window. A moment of silence followed.

'Brigg!' came the shout from an unseen man on the platform.

I heard the crashing of a couple of doors being opened. Harry opened the door to our compartment and organised the luggage with the help of a porter while we stood on the platform in a haze of bewilderment.

A passenger or two disembarked and disappeared so that the only noise coming from our train was quietly hissing steam.

We were alone in what was quite a different looking railway station. A curved sooty roof spanning the two platforms on either side of the tracks made it look like a miniature version of the railway stations that I had seen in London. But there were no echoing noises, no crowds and I could see that the bricks of the buildings had a yellowish colour instead of the grimy greyness of city buildings.

A black taxi, looking more like an ordinary large car, happened to be parked outside the station as if it been organised to wait for us. Harold motioned to the cab and gave the driver instructions and then proceeded to help him to load the luggage. We climbed into the soft, brown back seat that smelt of stale leather and cigarette smoke, but as it was my first time in a car since before internment, it felt like a final release from the restrictions caused by the effects of war. The forms of transport that I had experienced since internment had progressed from cattle trucks to army vehicles, railway carriages to the ultimate symbol of the end of the war, a saloon car. Even the London taxi felt not quite the same as the large black saloon that we entered outside Brigg railway station.

Twenty minutes later, the taxi drew up to a copse of half-grown oaks and came to a halt at a pair of closed wooden gates that were painted a bright red, the gate on the one side being larger than the other.

Standing about thirty yards beyond the gates was a small red-brick bungalow ornamented by two half-round bay windows protruding on either side of a red front door that was recessed between them. The two bay windows seemed disproportionately large for the little house that owned them. Behind the gates the drive curved immediately towards the left of the bungalow, the ground on the right consisting of a variety of small bushes dominated by a large spreading sweet chestnut tree. On the left, between the curve of the drive and the road, there was a small sunken area whose ambition to be a lawn was thwarted by shade, leaves and twigs.

Nadia did not notice the inadequacies of the area purporting to be a lawn. Instead she spent a few seconds grappling with the truth that presented itself in front of her.

'Good God, is this it?' she exclaimed quietly in Russian. The banality of the question did little to reflect the enormous flood of disappointment that must have welled up inside her. I heard what she said, but I didn't understand the full significance at the time.

That tiny brick edifice was to be her home! Not only was it to be a home for her and Harold, but for her two children and Harold's two children, not to mention both Harold's parents. She did not expect another Klosters but to her this could hardly be described as a home.

Harold said something that must have meant that we were home. It might have been something like 'Welcome to Redgates!'

The cab driver helped with our luggage while we walked down the short drive along the side of the house, devoid of windows except for one that nestled under the gable end of the roof. A tree was trained to spread itself on the wall below it. We came to a small raised patio lined by brick columns that formed the supports of a climbing rose pergola. Gingerly we went up the three concrete steps through the entwinement of foliage and pink roses, to be confronted by a half-glazed back door.

Harold and the taxi driver dumped the luggage and as Harold paid the driver, the back door opened and a woman appeared at the entrance. She wore an apron with a pattern of small flowers and her dark grey-streaked hair was flattened and gathered at the back to form a loose bun. A pair of wire-framed, eye-enlarging glasses rested securely on a straight nose. Her grey-blue eyes peered suspiciously at us. I thought she looked very old.

Harold gave her a quick embrace, turned round and made a sweeping motion with his arm to urge us to enter the house. As we entered she backed a little and seemed to screech 'Coom in!', though

I could only guess the meaning. Harold presented us and she responded with an English that sounded strange but that was neither friendly nor hostile, but I understood that we were being introduced to his mother.

We came into a passage lit by a long window placed on the left side of the door. On the left an open door revealed a boy standing on a table that stood in a dimly lit room. He was about six or seven and stood quite naked, holding a pair of scissors and a piece of cloth. A smaller, fair-haired boy in pyjamas appeared from nowhere and clung to the woman's flowery apron. Both boys stared at us without uttering a word.

Vera and I stared in a silence that was broken by a friendly greeting from Harold who presented Nadia and us to the boys. Harold's mother turned towards the table to help the larger of the two boys on with his pyjamas, but for some reason, perhaps the tension of situation, he had cut the pyjama legs off with the scissors while his grandmother answered the door. She uttered something that sounded unfriendly and disappeared to return with another pair of pyjama trousers.

Both the pyjamad boys stood in silence while their father pointed to the larger of the two boys and said 'Michael' and then pointed to the little boy clinging to his grandma and said, 'Philip'.

Vera and I simultaneously responded with our rehearsed 'How do you do?', which made me feel very awkward. The two boys stared at us in silence.

'This is Ivan,' said Nadia in a kind of English that sounded very clear, 'and this is Vera.'

For Philip the whole occasion appeared to be so bewildering and awesome that he preferred to remain half hidden behind his grandmother.

Clearly, the two boys had not seen their father for so long that he was as much of a stranger to them as Vera and I were. Harold turned to us and raising his voice a little, as if to be sure that we understood, he said, 'I'm their daddy as well.'

His mother watched him icily but said nothing. He then pointed to her and said, 'and that's Grandma.'

Nadia turned to Michael and Philip and said, 'You can call me

Mammy.' Michael smiled a little as if in agreement while Philip was still silent.

Nadia thought that the best way to relieve the tense atmosphere was to give the boys the presents that we bought in Holland and after a little rummaging came up with the brown parcels that were prepared before we set off on our journey that morning. Both the boys took the presents while Grandma fetched the scissors to cut the string. A broad grin of delight spread over Michael's face while she said something to him in a loud screechy voice.

Michael, still beaming with pleasure but with his head lowered, said something that sounded like 'thank you', as he held his model jeep. He then proceeded to wheel it on the red-tiled floor.

Grandma unwrapped Philip's jeep and handed it to him. He said nothing, put his jeep on the floor and then put his foot smartly on it, squashing the delicate model quite flat. Grandma shouted something at him. Then we all stood silent, dumbfounded by the unexpectedness of both the action and the result.

Grandma was first to break the atmosphere by speaking to Nadia with a loudness that suggested that she wanted to be understood and an inflection of voice that meant she was asking a question. Nadia replied by shaking her head, then gesturing and saying something that seemed to convey that she didn't want to cause any bother.

With that, Grandma ushered us through a door on the right into the living room that was one step up. We were motioned to sit round a table clearly set ready for our arrival. There were all the trappings of an English high tea, including a plate of ready buttered slices of bread, a cake, jars of jam, a pork pie and a large pot of tea hidden by a tea cosy.

Most of the far wall of the room was taken up by a large brown enamelled range, in the centre of which was a bright fire that kept a large shiny kettle steaming quietly. Above the range a horizontal oval mirror was suspended by a chain from a picture rail that ran along almost all the wall surfaces and served as a mainstay for several pictures, including two depicting multi-masted sailing ships in heavy seas. Apart from the door where we entered, there were three other doors from this room, which was obviously the nerve centre of the house.

Absorbed by my new surroundings I was too engrossed to notice that Grandma was shouting at me. Then I realised that she was pointing at the bowl of tomatoes, but before I could react, she picked out a tomato, held it close in front of my face, her spectacle-enlarged blue eyes staring at me and repeated in an even a louder voice, 'Do you want a tomaataw?'

Though I did not know the words the meaning was patently clear. That was my first practical lesson of English spoken directly to me by an English person in England. Nadia appeared to reply on my behalf as Grandma left the tomato on my plate before I could reply with 'thank you', or perhaps I should have thought of saying 'please'.

We children ate in silence while the adults talked loudly amongst themselves, Nadia pausing to help us to help ourselves to ready buttered and cheesed, cold-beefed and jammed triangular sand-wiches whose only requirements were the efforts of choice and con-sumption. Grandma, always starting with the milk, poured succes-sions of strong cups of tea and the sugar was limited to level teaspoons as it was rationed. We ate what we desired and we finished with a slice of Battenberg cake each. We felt satisfied and full without any after-effects, since our stay in Holland had done much to allow us to recover from camps.

While we were eating it occurred to me that Grandma dominated the tea table, but was I right in thinking that both of Harold's parents lived in the bungalow and if so, where was his father? The question burned within me and became so irresistible after we had finished eating that I felt compelled to ask Nadia. She in turn asked Grandma, who appeared to give a satisfactory answer. Nadia turned to me while Harold and his mother were engaged in another con-versation. The two boys had also finished eating and sat in silence, staring at us speaking a language that I was very much aware was foreign to them. I desperately wanted to speak English and to be English and to be rid of the foreignness at a stroke, but there was no choice. Nadia spoke to me in Russian.

'Grandma's husband is called George, but we are to address him as Grandad. He works at the steel works in Scunthorpe and works special hours called shiftwork. At present he is working from six in the evening to two in the morning, so he doesn't get home before three in the morning and this means that he has to sleep until lunchtime and we have to be quiet so as not to wake him up. We shall meet him tomorrow.'

It was quite late, really well past normal teatime, and the weakening evening light was beginning to make the room quite dark, so that the fireplace began to send out a reddish glow into the room, which made me think that perhaps someone should switch the light on. I looked up to the ceiling to find out where the light was, but couldn't see it. The adults continued to talk and then Grandma rose from the table and went through the door to the hall where we first entered the house. Soon I heard the sounds of a metallic pumping and a minute later Grandma returned with a hissing lamp that lit up the room with its glowing white mantle. The room smelt of paraffin. It had the smell of a house without electricity.

Harold rose from the table and walked to a wooden box-like construction that I recognised as being a radio from the vague memory of the one that we had at home in Semarang. When he turned it on the resulting crackles and hisses gave way to a man's voice.

'Daddy wants to listen to the news, so try to be quiet,' said Nadia to Vera and I while she must have been aware that nearly all the noise was coming from the conversation between the adults.

I wondered how the radio could work when there was no electricity in the house and wanted to put the question to Nadia, but as her last remark suggested that we were to be silent, I suppressed my curiosity. We continued to sit by the large table without interrupting the sound of the man's voice on the radio and the background hissing of the Tilley lamp. Harold switched off the radio when the news came to an end, which allowed Grandma and Nadia to start a conversation that must have been about how and where we were to sleep.

Grandma lit two small metal paraffin lamps, making sure that the wicks were burning well before placing the glass funnel over them and adjusting the wicks to minimise smoking. Grandma led the way bearing one of the lamps. Harold held the other lamp. By now it was almost dark outside and we followed behind in a tight, cautious line, afraid of tripping over something unexpected. She opened one of four doors that led from the living room where we had high tea. It led into a small room with a single bed. Another door led into a small hall, the end of which was marked by the front door between the two gables. A door on the left was quickly opened and shut to indicate the front room or lounge and the door opposite opened into a room that was largely occupied by a double bed and dresser, the master bedroom.

Harold concluded the flickering, dimly-lit tour of the house by pulling open a trap door in the ceiling of the hall. With a squeaking and rattling sound this action produced a neat wooden staircase which folded itself out with the aid of pulleys and wire ropes. We were told that that was where Grandma, Granddad and the two boys slept, that Harold and Nadia were to sleep in the master bedroom and that Vera and I were to have the little bedroom adjacent to the living room. Harold had acquired two army surplus camp beds which were allocated to Michael and me, his being up in the loft and mine downstairs with Vera while Philip was to continue to sleep with his grandparents.

The process of getting ready for bed, the use of the bathroom, changing into pyjamas and getting into our beds all took place using the small paraffin lamps for illumination both in the bathroom and bedrooms. Our shadows flickered on the walls and the air was dominated by the heaviness of paraffin vapour.

Nadia had put us to bed and tucked us up for the night and though the camp bed felt hard the events of the day induced a heavy sleep. I awoke some time later to the sound of movements of someone in the living room. Had Grandad come back from work? I found it hard to get to sleep again, wondering what he was like and thinking about what had happened that day. The sleep that finally followed was disturbed in some way with strange dreams. Suddenly I was aware of being attacked by forces that I could not describe. All I knew was that I was very frightened and rushed out of bed to find myself screaming, having buried my head in the seat of the utility armchair next to the radio in the living room.

'It's all right Ivan! I'm here!' said my mother.

Nadia was in her nighty. She had placed the little paraffin lamp on the table. I knew where I was but it took some time for my illogical fear to disappear. By the time Harold appeared in the room I was sitting on her knee trying to orientate myself back to sanity, while she stroked and reassured me. She told me that I must have had a nightmare.

12. Language

We woke to see the morning sun streaming in through the pale green flowery curtains. Sounds coming from the living room suggested that someone was already up laying the table, but as we did not hear any conversation Vera and I assumed that it was Grandma. There was no point in getting up until she was ready, and even then not before either the boys or Nadia or Harold were up. Being strangers in our new home, we felt it was appropriate to behave accordingly. We remained in our beds and talked about the events of the previous day and how strange it was to have to rely on paraffin lamps for lighting and we wondered how a radio could work without electricity. Perhaps the house had special electricity just for radios? Vera was surprised when I told her about the nightmare for she never heard me at all.

It wasn't long before we heard the boys talking to Grandma, at which point we decided that we could get up, but just as we did so, we heard Nadia say something followed by her entrance into our room. She was already dressed. She spoke in the usual Russian.

'Ah, you're awake, both of you. Did you sleep all right after your nightmare, Ivan? You're still suffering from the camps, you poor darling. Did you sleep well, V-erka?'

'Yes Mammy,' came the simultaneous reply.

'Good, you can dress now and have your breakfast. Michael and Philip are already sitting at the table.'

We dressed as quickly as we could and came to the living room to find Grandma helping Philip with a boiled egg while Michael was already eating his. The table was laid for seven, with a cosied pot of tea placed within easy access of the kettle that was comfortably simmering on the range fire. A centrally placed plate piled with ready-buttered slices of white bread dominated the table while a plate of cheese slices, open jars of red jam and yellow marmalade surrounded it like subjects paying homage to a king.

Nadia was in the bathroom next door and when she emerged in

her blue dressing gown she said, 'Good morning!' in English with a look that I knew was to elicit response.

'Good morning,' said Vera who was the quickest.

'Good morning,' I said with more confidence after Vera's response. Michael and Philip were silent.

'Harold!' Shouted Nadia.

He emerged in his maroon dressing gown, paused and said, 'Good morning!'

Everyone replied except Philip, Michael and Grandma, who after the chorus of 'good mornings' said something else.

'Yes thank you,' said Harold before disappearing into the bathroom.

We ate bread and butter with the egg and by pointing to the desired spread, Grandma would smear a thin layer on a slice of buttered bread. She stood hunched more than she sat, delivering re-fills of tea and milk and slicing more bread from the top of a verti-cally held loaf like a machine until we were all satisfied. At that point Harold and Nadia were dressed and had taken their places by the table with Grandma hunched in readiness to serve.

Michael was first to leave to return dressed in his short grey trousers and a pale blue jumper with a brown-striped turned-down collar. He was immediately sent to the bathroom by Grandma. She then took Philip upstairs to the loft to be dressed. Vera and I took it in turns to wash ourselves in the bathroom, using the driest available towel and avoiding the smelliest.

As I opened the back door the blinding morning sun made me take a step into the shade of the rose pergola where I stood to take my bearings. Michael joined me and indicated that he would show me the garden. Somehow, I understood what he said without knowing the exact meanings of his words. I followed him down the steps of the pergola to watch him opening the large door of the garage that stood separated from the house. The strong smell of grease and oil and the sight of a small black car chocked up by blocks of wood where the wheels should be gave me the feeling that this was a man's world and that the car was undergoing a major overhaul. The bonnet was open to leave the greasy complications of the engine exposed for whatever operation the car needed.

Michael closed the garage door and led me to a small greenhouse that stood behind it. Its open entrance greeted us with warm air already heated by the morning sun. Two fairly old bikes leaned against a long shelf that was strewn with plant pots, soil and string. On the other side of the greenhouse was the back border of the garden bounded by a simple two-barred wooden fence. The sight of three dense rolls of barbed wire pressed against the other side of the fence automatically made me look beyond to realise that their purpose was to enclose a large number of wooden huts of a military type, with pitched rather than rounded roofs.

Michael confirmed my suspicion that I was looking at a camp when he said something that included the word 'German' as he pointed to the huts. I stared in silence at the scene beyond the garden fence. Men in clothes that had a military origin lounged around. Some were smoking cigarettes, some leaning against the huts, others walking with some kind of purpose. It took some time for my nearly eight-year-old mind to absorb both the scene and the irony that came with it. All the signs of a camp were there, the watchtowers at the corners, the barbed wire, and the huts.

We had left Java and its concentration camp horrors, recovered in Holland where we got away from it all, we had come to our new promised land to find ourselves living next to a prisoner of war camp and it looked as though the prisoners were still being held! At the end of July 1946! Though I felt a certain amount of respect for the barbed wire and what it implied, I was not frightened, as I knew that there no longer was any war and that there weren't any Japanese lurking about. I was bursting to ask questions but the two people with whom I could communicate were still indoors and could hardly satisfy my curiosity.

Michael must have noticed my staring at the scene and said something in an effort to explain what lay before us and I nodded as if to indicate that I understood what he said. We walked a little way along the fence while I stared at the occupants of the camp. Were they really prisoners now that the war was over? If not what were they doing there? The only person I could ask was Nadia, and it was doubtful whether she was even aware that we had moved to a house that was next to a prisoner of war camp.

We moved away from the fence and came to another, this time a high-netted type that enclosed several chickens that were scratching about in the bare soil of their enclosure. Chickens! I hadn't seen a live chicken since before Ambarava! I simply had to get closer to one and touch it and when I saw a netted frame door into the pen I unfastened the latch hook and went in. Michael remained outside the pen and said something to me in a rather urgent voice, but I was set on touching a chicken and began to go after a brown leghorn that ran and clucked away in fright. All the other hens had begun a loud clucking in alarm. My antics were interrupted by a sharp tapping sound from the kitchen window. I looked up to see Grandma shouting at me, her voice subdued by the window and she was shaking her finger at me and was clearly angry. I immediately stopped chasing the bird and in the shame of my action I rushed through the entrance and closed the latch, pretending that I hadn't done what I had.

Michael smiled and motioned me to follow him around the rest of the garden that proved to be quite extensive and included small fruit trees and a small wooded border along the road.

As I was burning to know what the camp was all about I asked Nadia as soon as we came in, hoping to avoid Grandma in case she would reprimand me for my behaviour with the chickens. As luck would have it, Nadia was in the living room talking to Harold while Grandma was still in the kitchen. The cosied teapot was still on the table. She was quite surprised when I told her about the camp and immediately asked Harold what it was all about, while I waited for the explanation.

Harold told Nadia that at first it was a prisoner of war camp for captured Italian soldiers, but they were released after the Italian capitulation and German prisoners of war were taken instead. The Germans that were still there were not any longer treated like prisoners but many had to remain, as it was difficult to organise their return. Many no longer had a home to go back to and others had their home towns in the Russian sectors of Germany.

Michael showed me some wooden toys that the Italian prisoners had made. One was a very fine wooden lorry with wooden wheels that they gave to the boys through the barbed wire fence. It amazed me to think that though they were prisoners of war, they could communicate with the local inhabitants, which was unthinkable in concentration camps, as I knew them.

Michael must have been reminded about my almost total lack of English during my questioning Nadia about the camp, for he appeared with a nursery rhyme book with attractive coloured illustrations. He opened it and showed me the pictures.

'Goat,' he said pointing to the relevant part of an illustration of the story about the Three Billy Goats Gruff.

'Goat,' I repeated.

'This is a goat,' said Michael.

'This is a goat,' I repeated.

He continued, 'This is a boy' and I repeated all he said.

Michael proved to be a patient teacher. I felt at ease with him and he seemed to thrive on the fact that he had something to teach and something to give. When he had gone through a number of nouns in the nursery rhyme book I continued by pointing at various objects in the living room. I learnt to repeat the names of various objects in the room and to use the basic question form, 'what is?' At the same time I noticed that Philip had latched onto Vera and also began to coach her in English.

The bathroom door opened with the emergence of an elderly man. He had a purplish face and black hair that was greying at the temples and was plastered back on either side of a centre parting. His sagging jowls were bluish grey after a shave and a pair of broad braces that went over a long-sleeved cream-coloured undergarment buttoned at the front hoisted his dark-coloured corduroy trousers up a little above a bulging waist. He stood and paused a little.

''Ellaw,' he said with a little merriment in the tone.

''Ello Grandad,' said Michael.

'This is Grandad,' said Nadia, perhaps rather unnecessarily, but trying to make it a means of introduction. Grandma had come in from the kitchen and stood in the doorway.

''Ellaw, are yeh all right?' he asked, looking at me.

''Ello,' I replied.

'Say hhello, not 'ello,' said Nadia, looking at both Michael and I, while Grandma glowered at her.

I was about to say 'hhello, Grandad!' when Grandad had disappeared, the creaking of the staircase telling us that he was on his way up to the loft.

Before we knew it, it was time for the table to be set for dinner. As Grandad left for work at two, it was Grandma's custom to serve a main meal, known as dinner, at one o'clock. This usually consisted of slices of cold beef, mashed potatoes, cooked vegetables and thick brown gravy. The range, apart from being the main source of warmth for the house, was also the main source of hot water both for cooking and washing up. A Primus stove, hissing loudly in the kitchen, was used to cook the potatoes and vegetables. Dessert, known as pudding, usually consisted of a pie or crumble that was always served with delicious yellow custard. After that Grandad left with a packed box of sandwiches to catch the bus to the steelworks.

Saturday morning was spent at a leisurely pace and we were told not to get up too early. On Sunday we ate a real Sunday dinner. Grandma pulled a large roast out of the range oven and decanted into a white bowl the contents of a brown baking tray that took drippings from the roast above it. From the compartment above the oven she drew out a large tray that was filled with pastry, which was browned at the edges. We were told that we were about to have Yorkshire pudding. A large jug of brown gravy steamed on the table in readiness to be poured onto the squares of Yorkshire pudding that Grandma was busy cutting from the contents of the tray. The usual plate piled with slices of ready-buttered bread stood in the centre of the table. The aroma of roast beef and baked pastry made our juices flow, so that when I received my portion I began to cut up the first piece and was about to put it into my mouth when Nadia restrained me with her hand to make me wait.

'Get started,' said Grandma. 'Dawn't wait for it to get cold. 'Ave some bread and butter!'

I took a slice of bread and butter and waited for Michael to start his before I continued with mine. My first mouthful of Yorkshire pudding tinged with the thin, rich gravy from the beef was the most delicious thing I had ever eaten, so much so that it was difficult to remember to eat the bread and butter at the same time.

There was enough for a little second helping of Yorkshire pudding before the main course of slices of roast beef, mashed potatoes and peas with a slice of bread and butter to make sure that we were really full. I was almost too full to manage a slice of tempting plum pie and custard, but somehow it went down.

The summer was warm and dry and after exploring the large garden we ventured out onto the road and took a walk the two hundred yards or so, past the neighbours' bungalows, down to the crossroads known as Greetwell Corner, where there was a petrol station. As we stood at the crossroads, Michael showed us that the road at right-angles to ours was the Scawby Messingham road and Scawby was the village, some two miles to the east, where we would be going to school in less than a month's time. I gazed down the road wondering what school was going to be like, but my attention was drawn by shouts coming from a number of men running around in shorts in the prison compound. A fairly large ball was being kicked from one man to the other. Michael said that they were playing football, a game that I had never seen anyone play before, not even in Holland. I asked Michael whether they had been allowed to play football when the war was on and he said that he remembered seeing them play from the school bus and that was over a year ago.

This confirmed that there was no comparison to a concentration camp, where playing any game whatsoever was impossible owing to weakness, disease and the ways of the Japanese. And I was relieved to understand that the barbed wire next to our garden was not a token of starvation and suffering. Redgates, our home, was the last bungalow up the road known as Kirton Road, which led to a small town known as Kirton Lindsey about six miles away. It was the road linking Kirton with the principal town of the area, Scunthorpe. A copse of youngish oaks on our side of the road gave way to conifer woodland that was also bordered by the prisoner of war camp.

The land opposite our house and those of our neighbours, known as Greetwell Common, was what might be called wasteland, a jungle of high bracken, which gave way to sand dunes and heathland as one walked in the direction of Kirton. Michael told me that the army used this area of wasteland for their manoeuvres during the war and that their smoke bombs and shells were still strewn about. He remembered hearing the sounds of the explosions and seeing huge clouds of smoke, but as he didn't think the area was mined, it was safe to go there provided one was careful not to touch the bombs.

The last week of July gave way to August. During those first two weeks Vera and I learnt to understand most of what was said and most of what was said was in a mild form of a South Yorkshire dialect as both Grandma and Grandad were from Sheffield, the broadest variety being spoken by Grandad. We were also soon able to utter simple sentences and take part in conversations speaking a northern form of English.

This form of English, with its flat a's, dropped h's, the u-sound pronounced with the lips rounded that almost resulted in 'oo', was beginning to have its effect on Nadia. Not only did she sometimes find it difficult to follow a conversation, but her determination that we should learn and speak standard King's English made her begin to correct all the children with such frequency that it almost came to the point of nagging. And as we became more conversant in English it also became increasingly apparent that Nadia's own English was laced with a thick Russian accent. Grandma's face reddened with anger as she watched and listened to Nadia giving one of her linguistic outbursts, her pale blue eyes looking even larger behind her magnifying spectacles.

'No, Michael, not: she leeves in that 'ouse, but: she leeves in that hhouse. Say hhouse.'

'ouse' repeated Michael quietly.

'No, hh-hhouse'

'Leave the lad alawn,' said Grandma in a harsh tone, her mounting anger causing her face to change its colour from red to white.

'I am trying to improve you grandson's Eenglish, and you should be grateful.'

'There's nowt wrong wi 'is English. 'E speaks the King's English.'

Nadia said nothing, as her face also became red with both frustration and anger. Harold was not there to turn to as he had taken the bus to Scunthorpe to organise the resurrection of his building business. She went out to the kitchen to see to the laundry.

Washing clothes for eight people was no light matter, but she had promised 'mother', as she called her, that she would do the washing

154

after she had been shown the basics.

She piled all the linen and underwear into a large grey-enamelled copper, filled it with hot water with a white enamelled bucket that she filled from the kitchen tap, the water being plumbed from the range that heated it up.

The tense atmosphere seemed to die down and we left to go outside. As we went out through the door we heard Grandma saying, 'I'll give you a 'and wi' t' washing.'

The pervading smell of paraffin that received its daily boost in the evening became part of our lives. During the first week I went through two more nightmares of a similar type, making me extremely frightened for an unknown reason.

Michael and I formed a friendship that developed as one might have hoped when two boys of a similar age find themselves in the situation of being part of a new, united family. We were both perhaps a little reticent by nature, at the same time not lacking a sense of adventure when the opportunity presented itself. We found it easy to talk to each other, which made it easy for me to learn to speak English, at the same time as giving Michael a companion closer to his age. He would be seven that October while I would be eight in a few days.

He vaguely remembered his mother who died when he was three and his memories of his father, Harold, were almost equally as vague. The nature of his relationship to Grandma was not so close that she was a second mother; she was simply his grandmother. The effect was that while I had acquired a new father, he had to all intents and purposes acquired two new parents, which made it easy to regard each other as brothers. As luck would have it, Philip and Vera, who were even closer to each other in terms of age, had also developed a kinship, though Philip's relationship to Grandma, who had a soft spot for him, was closer. Consequently he found it harder to regard Nadia as his new mother and treated her with a certain amount of suspicion, but this in turn was mitigated by his inclination towards Vera. Accordingly, it was mainly through Philip that Vera found herself conversant in English. The result was that within a couple of weeks we were all as good as brothers and sisters, with Vera and me nearly fluent in the everyday English expressions used during play and in the basic essentials for communication with adults.

Nadia for her part no longer spoke Russian to Vera and me, but occasionally she did come out with Russian epithets that expressed displeasure with her new expanded family, and that not only included Vera and me but also Michael and Philip. If, for instance, Michael had not washed himself properly and left his dirt on the towel, she would exclaim, 'svinya nishastni!', unfortunate pig! Or if one of us had committed some misdemeanour she would exclaim, 'svollage tokaya!', what a scoundrel!, in front of the rest of us.

A rising tension was developing between Grandma, who ran the household in her own traditional Yorkshire way, and Nadia who had other ideas. Apart from that, Grandma was becoming increasingly irritated by Nadia's efforts to make us speak good English when she herself was so foreign.

Nadia told me that she noticed that Grandma favoured her grandsons, especially Philip, by secretly giving them sweets and biscuits. This seemed to increase her frustration which, as she had no other adult to talk to, was relieved to some extent by talking to me.

'You know that Grandma gives Michael and Philip sweets in secret?'

Before I could answer she continued.

'I can understand that she is jealous of me taking over the boys, but I do wish Daddy would help me. It's not at all like I expected. His business does not seem to be much. Grandad is not a real engineer. He told me that he was a fitter and turner and he seemed proud of it. What's a fitter and turner? Besides, real engineers don't do shift work, go to football matches and to the pub on Saturday nights. And how can we go on living in this tiny bungalow - eight of us?'

I could not answer to help her. I didn't even know what a pub was, let alone a fitter and turner.

Nadia went on to tell me about Grandma's attitude to her. It was not as if she were fond of Harold's first wife, whom she regarded as not much better than a whore, but it seemed that Nadia had more than fulfilled her prejudices against foreigners by trying to dominate the household with her foreignness. In addition, it seemed that to Grandma, her future daughter-in-law appeared to be doing her best to drive her estranged eldest son away from her. But Nadia told me that she only meant to raise our standards.

But as children we were only superficially aware of those tensions and the full meaning of Nadia's vented frustrations did not come to me until much later when I also understood Grandma's side of the matter.

We enjoyed our rural surroundings to the full, playing in the sand dunes of the Common, making castles and digging tunnels and coming home filthy. We played hide-and-seek in the copious bracken and jumped down into the soft sandy bottoms of the bomb craters.

We were so involved in playing out on the Common that the event of my eighth birthday seemed unimportant until the actual day. When it came in the middle of August we ate a special high tea that included cold dripping sandwiches and Nadia made a home-baked cake with eight candles that I didn't manage to blow out in one puff.

I felt secure and no longer suffered from nightmares. This was as well, since our preliminary sleeping arrangements proved to be impractical, especially as Grandad was on nights and had to trudge the creaking stairs to the loft while we were all asleep. The solution was that we children were all moved to the loft with Vera and me sleeping in the ex-army camp beds while Michael and Philip slept in the double bed previously occupied by Grandma and Grandad. Vera and I had no objection to our bedroom being taken over by Grandma and Grandad and we soon got used to carrying the paraffin lamps and enjoyed chattering in the dark prior to falling asleep. However, progress up the folding loft stairs was rather slow, as the stairs were steep and rickety.

One morning, Philip was first to get up and started to go down the stairs on his way to breakfast. We heard the usual rattling as he went down, which then suddenly gave way to a scramble and a shriek. We looked down to see Philip hanging from one of the hooks that guided the steel wires. He was caught and hung by the side of his jaw, suspended like a piece of meat hanging on a rail at the butcher's. Harold answered our shouts for help by rushing in and lifting him off. Philip was white with shock, too shocked to cry. There was a hole at the angle of his jaw where he had been hooked and a piece of fatty tissue hung out. Though the hole appeared quite deep, it didn't bleed. Grandma took him to clean it and put a plaster over it.

We did not see that much of the men in the house. Grandad was away during the weekday evenings because of his shift work and on Saturdays went off to watch the football match when Scunthorpe United played home games. Otherwise he tinkered with his chocked-up car during weekends. On Saturdays we had to be quiet while he was listening to the radio football results in order to plan out his football pool charts. It seemed that occasionally he won very small sums, which might have been larger if thousands of others had not been using similar forecast systems.

Harold came home from the building activities of his new firm tired, often late and sometimes irritable. He had acquired a black motorbike and sidecar that had the name 'Neale and Cook' painted on its side. We once saw Mr Cook bringing a load of timber tied onto the sidecar: a tall man in a black leather suit with black greasy hair and who didn't seem to say very much. It seemed that the sidecar was almost exclusively used for carrying building materials that were not directly delivered to the site and we never saw it used to carry passengers.

Not long after our arrival Harold had arranged the installation of a telephone as a necessary aid to his business. In practice this meant that the household had its own telephone and that we had our own number, Scawby 326, and the actual telephone apparatus, black with numbered dial, was the only thing in the house connected to an electric cable. If we had a telephone, why couldn't we have proper electricity, I wondered?

The telephone was placed on a small table in the front room, where Harold would often spend the early evening doing his paperwork and talking to customers. He was also his own draughts-man, drawing plans of houses on light blue linen paper that leaned in rolls against the wall. However, his hard work and all the worries associated with building up a business, were beginning to change him from a cheerful positive man to a grumpy background figure. He began to be irritated by the two women that fussed about things that seemed unimportant, which made his image as a father figure for both his own two sons and for Vera and me begin to tarnish.

The best way for Nadia and Harold to get over the strains and tensions of the week was to have a long lie-in on Sunday mornings.

Since their bedroom was directly below ours, this meant that we four had to be quiet in the loft bedroom, for what seemed to us was a very long time.

Grandma gave Philip a comic called *Dandy* with comic strip stories of characters such as Corky the Cat, Pansy Potter the Strong Arm's Daughter and Desperate Dan. These stories kept us all amused, and with the knowledge that we had to be quiet we enacted the stories on the double bed. It was inevitable, however, that we forgot ourselves and it wasn't long before Nadia shouted in a hoarse whisper up the stairs, 'Be quiet! Daddy's trying to sleep!'

As we were not allowed to go downstairs to the toilet, a potty was provided for us to pee in. Often it became so full that Nadia had difficulty in taking it downstairs without spilling the contents. We were finally allowed to go down at about ten, after perhaps three hours of reading comics and playing around on the double bed.

When we came down, sounds and smells coming from the kitchen indicated that Grandma was busy frying the Sunday breakfast, while Grandad was in the living room toasting slices of white bread in front of the range fire using a large brass toasting fork. After the Sunday breakfast banquet of bacon, eggs and fried tomatoes accompanied by generous amounts of Grandad's buttered creations, followed by toast and marmalade, we were ready to run out into the warm summer and play while the women attended to the washing up and the men read the Sunday papers. Grandad, a confirmed socialist, took the *Daily Worker* and *The News of the World* on Sundays. Harold, who believed in self-advancement without the interference of the state, read the *Sunday Express*. But to us the newspapers belonged to the adult world.

Grandma had a pretty tabby cat with a clear letter M patterned between its ears. During most of the daytime it slept in the living room utility armchair, curled up as if sleeping in the warm cooking smells of the nerve centre of the little bungalow and it must have been the next best thing to heaven. I did not know whether the cat was male or female and wasn't even sure of its name, if it had a name, for when Grandma called it from its night out she only said 'Tisst'. Often it was already waiting outside on the patio for Grandma to open the back door so that we didn't often hear Grandma calling it.

I grew fond of the cat, and would often stroke it and talk to it before it took its place in the living room and I referred to it as 'Tisst'.

Once Tisst came into the house with a baby rabbit caught securely in its jaws, a sight that was both sad and exciting, for though we had seen piles of rabbit droppings by their holes out among the sand dunes, I had not actually seen the rabbits themselves. Michael, however, said that he had seen rabbits many times and said that occasionally Grandad brought in a full-size rabbit that he had acquired from a colleague at work and that they were very good to eat.

After our Sunday roast dinner at the end of August, Harold and Nadia decided to take the four of us for a walk on the Common. Harold took a wicker basket and a walking stick as he said it was time to look for blackberries. In the basket he had several clean jam-jars for us to help with the picking. The warmth of the late summer made the air hum with insects and the patches of heather were alive with bees and grayling butterflies. We walked quite a long distance over heather and sand dunes until we came to an area of dense spreading bramble bushes interspersed with patches of grass so short that if it weren't for the copious heaps of rabbit droppings they would have looked as if they had been trimmed by machine. It wasn't long before Harold spotted some rabbits scampering into their burrows about thirty yards away.

'Just look at those rabbits!' said Harold. 'I ought to keep a look out for them in the garden and keep my shotgun handy. Here, help yourselves to these jars and start picking.'

'Where?' said Vera. 'I can't see any. Where?'

'They're all over. Look, there's one running over there,' said Michael.

'I can see one sitting by that blackberry bush,' said Philip pointing in the appropriate direction and I could see the vague shape of the rabbit that he was pointing out.

'Where? You're all teasing me,' said Vera, this time in a tone of dejection. 'I can't see any rabbits at all!'

'I can see them all over. Poor V-erka, you are short sighted. You have been ever since camp. I must take you to the optician's in Brigg before you start school,' said Nadia.

'Does that mean that I have to wear glasses?' Vera's tone was even more dejected.

'Yes, but don't worry, you will soon get used to it.'

Vera remained silent and out of sorts for some time while we began to pick blackberries. I tried a blackberry and found it to be quite sour, but a red one was much worse. The bramble tangles offered all stages from flowers, through green, red, dark red and black berries. I soon discovered that the sweetest ones were those that were not only black but looked swollen. By that time Michael had nearly filled his jar with black treasure while I had barely covered the bottom of mine. He had an amazing ability to gather blackberries, disappearing into a bush and filling a jar while Harold used the curved handle of his walking stick to draw bunches of ripe blackberries towards him. After about half an hour we had filled half the wicker basket, thanks largely to Harold's, Nadia's and Michael's efforts, and we all laughed at each other's mouths blotched with purple.

13. School

The idyllic summer began to fade like the petals of a flower before they fall onto the ground. During our first six weeks in England, I had experienced a bit of the North Lincolnshire countryside in the splendour of summer and learnt to recognise not only rabbits, but pheasants, French partridges, wood pigeons and foxes, Harold and sometimes Michael being the teacher. We had already met Mr Curtis, who sold us his milk direct from his farm about half a mile away on the road to Scawby. His shiny brown leather leggings seemed to emphasise his bow legs as he stood by his horse and cart to ladle out his milk direct from a churn. Now he was harvesting his wheat. Two horses drew a reaper and binder with the blades working like a mobile windmill in the field beyond the camp. The harvest was made up into sheaves that were arranged into stooks that looked like golden tents where we ran about on the straw stubble between them and played hide-and-seek.

The nights gradually grew colder, their passage marked by a heavy dew that festooned cobwebs, drenched the grass and remained suspended a few feet above the ground in the form of an early morning mist. The silence of such an early morning might be broken by the call of a pheasant that we could hear as we dressed before coming down to breakfast. As the days grew shorter the need to use paraffin lamps of various types started increasingly earlier in the evenings.

It was not just the seasonal changes brought about by the end of summer that began to encroach into our lives; it was the preparation for the start of school. I was already eight years old and had never been to a proper school before. As I already knew that at my age in England I should already be starting my fourth year at school, I wondered what they would do with me. Would I be placed with Philip and Vera in the first class? Would I be made to sit like an overgrown idiot amongst children nearly half my age? I was filled with a mixture of excitement and dread as the first week of

162

September drew to a close and the first day of school was about to begin.

Vera was already wearing her glasses, a silver frame supporting two small lenses that made her blue eyes look smaller. They were known as clinical glasses and didn't cost anything, thanks to Mr Atlee and his Labour government, and Vera's displeasure with her new appearance was mitigated by the fact that she could now see better than she ever remembered.

'Why didn't Mammy let me have new glasses before? I haven't been able to see for a long time,' she said.

Nadia took us shopping in Scunthorpe. We waited at the cross-roads to take a red double-decker bus like the ones I saw in London. But the excitement of visiting a new town soon petered out and changed to the sheer torture of being dragged for several hours round various clothes and shoe shops while Nadia tried to find the best clothes at the lowest prices. Grandma had already told her which shops were the most likely to provide the best bargains to enable her to spend both her money and clothes coupons in the best way.

At last we were back at the crossroads kitted out in new shoes, new grey short trousers, new grey shirts and pullovers, new navy-blue raincoats and school caps, this time waiting for the bus that ran from Scunthorpe to Brigg via Scawby. Nadia was taking us on our first day to be registered at Scawby County Primary School.

We alighted alongside a high stone wall that was dwarfed by the presence of several large trees that grew behind it. Nadia lead the way round the corner of what was one side of a T-junction while the wall gave way to a much lower brick wall, behind which the full length of the trees could be seen. She had noticed where the school lay when the bus passed it on her way to and from Brigg during her shopping tours. But finding the school after alighting from the bus would have been easy for a blind man, as we could hear the sounds of many children laughing, shouting and screeching to give me my first experience of the sound of a school. This was followed by my first sight of a school. Immediately behind the low brick wall a large horse chestnut tree grew to dominate the front of the playground that was somewhat raised above the level of the road.

'Could you tell me where the headmistress is,' asked Nadia, looking at one of the older children who stood near the chestnut tree.

'She's in there, missis,' she said, pointing to a corner of a brick building that was approached by a cemented passage on the same level as the road and thereby lower than the playground.

We went through an iron gate, up the passage and round the corner into a dark lobby with small low basins and rows of coat hangers. An open door invited us into a large room that was lit by a large gothic-style window at one end and two large windows along one side. The cream-coloured ceiling was very high and the windows were placed at such a height that we could only see the sky through them.

A woman dressed in a brown skirt and brown cardigan came towards us. She was about the same height and age as Nadia and had piercing dark eyes that seemed to absorb us within a split second. Her hair was nearly black and tightly done into a horizontal roll that ran along the back of her neck to make it look like a dark wig, such as worn by young men in the eighteenth century, rather than her own hair. Despite the intensity of her eyes, she did not give the impression of being severe; there was something kindly in her manner.

'How do you do? You must be Mrs Neale and these must be your children. My name is Mable Bowles,' she said.

She turned to one side and presented a taller, gaunt looking woman with greying hair and a large hooked nose.

'This is Miss Hazelwood, the deputy headmistress.'

There was an exchange of how-do-you-do's while we stood in silence.

'It was good of you to telephone me. It isn't often we get to know in advance who we are to have as pupils at the beginning of term. Now, I have the children's names written on the register, but let's see who is who. Of course I know Michael, he is still with Miss Everton, and Philip is just starting.'

She smiled at Vera. 'You must be Vera. You will be starting in the same class as Philip.'

Then she turned to me, still smiling while the intensity of her eyes had not diminished.

'This is Ivan,' said Nadia quickly.

'Welcome to our school, Ivan!' said Miss Bowles pronouncing my name almost in the same way as at home.

'Your surname is 'Kruys'. I understand that it is Dutch.' She pronounced my surname as 'crews'.

'Kruhis,' said Nadia, pronouncing it in the Dutch way.

''Crews' is the closest I can manage so 'crews' it will have to be,' said Miss Bowles apologetically and with some resignation. I realised that 'crews' was to be the future pronunciation of my name in English.

'Ivan can start together with Michael in Miss Everton's class and see how he gets on, though at his age he should really be starting with Miss Hazelwood. However, he has the advantage of just having turned eight, which means he will be one of the youngest of his proper year group. The children are grouped according to what age they are on the first of September before the start of the school year. Thank you for coming, Mrs Neale. Perhaps you might like to meet Miss Everton who is in charge of the infants across the road.'

'Thank you, Miss Bowles. Goodbye! Goodbye Miss Hazelwood!'

A 'goodbye Mrs Neale' came from both teachers almost simultaneously and as soon as we had left the main school building Vera halfwhispered, 'You're not Mrs Neale yet Mammy. You don't get married to Daddy until next Saturday!'

'It doesn't matter,' said Nadia as we crossed the road towards the infant section of the school.

Miss Everton was a smiling slim elderly woman dressed in a beige suit. Her grey hair was tinged a sandy colour, which suggested that she might have had ginger hair when she was younger. She had a light, slightly freckled complexion and her grey-blue eyes twinkled with welcoming warmth behind her brown-framed glasses. She introduced us to another elderly lady with white hair, called Mrs Gray, who took charge of Vera and Philip disappeared into the noisy classroom next door.

The classroom that was to be for Michael and me was a smaller version of Miss Bowles', the windows being not quite as large, the desks being smaller. I was so absorbed by my surroundings, the school posters of life on a farm, the almost life-size portrayals of foxes, badgers and squirrels, that I hardly noticed my mother saying goodbye.

The morning of my first day at school went by in an atmosphere of overwhelming bewilderment and excitement. It was a lesson that seemed to have more to do with our names on a register and where we ought to sit than the actual business of the three R's.

When Miss Everton announced that it was playtime all activity in the classroom abruptly ceased and I found myself joining the crowd of children shouting and screaming while we were running round and round the building in an aimless frenzy. After a couple of laps I was just beginning to grapple with the fact that I was the tallest and oldest child in the infant school when an even taller boy dressed in a neat grey suit caught my eye. He was standing quite still by the little wall next to the road. I broke off to join him. As I approached him I noticed how well-groomed he was. His light brown hair was neatly combed, not dishevelled like the other boys, and his brown shoes were neatly tied and polished to be shiny at the toes. He wore a light grey shirt and a plain navy-blue tie.

'Hello,' I said. 'What's your name?'

He continued to stare out onto the road without even turning towards me and before I could repeat my question, I heard someone saying, "Is name is Edward. 'E don't speak 'cause 'ee's shell-shocked. 'E cooms from Loondon and 'is 'ouse was bombed during the war.'

I was disappointed to learn that the only boy who appeared to be around my age was unreachable. On turning towards the main entrance I noticed a number of children, including Vera and my new brothers, clustered around a number of crates. Each child held the smallest bottle of milk that I had ever seen and was sucking the contents through a paper straw. I took a bottle from one of the crates, pressed in the round punched centre of the card-paper top and inserted the straw to imbibe the rich and refreshing creamy liquid. Edward was still standing by the wall.

Miss Everton came out ringing a small hand bell to signify that my first playtime at an English school, Scawby County Primary School, was over.

My first lesson in mathematics, commonly known as 'sums' was about to begin. I was not placed to sit next to anyone. Instead I sat on my own at a desk at the extreme end of the front row. Both the desk and seat felt too low but when I looked round I observed that when we were seated my large size was not so obvious. Miss Everton had chalked some simple additions on the blackboard and taught us how to set out a sum with the plus signs and lines. Using pencil-shaped solid pieces of slate we had to copy what she had written on square pieces of slate that had simple wooden frames: slate against slate. As I wrote down the figures, I remembered my efforts to write on the hard baked dry soil of Ambarava. If only we had this writing equipment in camp! As it could be used countless times over, it would have solved the problem of the lack of paper, and so easy to erase just by rubbing with the finger or the side of a hand!

I soon understood the basics of addition and had no trouble in solving Miss Everton's tasks, counting on my fingers as a check.

Lunchtime, called dinnertime, began when we were told to walk in pairs from the school with the first class leading under the guidance of Mrs Gray. We went past a terraced row of old cottages and round a sharp corner along a road that ran diagonally behind the infant school. After five minutes we came to a building that was built of bricks of the same colour as the school and about as tall. Like the school, it had a dark slate roof. All the windows, however, were long and narrow and rounded at the top, which gave the impression that at one time the building had another purpose that had nothing to do with the school. Once inside, we walked on the bare wooden floor along an aisle between long tables placed at right angles to the aisle and grouped in pairs. Mrs Gray was already ushering her brood to queue up along a counter at the end of the aisle where large round metal containers were steaming out smells of boiled potatoes and vegetables.

A red-faced woman with white hair and an almost white apron was handing out plates onto which she ladled out mashed potato and vegetables after asking each child a question. Another, smaller, middle-aged woman beside her dealt out slices of what looked like cold beef. While we waited in what was now a queue along the whole length of the building, I could see Vera and Philip already taking their places at one of the tables nearest the serving counter that were designated to take Mrs Gray's class. All the tables were already laid with knives and forks, spoons and drinking glasses. Instead of eating straight away I noticed that everyone on the table was made to wait and Vera was taking some time inspecting her portion with a look of disgust on her face.

The queue seemed to move quite rapidly, so that I could soon see in detail the routine of how every child received his portion, allowing me to know how to react when it came to my turn.

'Mash?' asked the woman with the red face, her brown eyes burning like coals in a glowing fire.

'Yes please.' I was given an appropriate portion for a growing boy.

'Cabbage?' she asked in a voice that I noticed was high-pitched and bubbled as if she herself were a boiling cooking pot.

'Yes please.' A steaming, greenish, amorphous mass landed on my plate, which made me wonder if it really had been cabbage at one time. I thought the cabbage that Nadia cooked at home looked more like a chopped up version of the original vegetable. That little cerebral detour caused me to forget to say 'thank you' on receiving my portion of the canteen's version.

By the time I realised my omission the smaller middle-aged woman asked, 'Meat?'

'Thank you,' I replied, instead of saying 'yes please'. She put a slice of beef on my plate while looking at me as if she knew that I was one of the new foreigners that started at the school.

When we had all seated ourselves at Miss Everton's two tables, and that included Miss Everton herself, she said in her quiet reassuring way, 'Hands together. Eyes closed. '

I did as we were told and heard Miss Everton start a prayer that we were all meant to say, 'Thank you, Lord, for the food we eat', to continue with thanks for a whole list of things and ending with 'thank you, Lord, for everything.'

With that, the table clattered with the grasping of cutlery. To the general background of sounds, there was also the sound of voices asking 'pass the gravy' while a large white jug was grappled with around the table, its contents browning and sometimes drowning various portions of meat, mashed potato and the greenish mass that purported to be cabbage. The gravy, with its slightly salty flavour, turned out to be an asset. It imparted some flavour to the cabbage that would otherwise have been tasteless and would have been difficult to identify as such, had it not been for the faint cabbage smell that still remained, despite the cooks' efforts to destroy it by prolonged boiling.

By the time most of us had finished our main course the last people in the queue, the largest and oldest in the school, Miss Bowles' class, were receiving their portions. We were not allowed to get up and fetch our puddings until we had eaten up our main course, which meant that the boys, being less finicky eaters, were usually first in receiving their dessert. Most of Mrs Gray's class was already eating what looked like a chocolate pudding with yellow custard but Vera was still struggling with her portion of super-boiled cabbage. When Miss Everton had stacked our empty plates, I followed Michael to collect our dessert and on handing him his portion, the head cook peered at Michael and asked, 'With or without?' The word 'without' came out in a series of high pitched vocal bubbles. On saying 'with', Michael received his dollop of custard and I decided to follow his example to receive mine.

Vera's struggle with her cabbage was finally put to an end by Mrs Gray who allowed her to leave most of it uneaten so that she could eat her pudding and catch up with the class who were waiting to go back to school.

When we had finished our dinner, for that was what it was called, I walked back with Michael. He told me that the school canteen was a converted chapel and that the white-haired head cook with the high pitched bubbly voice was called Mrs Harley, who had two children at the school. The walk back to school in pairs with our teachers seemed a little more relaxed and we were allowed some time to play before the start of classes.

Back in class, Miss Everton made us practise our handwriting in small ready-lined notebooks with the printed model letters, both capital and small, to be copied on the blank lines. It was my first writing exercise on paper, which made me realise that the slates were used mainly for arithmetic, presumably because there was a lot of rubbing out.

A short break in the mid-afternoon was followed by a reading lesson and the day ended by Miss Everton reading us a story from

Hans Andersen, which was already familiar to me as Nadia had told us a similar story in camp.

The end of my first day at school came with, 'Will you all stand. Hands together, eyes closed.'

I was tempted to peep to see if anyone was cheating but realised that it would be futile as I was standing at the front. Miss Everton 'Thanked God for the day' and I tried to keep up with the rest singing 'Now the day is over.'

Miss Everton saw to it that all who had to catch the bus home were safe across the road, though there was hardly any traffic. We joined Miss Bowles, who waited with a group of children of mixed ages for the school bus to arrive. While we waited Michael and I chatted about the events of the day and both agreed that Miss Everton was a good teacher, by which we really meant was that she was a nice person. We had no notion of what it took for a teacher to be good at her job.

A green bus drew up, its motor throbbing loudly under its protruding bonnet. Mr Jessop, the driver, a smiling squat-faced man in a cloth cap, turned to meet the little crowd of eager passengers while Miss Bowles opened the door and leaned in to talk to him, presumably to give him a report on the passenger situation. When she had finished, she tried to stem the rush for seats by making the children stand in line, but the end of the school day had affected both her resolve and the children's obedience. The bus itself was smaller than the usual service buses and because it already had children from the Brigg direction, it soon became full. The concentrated din of chatter, shrieks and shouts made it almost impossible to hear ourselves talking and as neither of us had a tendency to shout, we sat without attempting to say anything.

The novelty of the first few days' school gradually faded into a routine. In the mornings the green school bus picked us up opposite our red gates and in the late afternoons Nadia always knew when we were home because she could hear it approaching by the sound of the crescendo of the voices of its passengers above the noise of the engine. She knew when we had alighted and were on our way up the drive by the whining sound of the acceleration of the engine, the gear changes and the resulting diminuendo of voices. Consequently

170

she often stood in front of the open door ready and eager to hear our accounts of the day at school. Nadia had a genuine deep interest in all that we could tell her about the events at school.

Most of the events of the day, however, were recounted while we were having our high tea. Philip and Vera seemed to enjoy each other's company and that of their classmates, but Vera was not especially fond of Mrs Gray. She said that she was too fussy and that they were made to put their heads on their desktops to have a sleep in the middle of the afternoon, just when she was not at all sleepy. Vera also considered that her school meals were often an ordeal, especially the over cooked greens. The products of the school canteen often caused divided opinions amongst us. There were those, including me, who liked sago pudding, popularly known by all as 'frog spawn' and others, such as Vera, who could not stand the sight of it, even though at that time we both had not seen the origin of the epithet.

It soon became clear to Nadia that I had no difficulty in learning the basics of the three R's and that it would not be long before I would be able to start in the junior section of the school with Miss Hazelwood.

As, after the first few days, it became apparent to the teachers that the school was not the right place to help Edward, he was transferred to an institution, which gave me the dubious status of being the tallest boy in the infant section of the school. This made me even more keen to be with my peers across the road, but at the same time I felt a growing fondness for Miss Everton, who seemed to understand me in ways that I could not always define. Above all, she had the ability to bring out the good aspects of her pupils, which in my case resulted in the writing of simple rhymes, drawing, and modelling in grey clay. During my first experiments with modelling clay, which was not plasticine, but light grey water-based clay, I modelled a camel as I remembered it from Port Said. She was so impressed, that she said that she wanted to save it for later use and that I could have it afterwards. She praised my arithmetic in a way that suggested that there was nothing remarkable in my performance as it was only to be expected if I were to move up next term to be amongst children of my age.

14. Winter Clothing

On the Saturday that followed our first week at school Harold and Nadia became man and wife in the eyes of the law.

In our eyes, however, they were already our parents, Michael and Philip having accepted Nadia as their mother, which was perhaps not so surprising, since not only was their biological mother deceased, but they hardly remembered her when she was alive. Vera and I had already been predisposed to having Harold as our father when we were still in Holland. We did, after all, call him 'Daddy' as soon as we arrived in England. Nevertheless, the fact that we were officially a united family living in the same house was important to me, perhaps also to Michael, if not so much to Vera and Philip who were too young to accept the family situation in any way other than just a matter of fact.

The wedding itself was the simplest of weddings, being a basic paper exercise at the Scunthorpe register office. There was no fuss, no guests, no family and no people other than the witnesses and the bridal couple. Nadia was dressed in a simple dark-coloured close-fitting dress and Harold wore a grey suit. The event took place so unobtrusively that we were dressed in our old clothes and went out to play on the Common as if it were an ordinary weekend.

As the weeks went by the days grew shorter and colder. Leaves began to fall in brown and golden flurries, whipped up by the breeze into small heaps that collapsed into dark soggy masses with the autumn drizzle. The damp autumn air smelt like a mixture of cold tea and honey.

The sweet chestnut tree at the front of the garden had four trunks that were the result of a coppicing that must have taken place after the First World War. They grew out at an angle of about forty-five degrees to make the tree spread out like a giant bush, which must have been the standard way to grow chestnut trees, and the effect was to produce a very large crown that was easily reachable. The whole aim was to harvest those intensely spiky green hedgehogs that

172

were occasionally blessed with fat ripe chestnuts. We enjoyed both climbing the trunks and looking for chestnuts among the many that were empty or merely contained flat apologies for nuts. We ate them raw after peeling them with our teeth and fingernails, often with little patience to do the job properly, which resulted in pains in the stomach later. But we soon discovered that it was better to resist eating them raw and to save them to be roasted in front of the range fire, to let them burst open with the heat and convert their hard rawness to the soft sweetness that gave rise to their name.

Just as September meant blackberries and pies, October meant chestnuts by the fire.

September and October also meant fun with those astonishingly highly polished wonders that came from spiked cases that were as soft and inviting as the covers of sweet chestnuts were not. They reminded me of the tropical fruit on display in the markets in Java. I saw that the older boys across the road at school threaded them through with pieces of string and played games with them. The large tree that grew on their side of the wall was a generous source that dropped its harvest during a windy day. After I learnt that these were called conkers I was told that they were more properly called horse chestnuts. Was it because only horses could eat them? What was it about the use of the word 'horse' that meant something was either inedible or nearly so, like the horseradish we had with our roast beef at the weekends? Almost subconsciously I began to wonder about the vagaries of the language that I was so keen to learn but which had so many pitfalls.

Michael's birthday happened to be in October. In fact it was the only one of our birthdays that could be celebrated at a time of year when it was most suitable to have a party. Vera's in June was at a less suitable time and those of Philip and I, being in August, were in the summer holidays. Nadia decided that Michael should have a birthday party and that if we invited a friend each, a total of eight children would be just right in our small front room. Michael invited the boy he sat next to in class, Vera invited a girl called April who lived on a farm about a mile away, Philip a friend who lived in Scawby and I realised that I had no friend that I could invite. I was too old to make a real friend from the boys in my class and I knew no others.

It was a small party after school for a total of seven children. The guests took the school bus with us to Redgates and we arrived to find Nadia and Grandma presiding over a table that was as inviting as a fairground. There was an iced cake with seven candles, two large jellies moulded in the classic form, one red and one yellow, two large plates piled with prepared sandwiches, biscuits of various kinds, glasses filled with lemonade and the usual large teapot waiting to serve the empty cups and saucers. We stood and gaped. Suddenly Michael started to cry in quiet sobs with copious tears running down his face.

'What is the matter, Michael?' wondered Nadia.

'I dunno,' he sobbed. 'I've never 'ad a party before. I'm...' He couldn't say more, but it was quite clear that he was overcome with emotion.

Nadia dried the tears on his face and directed us all to our seats and we began to wallow in the festivity offered by the sandwiches, first with fish paste, then with jam. This was followed by trifle and jelly with second helpings, all of which led to the big moment of lighting the seven candles on the cake for Michael to blow out.

He drew a deep breath raising his shoulders, then his cheeks became two pinkish balls on his face as he launched an attack on the candles. The seven flames succumbed as Michael blasted out and everyone joined in the cheering and the clapping and the singing of 'happy birthday to you' with Nadia being the initiator.

We were led into the front room, less frequented by members of the household. The furniture consisted of a three-piece suite with thick rounded arms and backs and covered with a soft brown and green pattern that was quite noticeable without being too loud. They stood on a neutral beige carpet that covered most of the wooden floor. The roundness of the furniture and the bay window reflected the mellow modernity of the 1930s. Though the room was lit by the large bay window during the daytime, the eye homed in on the red-brick fireplace which, in contrast to the roundness of the furniture and the bay window, was square. The mantelpiece was adorned by a foot-long model Columbus' *Santa Maria,* beautifully made by Harold when he was fifteen, together with a seventeenth-century flintlock pistol that might have been genuine. The hearth was made complete by a brass-handled poker on one side and a pair of sixteenth-century style bellows that were also made by Harold when he was in his teens. These bellows and the model ship gave us an insight into the skills that Harold possessed as a fine craftsman and we therefore avoided playing with them in case we damaged them, but we felt freer to play with the flintlock pistol. On the odd occasions when we came into the room we pulled back the hammer and made it strike the plate by squeezing the trigger, fascinated by the thought that perhaps two hundred years ago the squeeze of the trigger would cause an explosion that might have caused someone's death. Was it a high-wayman's pistol? Did it belong to a pirate? Was it used in battle? Harold could only reply that it might have been used under any of those conditions but we never asked him how he came to own the weapon.

As it was almost dark outside, we were led into the front room by Nadia holding the Tilley lamp and were amazed to see a long row of objects suspended on a piece of string that stretched across the whole room. Harold's business papers and architectural drawings were removed to make way for the party. Some of the objects glittered in the bright light to reveal that they were sweets while others were small mystery brown paper packages. We were blindfolded in turn and given a pair of scissors to try and cut a desired object off the string. Michael, the birthday boy, was first while the rest of us were given pieces of paper of various lengths to draw to determine turns. Michael's attempt yielded a toffee, while Philip managed to cut down one of several small toy farm animals. The guests seemed to be luckier than the hosts, which, Nadia told us, was how it should be, but we all cut down something to please us. This was followed by several party games such as 'I spy' and 'blind man's buff.' I was so absorbed in the activities and the whole atmosphere of the party that the feeling of being the oldest was totally absent. It all seemed to pass so quickly that I felt a mixture of surprise and disappointment when it was time for the guest children to catch the bus home. Nadia told us later that she had used up the week's sugar rations for the whole family.

The beginning of November was marked by a change. When it was time to get up after our forced confinement in bed the first Saturday morning in November, I looked out of our loft bedroom window to see the whole ground veiled in a tinge of white. Instead of being straw-coloured and green, the grass looked as if a fine layer of sparkling flour had been carefully and evenly spread on it. The same was true of the autumn leaves, except that the edges were whiter. I had heard of snow and that sometime in the winter we would see the ground covered by it, but this was unexpected. It was on that occasion that Michael taught me the meaning of the word 'frost' as we both stared out to survey the change in the appearance of the countryside.

While seated at the breakfast table we talked about the frost and how much colder it had become. We said that our knees felt cold and Nadia thought that as it was too cold to go about in short trousers, she would make us some new trousers that would be suitable for the coming winter. As we already had knee-length grey socks, she designed trousers that bagged over where they fastened just below the calf, using material that came from the welfare clothes that she had received from Holland.

Harold, on the other hand, was more preoccupied with an entirely different matter. He explained that we should put on our playing clothes and help him to gather branches and twigs as he cut them in order to build a bonfire. He told us that Tuesday was the fifth of November which was when we were to light a bonfire in commemoration of a man who was caught in the act of detonating the Houses of Parliament. He also promised that there was more to it than just lighting a fire. That spurned us on to help him to build the bonfire by gathering branches and twigs to form a heap that was soon made to become a respectable size by Harold's addition of timbers that were cast-offs from his building business. He then erected a post, a plank on two sawing benches and hammered a pipe into the ground and when we asked him what they were for he smiled and said, 'Wait and see'. He also filled an old hessian sack with paper and straw and tied string round it to produce a sort of effigy which he clothed with an old jacket and one of Grandad's old hats. When he placed it on top of the bonfire we were told that it was meant to represent the man called Guy Fawkes and was simply called 'the guy'. Though he lacked trousers, to me he looked just like a condemned man, his head hanging down, and his hat covering the guilt on his face.

The blazing fire masked the real darkness that followed dusk on the fifth of November, the flames reaching the guy in a matter of minutes. We held our breath and then cheered as the flames engulfed him and as if we could add to that blaze, we were each given a sparkler to hold and whirl around. This was followed by Harold announcing that we were about to see a Roman candle that first glowed after he lit the object that he placed on the plank. Then it fizzed with a shower of sparks, followed by the pop of a green glowing ball that shot up into the sky. Shooting comets and blazing volcanoes that he lined up on the plank followed. The display on the plank became the centre of attention as Harold lit one at a time. The fact that we were made to stand a safe distance away made the procedure of lighting each new piece even more exciting. Harold became a wizard, a master of timing, lighting the few fireworks in such a way that we could appreciate each item at its best, including the bangers and the Chinese crackers. Just as we wondered what was to follow, a Catherine wheel set up on the post fizzed and spluttered out its whirling fiery colours, and just as we thought the whole display was over a rocket whooshed out, cracking out its unbelievable shower of colour in the dark November sky.

On the following morning we saw the remnants of the night's festivities as we went to the road to wait for the school bus. The still smoking ashes, the constructions that Harold set up, the burnt firework cartridges, all reminders that Bonfire Night was something that could only happen in England.

We returned from school to find Nadia busily stitching our new winter clothes with the help of Grandma's treadle sewing machine. She said that she had been at it for most of the time. The result was that a few days later each one of us three boys was provided with a new pair of tweed plus fours. Mine was a light brown while Michael's and Philip's were made of a grey herring-bone tweed. We thought that they looked very smart. When we tried them on we looked liked pre-war young upper class gentry and felt quite proud of our smart new and warm trousers.

The Monday morning that followed was chilly from a biting east wind that blew over from the North Sea, but as we waited for the school bus we felt the secure warmth provided by our new winter trousers. Vera's legs were protected from the cold by her full-length stockings. The bus drew to a squealing halt, only the squeak of the breaks dominating the din made by its passengers, but as we mounted the bus the loud chatter began to die down, followed by silence. Then the long moment of silence gave way to a few titters and giggles. I felt very self-conscious. Was it our trousers that caused the reaction on the bus? When I noticed the resumption of the normal ear-bursting chatter I decided that it was better not to worry about our appearance. I preferred to concentrate on the day before us. When Miss Everton remarked about the smartness of our new trousers, my misgivings disappeared altogether and I was able to take part in classroom activities without giving my trousers another thought.

We rushed out at playtime, as we called it, Michael and I taking our milk from the crate that stood by the entrance. As we stood sucking up the cold creamy contents through our paper straws we were distracted by the sounds of raucous boyish laughter:

'Ha, ha, haaa, shit stoppers! Shit stoppers! Shit stoppers! Shit stoppers!'

The voices grew into a chorus made up mainly of boys from our class, some squatting and jumping up and down like apes and pointing while shouting the description of what was obviously aimed at our new trousers.

'Anyway, they keep us warm,' shouted Michael bravely when the mockery began to die down.

'Leave 'em alawn,' said a girl who was one of those sensible motherly types to the leader of the mob. The one who started the teasing about the trousers was a boy called John Anderson who travelled on the same bus as us. He got on at the crossroads together with his sister April, the girl whom Vera had invited to Michael's birthday party.

Michael seemed to be able to tolerate the teasing better than I could, for I was shattered. All my efforts to be the same as the rest of the children, to speak the same language, to look the same, to be English, were thwarted because of those plus-fours that my mother

178

made to keep off the cold. To me those trousers meant that I was branded as a foreign oddity. The only small consolation was that both Michael and Philip had similar trousers. To me, however, it seemed as though they were made to look foreign as well. I spent the rest of the day, including the walk to the canteen that seemed much longer than usual, deeply ashamed of my trousers, as if I had peed in them.

That teatime we told Nadia about the effect the trousers had on our classmates and how they teased us, calling them 'shit stoppers'.

'I don't want to go to school in them tomorrow,' I said, recalling the day like a nightmare.

'You don't want to take any notice of a few stupid boys,' said Vera. The maturity of my nearly three-years younger sister made me feel quite inferior.

'I'm not going to school in those trousers tomorrow,' I said, determined to assert myself.

There was little silence round the table. Grandma seemed to enjoy being a bystander, her eyes twinkling with amusement.

'D'yeh want soom maw tea?' she twinkled at me, and proceeded to pour before I could reply.

'I'm going to carry on wearing mine,' said Michael. 'They look good and they feel warm.'

'Me too,' said Philip. He didn't see Grandma give him a disapproving look.

With that, I had no choice but to revoke my declaration. 'All right, I'll see what happens tomorrow.'

It was almost as if I wanted the titters on the bus and the teasing on the school playground to resume, so that I could prove to the world that my plus-fours were really odd and quite unsuitable attire for an English schoolboy.

But there was no more ridicule. The high volume of chatter hardly died down when we mounted the bus that following morning and life at school went on as if our clothing was nothing more remarkable than any of the daily sights at school. Furthermore, it seemed that our trousers were not only accepted, they were even admired as the weather grew colder. John Anderson, the boy that initiated the teasing, came up to me and said that he wished that his mother could afford to buy such a fine pair of trousers for the winter and when I told him that my mother had made them, he merely said, 'Cor!'

As we lived next to Greetwell Common, it was not unusual for us to see some of the wildlife that had come into the garden. Dusk was the best time to see the occasional fox or badger that we might see if we sat near the window away from the glare of the Tilley lamp. In the evening we noticed rabbits scampered along the fencing, often tunnelling under the barbed wire and into the camp. The sight of them tempted Harold to bring out his double-barrelled twelve-bore shotgun, but when he opened the window even the slightest sound would make them disappear in a flash.

Saturday mornings were the best times of the week. They were mornings free from compulsion, free from the thought of having to go to school and we could lie in our beds without being forced to stay there as long as on Sundays. On one such morning we were suddenly startled by a series of unearthly screams that sounded as if they came from some creature outside. When Michael opened the window he exclaimed, 'It's the Hudsons! They're sticking their pig!'

I already knew that our neighbours kept a pig and now I presumed that what Michael said meant that they were killing it. By sticking knives into it? The thought was both frightening and revolting. Michael explained that he had seen them doing it before. First they tied the pig's feet, then they hung it up head down from a large tripod made up of three posts, and then they slit its throat and let the blood run into a bowl. He said that Grandad said it was the best way to kill a pig, though I couldn't understand why it took so long for the pig to die.

The screaming continued while we dressed and continued while we washed ourselves and it didn't stop until after we had started breakfast, when Grandad came in looking sweaty and breathing heavily, his vested belly blowing in and out behind his trousers.

''Ee was right 'eavy,' he said. 'Frank an' me was sweatin' like pigs oursells to get 'im 'oong oop.'

I then realised that the screams were produced while the pig was being caught, tied and hung and not during its throes of death. That seemed to mollify my worries about the whole matter of sticking a pig. But I sometimes wondered when eating a slice of pork pie or ham whether the production of that meat entailed all the screams

180

and fuss, or could pigs be put to death more quietly?

One evening after tea we heard a loud bang that came from the kitchen. We rushed in to see Harold holding his still smoking shotgun with an expression of excitement on his face.

'I've just shot a cock pheasant. I saw it strutting along the far fence and took a pot at him.'

He went outside to return with a large cock pheasant that he held by its feet and lay on a newspaper on the kitchen table. Nadia fetched the Tilley lamp so that we could see the beautiful black-barred copper feathers of its tail, the stunningly red wattling on the face and the white ring dividing the shimmering blue-black upper neck and tufted head from the rest of the coppery body. Though its eyes were closed to show that its life had been shot away, it was the most magnificent thing I had ever seen.

'Colonel Nelthorpe won't be pleased eef he knew that you had shot one of his pheasants,' said Nadia with a grin.

'It was on my land, wasn't it?' said Harold.

'Can I have a tail feather?' I asked, without directing the question to anyone in particular.

'May I have', said Nadia automatically correcting me. 'I'm thinking of using them for a hat.'

'I'd like one too, to put in my beret,' said Vera.

'Wait until it has hung for a couple of days. It will then be easier to pluck and the meat will be tastier. Get me a piece of string,' said Harold.

When Grandma gave him the string he tied the legs and took it into the pantry to hang it up. Harold showed us the red cartridge, the brass end being still warm from the explosion, but we had seen and collected so many from the Common that even that fresh cartridge had little appeal.

The pheasant was allowed to hang until the weekend when it was plucked, put into the range oven, carved into small portions that were given the status of roast beef and eaten with all the trimmings, including cranberry jelly. Somehow I found that eating meat with jam, which was what cranberry jelly was to me, was difficult to accept, whatever the flavour of the meat. However, it was exciting to eat the quarry that was taken in our own garden and having been warned about the lead shot we ate our small pieces of meat slowly to find the shot and line them up on the edges of our plates. Michael won the most-shot competition.

One Saturday morning Michael and I were about to cross the road to go to the Common when we saw something lying on the road some distance away. Our curiosity drove us to approach the mystery, which as we drew closer began to look like a dead animal. It was greyish, it looked as if might be a cat, it could be Tisst! It was Tisst!

We were confronted by the unbelievable sight of the body of our cat distorted by the effects of being run over. His head was intact but the rest of the body a tangled mass of grey fur, entrails and blood. I couldn't believe that an animal so alive and part of our lives could become the horror that we saw and the shock of it made me bawl loudly, unaware at the time that Michael was also crying. We then recovered our senses and went back to the house and Michael reported the accident to Grandma who took it almost as if it were something to be expected. She took hold of a shovel and went off to deal with the remains, while I realised that it was the first time that I cried on the sight of a dead body, despite the horror of the dead in camps.

15. Winter

Frosty mornings became more frequent as November wore on. Thanks to the plus-fours our legs were almost as warm as our bodies which were adequately covered by a singlet, shirt and tie, jumper and overcoat, but the tips of our ears and our cheeks stung as we waited for the bus in the cold. I was fascinated by the clouds of steam that we breathed out and wondered if it would get cold enough for the air to make crackling noises when we breathed out, like Nadia said happened to her in the freezing winters that she experienced as a child in Manchuria.

It didn't only become colder outdoors. Inside the house the fire in the range seemed even more essential as there was not a source of warmth anywhere else except from our own bodies. Nadia told us that when she was a child in Harbin the winters were so cold that they had central heating in even the simplest of homes. She couldn't understand why the vast majority of homes in England lacked central heating, for though it was not as cold as in Manchuria, the dampness of the Lincolnshire air in winter made it feel as cold as the dry air of Manchuria at thirty degrees below. The bedrooms were ice- cold. We shivered as we put on our pyjamas and looked forward to the warmth provided by the earthernware hot water bottles that Grandma put into our heavily blanketed beds. We shivered as we got up in the morning to inspect the beautifully formed leaf-shaped patterns of frozen condensation on the inside of the window and we ran our fingernails through the shapes to make lines that rasped their way through the ice.

Though John Anderson did not come to school in plus-fours he did keep his head warm and almost hidden in a loose-fitting woollen balaclava, his breath coming out like smoke from a small smoulder-ing woollen sack. We mentioned John's balaclava to Nadia that teatime and thought it would be nice if she could knit us one each. Instead, Grandma said that she had already knitted one for Philip, one that he wore in bed during the winter and had nearly completed one for Michael, whereupon Nadia said that she would knit one for me. Vera had to make do with her longer hair topped by her red beret, into which she had inserted one of the shorter pheasant's feathers. The insertion of that feather into her beret was an expression of her individuality that no one dared to question when she wore it at school, instead it became the source of some admiration among her classmates.

Balaclavas and, for our part, plus-fours, were not the only garments that signified the onset of winter. Some of the older boys across the road at school had taken to wearing leather helmets with flaps covering the ears, which made them look like Battle of Britain pilots, while others braved the winter chill of Lincolnshire either bare-headed or wearing caps with small peaks. While we continued to wear stout shoes, some of the boys that were from families out in the country had black hobnailed boots that made noises like a full-speed goods train as they ran and then slid over the concrete entrance into the school.

One morning in early December, when it felt colder than just an ordinary frosty morning, we arrived at school to see a crowd of the older children across the road shouting and cheering. When we came closer, we could see some boys hurtling down an icy slide about ten yards long down towards the wall on the slightly sloping school-yard. One of the older boys who lived in the village must have poured a line of water on the yard the night before. The girls did not take part and were content just to see the spectacle of competition between the boys as to who could slide the furthest and to watch the tumbles that inevitably occurred. We from the infant side watched at a distance from our side of the road and I longed to be amongst them.

The school preparations for Christmas consisted of rehearsals for the nativity play and decorating the crypt, and my camel took pride of place among the animals that decorated the central figures of Joseph and Mary. We sung Christmas carols and hymns and painted Christmas pictures that were pinned up on a dark brown wooden rail that ran round the wall. The whole build-up to Christmas was a festivity in itself and made Christmas seem to last much longer than what we had ever experienced before. It all culminated just before we broke up for the holidays when the school Christmas concert was held in the ramshackle wooden building that purported to be the village hall and lay some distance beyond the school canteen. Members of my class performed the nativity play. Michael was one of the Three Wise Men but Miss Everton had decided to leave me out as she said that I was perhaps a bit too tall to fit in. I was much relieved by her decision.

The concert began with carols to be followed by a short play performed by the first class about a maiden with a broken heart. Philip was the doctor who could repair the heart, but when his cue came he entered the stage without his Gladstone bag. He stopped mid-stage, turned quite red, rushed back to the curtain to return carrying his doctor's bag containing a new bright red heart and Vera who played the girl with the broken heart was saved. The audience laughed and cheered. This was followed by performances by the older children, mainly girls, including one that sang 'You Are My Sunshine' and another that played 'The Blue Danube' at half pace on the echoey piano.

The school concert ended with a few more carols and a solo performed by a boy of my age in Miss Hazelwood's class. His red face burst with song that seemed to be in tune but the higher notes had a stringent quality that did not sound quite right. Michael told me that his name was William Harley, the head cook's son and that he was one of the best boy singers in the church choir. I noticed that his face was almost as red as his mother's was.

The end of the concert marked the end of the autumn term. The last day of the autumn term also overshadowed Harold's thirtieth birthday, which happened to be on the same day and which went by almost unnoticed as far as the children were concerned. For me the end of my first term at school was the end of the beginning of school, since Miss Everton said that I was ready to join the children of my age group in Miss Hazelwood's class. I looked forward to being with people of my age, of being less of an oddity. Nevertheless, I had the uneasy feeling in the back of my mind that my limited English would make it hard to keep up with my peers. Leaving the security of Miss Everton's class and her encouragement was also unsettling. However, the prospect of spending my first Christmas at home with my new

185

family was a quick antidote to any misgivings about school in the spring term.

After all the excitement of the end of term, the run-up to Christmas was an anti-climax. Nothing seemed to happen at home and it wasn't as if there was much point in going outside to play, as the first days of the Christmas holidays were raw, grey and uninviting.

Grandma said that it was going to snow. She found a pile of old comic strip magazines like Hotspur and Adventure that belonged to Uncle Cedric, Harold's younger brother. Cedric would not be coming home for Christmas as he was still doing his national service out in India, but he might be demobbed in time for the New Year. Though it was clear that the comics were really meant for older boys and contained adventure stories that were too advanced to read, the illustrations were quite fascinating, especially when we had little else to do as we all had finished looking at our pile of comic magazines consisting mainly of 'Dandy' and a new comic called Beano' To us characters like Desperate Dan, Corky the Cat, Lord Snooty and his friends Biffo the Bear and Pansy Potter the Strongman's Daughter were part of us and often featured in the games that we resorted to during our enforced stays in bed on Sunday mornings. Though Michael, not Vera, was often chosen to play Pansy Potter as we considered him to be the strongest of us all, which also made him suitable as Desperate Dan on other occasions.

On the morning of Christmas Eve we faced another grey day. We pressed our noses against the living room windowpane after breakfast wondering what the day had to offer apart from books and comics and went back to looking at comics and books until after dinnertime when Philip suddenly said,

'Look! It's snowing!'

After a few moments of staring we could make out an occasional white flake looking like a small flat piece of cotton wool coming out of the greyness above, but after a few seconds on the ground the flake would shrink and disappear. But the number of flakes coming out of the sky began to gradually increase so that it wasn't long before they were spread on the ground and I was witnessing for the first time in my life the process of snow 'settling'.

'It's snowing, it's snowing!' cried Vera.

'Alley, alley aster, snow, snow faster,' chipped in Harold. 'That's what we used to say when I was a boy.'

'Alley, alley aster, snow, snow faster,' we all chimed in unison.

The rest of the day was spent watching the snow gradually cover the garden with a white blanket that made us want to go out and play in it, but Nadia would not let us go out as she said that we didn't have the right footwear.

'You can go to the back door and feel it, but don't go out into the garden,' she said.

The snow was about an inch deep by the back door. When I touched it lightly at first there was little to indicate that it was cold, instead it felt slightly wet and it didn't feel much colder when I pressed my hand into it, leaving a dark half melted handprint. Michael picked up a handful, pressed it into a snowball and threw it against one of the pergola pillars, making a dull thud as it hit the brickwork and leaving a lumpy white mark. Making snowballs was fun and whet our appetites to go out and enjoy it to the full. After begging Nadia that since snow was the best thing in the world and that if we were careful not to wet our shoes and stick to the path she surely would allow us to go out to play in it. She couldn't refuse, but the result was that throwing numerous snowballs at various targets and learning that we could roll large snowballs and make snowmen, we forgot our restrictions and when Nadia called us back at dusk we returned soaking wet from snow and sweat.

The limited supply of hot water from the range was emptied into the bathtub and Vera, being a girl and therefore considered cleaner, used it first. Then we, the boys, who were naturally dirtier, used the same bath water afterwards with additional supplements of water from the kettle. It was a weekly routine to which we became accustomed. But that bath day was special. It wasn't just that we had played in the snow, for Vera and I for the first time in our lives, it was also a special bath before Christmas Day the day of our first Christmas as a united family in England.

There was the excitement of anticipation when shouting our Christmas wishes up the range chimney and receiving our stockings to hang up at the ends of our beds. We speculated as to whether we

would see Father Christmas when he visited us, which made it hard
for us to get to sleep, despite all the exertions of the day.

At about four in the morning came the earnest whisper from
Michael; 'Are you awake?'

'Yes, I hissed.'

'I've seen Father Christmas!' said Michael.

We didn't really believe him but replied by rummaging for our
stockings at the end of our beds.

The result was the discovery of nuts and fruit and exciting things
in bags that rustled with an ever-increasing loudness caused by our
efforts to discover their contents in the dark. We forgot to confine
our voices to whispers, which soon changed to a babble of childish
excitement, which made a tired Nadia come up the loft stairs holding
a lighted paraffin lamp to allow us to see what Father Christmas had
left in our stockings.

Excited exchanges of 'Look what I got!' as we showed each other
our small toys and sweets died down when Nadia said,

'Maybe Father Christmas hasn't had enough space to put all the
presents in the stockings. You ought to look under the beds.'

We looked, we saw; we shouted in amazement to see large packages
lying under our beds. I had a large box-like parcel that soon lost its
brown paper wrapping to reveal a wooden case with aluminium top
and base beautifully made to hold a small saw, a hand drill, hammer,
screwdriver and a pair of small pliers. A beginner's tool kit! Once
again we showed each other our surprise gifts with an excitement
that reached such a pitch that any hope of sleep that Nadia might
have had was crushed.

Michael had also received an identical tool kit and Vera and Philip
discovered that each had received a scooter made out of wood with
solid rubber and metal wheels. Vera's was painted a bright red and
Philip's a dark blue. Where did Father Christmas get these presents?
We never saw anything like them in Scunthorpe and how did he get
them down the chimney?

When we finally came downstairs to be ushered into the front
room another miracle presented itself in the form of a glittering
Christmas tree. How did that get there and who decorated it? All
these Christmas questions remained unanswered until some time

afterwards.

After Boxing Day the snowing resumed and became almost incessant so that the white Christmas turned into an even whiter New Year. Nadia took the bus into Scunthorpe and bought us shiny black new wellingtons that had the aromatic smell of new processed rubber. This allowed us to play in the cold soft whiteness that lay a foot deep around the house, though as the snowing continued, even our new wellingtons were not high enough and we were forced to dig our way through the new medium covering the landscape. Having seen a picture of an igloo, we made snow dens out of large rolled balls but as we could not make a roof we had to be content with a half-open construction.

The occasional lorry that passed the house kept the road useable, but only for heavy vehicles. Harold could not travel to his building jobs with his motorcycle and sidecar without the likelihood of slithering off the road. Instead he stayed at home and spent a couple of days working in the garage. The result was another wonder of his craftsmanship in the form of a sledge made in the classic style with rounded metal runners that curved upwards to form two small loops that formed fasteners for a drawing rope. Two of us could squeeze onto it but then it was too heavy to pull. Instead two of us took it in turns to pull, one to push and one to ride on the compacted snow of the road. We then took the sledge a couple of hundred yards up the road where there was a small hill to hurtle down and where crashing into the verge was painless fun. When we were confronted by the fairly rare prospect of an approaching lorry, we learnt to control the sledge by leaning towards the verge.

It was just when we were coming to grips with tobogganing that Uncle Cedric arrived from India. He was demobbed in time to celebrate the New Year with us. At the age of nearly twenty-one, he was over nine years younger than Harold was. He was six foot tall and lanky, his brown eyes twinkling with humour and he laughed with his head thrown back as if he had heard the funniest thing in the world. Cedric took us out on the sledge and gave us a real sensation of speed when he used his long agile body to push us down the little hill.

He had a natural ability to tell stories, making them alive by making the right sounds and gestures at the appropriate moments. He told us a little about India and the gurus and other holy men that he saw and he imitated the sounds that they made by stretching his long neck and making a long 'ahhh' sound at the same time as drumming his hand lightly on his Adam's apple. We all laughed, including Cedric, until tears ran down our cheeks.

The unbelievable Christmas holidays, the presents, the snow and the arrival of Uncle Cedric all dominated an event that might otherwise have given me more to think about: namely the start of the spring term. Consequently it wasn't until the actual morning of the first day of term as we waited in the snow for the bus to arrive that I began to really think about my new status in school and what it would be like to be among people of my own age.

As I was well aware that classes would be more difficult, I doubted whether Miss Hazelwood would match Miss Everton in kindness and understanding. Her gaunt features, her wiry grey hair, her aquiline nose supporting her thin-framed glasses all contributed to an image that was more teacher than human. Though she must have been under forty she looked as though she would look the same until after she retired. Her classroom in the main school building opposite the infant school was more airy with a higher ceiling and the windows were designed to give light but were placed high enough not to allow anyone to be distracted by any happenings outside. A glowing fire with a guard kept out the winter chill and beside it there was a door that connected the room with the top class, that of Miss Bowles. A blackboard supported by an easel faced us from the corner between the two doors and Miss Hazelwood's high desk loomed over us from the middle of the space between the assembly of desks and the fireplace. I was given a single desk at the front and closest to the door. In the far corner, next to the window stood a brown piano.

Once again I found that the main business of school was to achieve a certain standard in the three R's. In fact the actual content of the subjects proved to be no great step forward from Miss Everton's class. The biggest change was that I no longer used a slate. Arithmetic was merely a matter of copying countless additions and subtractions of columns of two-figured numbers and entering the answers in pencil in an exercise book with squared pages.

The first playtime in the snow, the first playtime in the junior section, was entirely dominated by the oldest boys who organised two waist-high walled fortresses, built of snow on opposite corners of the front playground. Two generals were chosen and they in turn chose boys to join their 'armies'. I felt really proud when I was actually chosen, along with other boys in my class to join the army led by a boy who always looked well groomed and decently dressed compared to most.

'Ivan, you can join us,' he said. He knew my name! I ran to join him in his fortress where my task, along with others of my age, was to gather as much snow as possible and make snowballs ready for the battle that ensued. There were neither winners nor losers, just a salvo of snowballs flying in both directions until the bell rang to call us into class.

We were given slightly more advanced reading books whose content was unremarkable, if not boring. In fact, Miss Hazelwood herself us read the most interesting stories. She had the most amazing ability to use her nasal voice and express it in such a way that even the most inattentive children sat spellbound when it was story time. She read quite frequently from a wide range of books, including Kipling's 'Just So' stories. Through Kipling and Miss Hazelwood's voice, we found out how the elephant got its trunk and leopard its spots but apart from Kipling, the most popular were Epaminondus stories about a rather naughty but likeable West Indian boy and his pranks. At the right moment, at the crux of the story, she would exaggerate the pronunciation of his name to Eeepaminondus, whereupon we would wait for the way he committed his next misdemeanour.

The first arithmetic book was the Yellow Book, which I found so easy that I was anxious to work through it as quickly as possible so that I could begin the Red Book. The Red Book was really the same as the first except that the sums were three-figured.

The snow was no longer a novelty and as the weeks went by the ground continued to be thickly mantled, any melting snow being replaced by new layers. We became quite expert at tobogganing with Nadia sometimes joining in the running and riding. In about the middle of February Nadia told us that she was expecting a baby some time in August, but she at that time didn't appear to be at all pregnant. She looked and behaved as before and even continued to go with us for frolics in the snow, sometimes making us worried about whether we would have a baby brother or sister at all if she slipped and fell awkwardly. But all was well and life continued as normal, including the snow. I found out that my first winter in England turned out to be one of the snowiest in living memory, the ground being covered by snow until the beginning of March. One morning a boy found a starving green woodpecker hanging on the trunk of the horse chestnut tree. A short time after he brought it in to be shown to Miss Bowles, it died instead of recovering in the warmth of her classroom. We did, however get the opportunity to see the beauty of its green plumage close at hand and its fresh greenness reminded me of the fruit pigeon that Jan shot in Java. It was the greenest thing I saw that winter.

16. Upheavals

The interminable white blanket of snow had suppressed the beginning of spring but when it finally relented, the vigour of growth burst like water being released from a dam.

As the snow melted dark grass-like spears penetrated the remaining thinning white crusts of winter and they soon began to hang with a burden of white bells. The flowers that Michael told me were snowdrops were soon followed by the blazing splashes of colour that gave me new names like crocuses and daffodils and these heralded the onset of Easter.

Cedric, who slept on a camp bed in the front room during the first two weeks of the new year, sought lodgings in Scunthorpe where he went to night school to study building technology. He had also joined Harold in his building firm. At weekends he came over to help Grandad put the Austin seven on the road by overhauling the engine and by refitting the wheels. This meant that Grandad was no longer dependent on the work buses and that Cedric could borrow the car to court his girlfriend in Scunthorpe.

Going to school became a routine. Moreover, staying in bed on Sunday mornings in order to allow Harold to recover from the stress and frustration of running his own building firm became a routine that we found increasingly harder to endure. It was an ordeal for us not only because we wanted to be out and about, but also our adult size potty was full to the brim. It became too full for further use and the only solution was to carefully tip the contents out of the window onto the wall-trained cherry tree that grew below. One Sunday morning in the late spring I decided that it was much easier to kneel on the window sill to pee directly out of the window instead of trying to dispose of the smelling contents of our overflowing urine container. Michael and Philip followed my example, which left the potty to become Vera's domain and thereby much more manageable.

As we grew more used to each other, our Sunday morning rampages on the bed became noisier, forcing Nadia to appear in the

193

loft opening with,

'Be quiet! Daddy's trying to sleep. If you can't be quiet he'll come up with his belt!'

We quietened down long enough for the threat not to be put into practice and we learnt more or less how far we could go on Sundays. The window, however, continued to function as a relief for our bursting Sunday morning bladders but we did not tell Nadia about it and no-one had noticed the bloom of green algae around the base of the cherry tree that now had the benefit of extra nutrients..

The arrival of warmer weather had widened the range of possibilities that the school playground had to offer, compared with the restricted forms of recreation brought about by the snow. Someone realised that the popular song of the time included the sound of my surname: 'Cruising down the river on a Sunday afternoon' It wasn't long before two or three boys in my class insisted on chanting those lines while looking at me with scorn expressed on their faces. But as I liked the tune I sang along with them, which took the wind out of their sails.

The girls tended to keep to themselves with their skipping rope games, hopscotch and activities that involved various kinds of chanting and singing. They also tended to confine themselves to the area of playground closest to the large horse chestnut tree at the front. The older girls monopolised the best open places while the younger ones were either spectators or kept to less desirable areas, corners and the smaller area divided at the back of the school by a creosoted fence.

Beyond this creosoted fence there was a larger level area that was totally dominated by the boys playing football. While I was standing by the fence wondering just what football was all about I was surprised to hear my name being shouted by one of the oldest boys, the same one that asked me to join the snowball battle. I found out that his name was Thomas Smith though he was commonly known as Tommy.

'Ivan! Do you want to play football? You can be left-back if you want,' said Tommy with a kind expression on his face.

'No, I think I'd like to join you,' I replied not wanting to be left out. But I didn't have much notion about the point of the game, except that half the boys cheered when the boy standing closest to a low brick building failed to stop the ball rolling between two heaps of jackets.

'Good,' said Tommy smiling and pointing to a spot to the right of the two heaps of jackets. 'It's one nil to them and we're short of a man.'

I thought I began to realise what the expressions meant. The opposing team had a 'nil,' which I guessed must be 'nail ' when not pronounced in the Lincolnshire dialect. I was to stand more or less where Tommy pointed and help to prevent them scoring another 'nail.' Once again, I felt proud to be called to join the older boys, this time as 'a man'.

I was so enthralled in my new status that I failed to react quickly enough to tackle an opposing player who shot the ball past the boy between the two heaps of jackets.

'Goal!' Came the shout from several boys on the opposing team.

'Oh! They now have two nails,' I gasped, trying to pronounce the words in the best, only slightly Lincolnshire way. Tommy stared at me as if I was an idiot.

I was completely bewildered. Before I could recover from the shame of having let my side down, Miss Bowles rang the bell for the end of playtime and for us to go back to class.

On the way back home while waiting for the green bus, I told Michael about my first experience of football. Was it called a 'nail' when the ball was kicked between the two heaps of jackets? He explained a little more what football was all about and told me what nil really meant and that one scored goals in football and that the person defending the space between the two heaps of jackets, known as the goal, was known as a goalie.

Nadia reacted with a snort when I told her that I had tried to play football at playtime.

'Football! That's what Grandad is interested in! That's a game played by the working class!' she hissed.

Her whole tone implied that she wanted neither me nor Michael nor Philip to develop an interest in football, though she did not actually say so. From that day on it not only became clear that football was a topic not to be mentioned at home, but my unsuccessful initiation in the game guaranteed that I had no reason to mention it for I was not invited to join the football games at playtime again.

It was not just that Grandad took over the living room on Saturday afternoons to listen to sport, thereby football, on the radio. Nadia's aversion to football turned out to be a symptom of an accumulation of tensions that had built up since we came to England.

Much to Grandma's disapproval, she took over the management of the household and it went without saying that she did things in her foreign way. Now it was Nadia who did most of the shopping and it was she who filled the pantry with food. She would notice that a biscuit or two might be missing and as Philip was known to visit the pantry sometimes, she turned to him:

'Philip, did you take a biscuit from the pantry?'

'No, I didn't, Mammy,' he said sweetly.

'Philip, why do you lie to me? I know you took a biscuit from the pantry.'

'I didn't,' he said quietly.

To Grandma and us he seemed to be telling the truth and we felt he was being victimised. I wanted to say something in his defence but bit my lip. Instead it was Grandma who spoke:

'If the lad says 'ee didn't do it, then 'ee didn't do it. Leave 'im alawn.'

'It's bad enough when he steals, but I can't stand it when he lies to me,' said Nadia.

Grandma was red with anger.

Philip had told Vera once that he actually did take a biscuit from the pantry and lied about it but at other times he was wrongly accused of stealing and was punished unjustly.

Another contribution to the strained atmosphere in the house was Nadia's demand that we children should all speak good clear English. She corrected our dropped H's, insisting that we pronounced vowels in the southern instead of the northern way and she was adamant that we pronounced our gerund i-n-g's correctly. She had a correct English language bee in her bonnet while she herself had a strong Russian accent, which added grist to the mill of tensions that grew between her and her new parents-in-law, especially

Grandma.

We children were aware of these tensions but as we enjoyed each other's company, we played together so much that adult problems were left to the adults.

However one Sunday morning when Nadia shouted 'boys' at the top of her voice to call us in for dinner things came to a head. The word 'boys' was the word she used to call us all, including Vera. We had been playing in the sand on the Common across the road and were not the cleanest looking children.

'You're all filthy! What have you been doing?'

'We've bin playin' in the sand,' said Michael.

'PlayinGG', said Nadia - 'Say it!'

Before Michael could reply, Grandma screeched in, 'You leave the lad alawn!'

'It's none of your business, mother!' said Nadia turning white with anger.

Grandma picked the carving knife that was lying on the living room table and pointed it at Nadia.

'Oh yes it is! If you torment those boys again I'll kill yeh!'

'Put that knife down, mother!' boomed a man's voice.

Just at that moment Harold came into the room and wrenched the knife out of Grandma's grasp.

'Nadia's in charge of all the children now.'

He didn't say anymore. The two women glowered at each other in the charged atmosphere. Finally Nadia broke the silence.

'Go and wash your hands, boys,' she said.

She then turned to Harold, 'Either they find somewhere else to live or I go. It's up to you.'

He still said nothing.

As luck would have it, there was a house for sale at Greetwell, right next to the bus stop by the petrol station. At around a thousand pounds it seemed reasonably priced and with Harold's help it wasn't long before they arranged a mortgage and Grandma and Grandad were to have a little bungalow of their own.

It was early summer when they moved. Harold seemed as relieved as Nadia and though our mother's nagging didn't cease, the atmosphere in the house improved markedly.

On the Monday evening after the weekend taken up by the move, the green bus had deposited us by the red gates as usual. However, Nadia was not her usual cheerful self, anxious to hear our school news. She was not waiting for us by the door smiling. Instead she greeted us with a scowl.

'How long have you been peeing out of the loft bedroom window?'

'We only did it when the potty was full on Sunday mornings,' I said after wondering how long we had been doing it.

'Well, you'd better stop doing it now because Mrs Hudson has been round to complain. She can see you doing it from her window and she thinks it's disgusting and so do I. Not only that, she said that you have been doing it for some time.'

'Can we have two potties, then?' I asked.

'That won't be necessary because Vera is going to sleep in her own bedroom, which means that the three of you should be able to manage with the one that you have.'

The Hudsons were an elderly couple who seemed to keep to themselves and normally the only real signs of life that came from them were caused by the death of their pig. Like us, they lived in a similar bungalow with a large garden, large because the house had two plots of land, which was why we were never conscious of being observed when emptying our Sunday morning bladders. Their house was more than fifty yards away.

Nadia was becoming ample with her pregnancy and allowed us to put our hands on her swelling belly to feel the kicks produced by our future brother or sister. Vera said that she hoped that she would have a sister, as she was tired of being surrounded by boys. Nadia reminded her that she at least she now had her own bedroom.

Grandma and Grandad's move not only provided more space in the house, it also gave Nadia more freedom to run the household, but the house itself limited her scope. One problem was the range in the living room. Though it provided hot water that was piped to the bathroom, the supply was far too inadequate to allow us to have a bath without boiling several kettles on the Primus stove and the kettle on the range fire itself was a meagre supplement. Nadia felt very frustrated

The solution presented itself in the form of a gang of men that started digging a large hole next to the fence that divided us from the prisoner of war camp. They were digging a hole to set up a pole that would support a relay box and electricity cable. We were soon to have electricity! Harold soon arranged for an electrician whom he knew through his building business to wire up the house and we were connected to the mains within two weeks of the arrival of the cable. The days of darkness and smell of paraffin were gone and we had light bulbs hanging from the ceilings by small, brown, twisted cables attached to brown Bakelite fittings.

The new source of power was like breath of fresh air blowing away most of what was old and stuffy and left behind by Harold's parents. The old washing copper was sent to the scrapyard and replaced by a new Thorn washing machine and the paraffin lamps were put away to be stored. Grandad took his old accumulator powered radio, which Harold replaced with an impressive new glossy mahogany coloured apparatus with a gold-coloured metal mesh that covered the speaker. The accumulator deliveryman who came with recharged accumulators every Tuesday belonged to the past.

It wasn't just the arrival of electricity that initiated this modernisation. Nadia was very much a driving force, driven by her will to have a proper home and driving Harold to provide it for her and the new family. Nadia was not slow in persuading Harold to replace the range in the living room with a nearly new Rayburn cooker that he and Cedric installed in the kitchen.

We came home from school one day in June to find a huge hole in the living room where the range once was. A tall young man with a peaked cap like those worn by the Germans in the camp next door was standing on a large heap of rubble and busy chipping away loose plaster from around the gaping, dusty emptiness once occupied by our source of warmth and hot water.

'This is Otto!' Chirped Nadia as we stared at the results of his work.

Otto looked at us and nodded with a broad smile that spread through his dusty face. I suddenly found it difficult to look at him directly because one of his eyes was bright blue while the other was brown. I first wondered if that was a common occurrence in Germany but soon dispensed with that thought and dwelled instead on whether he missed his home and his family. Despite the fact that the war had been over for more than two years there were still many Germans left in the camp. Would they gradually settle in England?

Otto joined us for a cup of tea before returning to camp and told us that he would return to his home land as soon as he had the appropriate papers from the occupying authorities responsible for the sector where his family was. He had an accent that sounded quite different from that of my mother. The bureaucracy that the Allies had organised was the reason why so many German prisoners of war had to wait a long time to return and many, including Otto did not know whether they had a home to return to.

For our part, the temporary chaos caused by the absence of the range meant that we had to wash in the kitchen with water boiled on the Primus stove. This became our routine for a about a week until Harold did the plumbing connecting the Rayburn to a new cistern in an airing cupboard that he had built next to where the range was. The absence of the range left a blank wall that had the effect of making the living room larger. Harold had also dug up the floors of the living room, the front room and the two downstairs bedrooms to pipe and connect radiators to the Rayburn. He removed the old linoleum from the living room floor and replaced it with new woodchip tiles and he bought her a new floor polisher that had three revolving disks for the polishing pads.

All this came in time to make life more comfortable for Nadia before the birth of the baby. Harold had seen to it that she had all the gadgets of a modern home while we enjoyed the luxury of copious and easy lighting. As the new building business was not established enough to provide a steady income, Harold had to cover these costs by arranging a mortgage.

She had also made other changes to the running of the household.

The fact that not many people owned a car and most housewives living in the country would only travel to town either on market days or Saturdays was the basis for a thriving trade of various kinds of delivery services. The baker's van came on Mondays and Thursdays and there were various traders that came on other weekdays to sell necessary household items and groceries. The grocer that usually stopped to deliver Grandma's items had a fine brown van in which his goods were neatly arranged but he turned out not to have many of the items that Nadia wanted. However, not long after Harold's parents had moved she turned him away as she found an old grocer in Brigg who also made deliveries of the very items she wanted, even though his van was rather ramshackle and coughed with smoke as it drove away. Despite visiting tradesmen, Nadia found that visits to the market on Thursdays were well worth the time and bus-money and she often came home with cheap greens and groceries. One Thursday we came home from school to be led into the kitchen to peer into a box where there were four small, peeping, yellowish-grey fluffy things with webbed feet.

'Goslings,' she almost whispered. 'We're going to fatten them up for Christmas.'

Harold made a coop for them at the weekend, but they seemed to keep to the garden near the house without us having to pen them in. They grew very fast and soon replaced their fluff with feathers and their peeping with gaggling noises.

As we didn't have any chickens after Grandma had taken hers to her new home, Nadia would send us to her to relieve her of any surplus produce of eggs. Despite all the aggression between them, Grandma refused to take any payment for them.

On one of her weekly trips to Brigg Nadia discovered the green-grocer she preferred and became ecstatic when she found out that he even stocked garlic. Cloves of garlic not only had an impact on the taste of our Sunday joint, especially lamb, it also affected my rela-tionship with Miss Hazelwood.

'You smell of foreign,' she honked at me as I came into the classroom one Monday morning. 'I won't be surrounded by the smell of foreign foods in my classroom! As I can't stand the smell you had better change desks with Mary at the back of the room.'

She never mentioned the word 'garlic' because she presumably had never heard of it.

Once again I was made to feel like a foreign oddity and when I told Nadia about it that teatime she laughed, 'What nonsense! Garlic is good for you and besides, as I know you like the taste of your mother's cooking, Miss Hazelwood will just have to put up with it.'

It seemed that I was the only one treated in that way, for though the other teachers might have detected the smell of garlic on the breaths of Michael, Philip and Vera, they did not express any feelings they might have had against it.

I felt at first as if I were marked as an oddity, a foreigner, but it wasn't long before I realised that apart from obnoxious smelling foreigners, either the most reliable pupils sat at the back or those that were regarded as totally unteachable but not unruly. One of those 'unteachables' was a girl called Glenda who belonged to a large family that lived in a house known as the Black House that stood at a T-junction on the way to Brigg. Several of the brothers and sisters were at the school and they all seemed to have simple minds. Glenda sat at the back of the class with one desk between us, doing nothing except just sitting quietly at her desk with a broad grin spread across her red country face. She could neither read nor write and when she tried to put pencil to paper the result was just a mess of squiggles. The best thing she could do was to sit and smile.

Miss Hazelwood was content to leave it at that, for she had no patience to try to teach her anything. Being placed at the back of the room made it more difficult for me to see the blackboard clearly. But that did not matter much, as she hardly used it. When she actually taught she did it individually, from desk to desk, telling Glenda that she was being a good girl when she passed by.

The only times she took on the class as a whole was during singing when the tune she played on the piano sounded so much more melodious than her coarse, nasal voice. But it was when she was reading us a story that her voice became the best of her talents. It was just during such a story time when we listening to the deeds of Little Black Sambo that a 'psst' sound came from the boy sitting in the desk next to me. He had a broad grin on his face and was pointing at Glenda, his pointing finger below the level of the desk. Glenda sat facing us with an even broader grin on her face, her arms placed in such a way as to lead the eye downwards. She was sitting with her legs apart holding her knickers to one side to reveal her rosy fleshiness, the basis of both her femininity and our masculine curiosity. We gawped. Suddenly, Miss Hazelwood's voice took on a different tone. Sharp and to the point:

'Turn round Glenda. There's a good girl!'

Embarrassed, I also turned to face the right way while Glenda continued to smile.

When on the way home I told Michael about Glenda's display he said that she had a little sister in the first class that wore no knickers at all.

A few months later Glenda and her brothers and sisters disappeared, perhaps to be taken care of by the social services.

Playtime was not only time to drink small bottles of milk; it was time for rushes to the post office not to buy letters or stamps but sweets. The black windowed door opened inwards with a jingle into an Aladdin's cave with a floor that was lower than the pavement outside. As sweets were on ration a whole plethora of alternatives were available as refreshments to be consumed at playtimes. There were greasy packets of broken crisps at a ha'penny each, black sticks of liquorice as long as a finger and half as thick at four for a penny. They made people's teeth and mouths black. There were beige-coloured dried chewing roots that were bright yellow inside and tasted a bit like liquorice. I followed the prospective purchasers to look at the counter by the post office grill and saw what they bought, was given a sample to taste by a boy in my class and wished that I had a ha'penny to spend.

On the bus home we talked about the post office tuck shop and decided to ask Nadia for pocket money to spend at playtimes, though we knew that children in Vera and Philip's class were not allowed out except to lunch.

When we described the post office and its attraction to nearly all the children in the school, Nadia understood that we must also have a little money to spend. She therefore decided to give Michael and me three-pence and Philip and Vera two-pence a week pocket money, which we were allowed to spend as we wished.

This resulted in almost daily purchases of sticks of liquorice and chewing root, black and yellow with the sweet taste of liquorice. No sugar because it was rationed. There was also a white powder that fizzed and bubbled in the mouth to give off a kind of fruity flavour and it came in small sealed paper packets whose outlet was a paper straw. The old lady at Scawby post office raked in the pounds, shillings and pence by selling various kinds of sugarless sweets. They were sugarless until some loophole in the regulations allowed the selling of a yellow powder that contained sugar, but as the sugar made it heavier it was sold in small cone-shaped packets to be poured out into the palm of the hand and licked. This product was known as Kale-eye and was the beginning of the post-war surge of sugar into the mouths of children and a contribution to the cause of mass extractions that Mr Picton had to carry out in his dental surgery in Brigg.

Our pocket money began to help to fill the pockets of our local dentist, Mr Picton, a smiling white- haired gentleman who smiled at us while he gave us laughing gas, anoxia and nightmares because we developed abscesses in our Kale-eyed teeth.

Nadia, realising that our pocket money was being spent in a way destructive to our dental health, forbade the purchase of sugary things and we went back to those goodies that were black or yellow and without sugar.

The spring term gave way to summer, the summer of 1947. Sounds of summer came not only from birdsong, it also came as songs through the wall of my classroom. The children in Miss Bowles' class sang so beautifully that I just listened instead of concentrating on my exercises. 'In June they change their tune. In July away they fly'. They were singing about the cuckoo that we could hear calling across the Common at home. They were big children. They were in their last year at Scawby School. They seemed to be nearly grown-up! One of the boys even had long grey trousers instead of shorts, even when it was warm! Just like a man. At school they also did grown-up things like gardening in the school plot next to the playground and during games the boys played grown-up games like cricket in the park while the girls played something called rounders. It was hard to believe that in the autumn term I would be old enough to start in the top class.

Of those that left school a record number of seven had passed an examination known as 'The Scholarship', which meant that they were given the privilege of going to better schools known as Brigg Grammar School for Boys and Brigg Girls' High School.

I already knew that that the grammar school was what Nadia had in mind for me.

One Saturday morning, the postman came with a heavy parcel,

larger than a shoebox. The stamps indicated that it had come from China. Nadia opened the parcel without a word, the only noises coming from the scissors as she cut the string and brown paper.

Then she exclaimed in Russian, her eyes full of tears:

'My parents have sent us a tin of ham! How did they know where we live? They must have thought we were starving after the war! Oh! My God! I must write to tell them that we are well! '

She then collected herself and explained who sent the parcel and that she felt happy to know that her parents were still alive, and was amazed that they managed to locate her.

She wrote back to them and we ate the ham, but we never heard from them again. Nadia guessed that the Communist Chinese had sent all the Russians back to their country and that they must have ended up in a forced labour camp somewhere in Siberia.

17. Squatters

It was a long and sunny summer. Longer for Nadia who was weighed down by the ever increasing burden of her pregnancy.

Alexander Harold was born on the 14th of August at the infirmary in Brigg, two days before my ninth birthday and just over a year since we moved to England. To us boys he was just a baby that made baby noises and created heaps of smelly nappies and lines of nappy washing. To Vera he was a future boy and thereby a future pest. His chosen name, Alexander, being too long to be practical was soon shortened to 'Lex' and Lex he became.

His parents, already burdened by four children, work and worries about the family income soon became even more worn by his arrival, the fifth child. It was in this atmosphere that Harold succumbed to Nadia's argument that if the household were to maintain some standard and Nadia to keep her sanity, the employment of some kind of help would be necessary, despite the extra cost.

She went down to the petrol station, the hub of Greetwell, to ask the proprietor whether he knew of any domestic help and he put her on to a young woman called Marge who worked for several households in the district. The result was that a cheerful efficient young woman in her early twenties relieved Nadia's household burdens. She came to help twice a week. The problem was that though she lived locally, she had to rush off to catch the bus in order to reach her next client. Not only that, she was expensive. As Marge already had enough work to do apart from our house, she agreed to put Nadia on to an eighteen-year-old, who she said would be cheaper and more flexible but who had a minor physical handicap. Nadia agreed to try her and Marge would contact her.

Betty lived with her parents in one of the semi-detached cottages that belonged to Curtis farm, which, being less than a mile away, was conveniently near. We happened to meet her after school on her second day. She was thin and quite tall, at any rate much taller than Nadia and was so short-sighted, that her pink-framed glasses made her eyes look like two small blue bull's-eyes in glass targets. Her face was red with the country air and she uttered her 'pleased to meet you' with a nasal quality to her voice, which was otherwise soft and mild. But the most striking thing about her was that her right forearm ended in the form of a small pink blob instead of a hand.

Betty was amazing. She quietly changed Lex's nappy in a matter of seconds, her good hand deftly working at high speed while her blob wove in and out to give the right support. She could do all that Nadia asked her to do quickly and well.

Lex who was looked after both by Nadia and Betty became a part of our home and the background of our lives. For the first few weeks of his life Nadia breast fed him and her breasts became heavy with milk, sometimes so much so that she had to squeeze away the excess. Once, while she was feeding him, she called us into her bedroom and let us try a few drops of her milk. We were amazed by its sweetness and wondered where all the sugar came from when its availability was so restricted by rationing.

As Nadia was only able to breast-feed Lex for the first ten weeks of his life, she had to buy powdered milk that the National Health Service provided and that came in large tins with tight-fitting lids. When emptied, the tins were used for storing all kinds of things from dried foods and flour to providing an extra Sunday potty for our growing Sunday morning bladders. Judging by the large number of empty tins, Lex must have drunk an enormous amount of milk in only a few months.

To Nadia, Betty was a treasure. To us she was something else: she taught us how to ride a bike. After she had finished her work at about four, she asked us,

'Can yeh ride a bike?'

'Ah can teach yeh if yeh like,' she said when we replied that we couldn't.

'Yeh can try mine.'

Her bike was an old ladies' sit-up-and-beg type with a black frame, the polished brown seat and the chrome handlebars being far too high and far apart even for me to reach.

'Ivan, you can stand on the pedals and pedal while I hold the saddle,' she said with half a smile. In order to be sure that we understood she seemed to make an effort to speak more correctly.

I stood on the pedals while Betty stabilised the bike which began to move forward on the side of the road as I started to pedal and she gave us all a turn at doing the same thing. We laughed as we watched Philip, who was the smallest, when he bobbed up and down like a yo-yo with the rise and fall of the pedals, while Betty held the saddle which was as high as his head. We all wanted to continue but Betty said that she had to get home but would let us have another go the next time. She let us try her bike in this way several times after she had finished helping Nadia for the day.

It wasn't long before she let go of the saddle while Michael was pedalling, and he wobbled his way along the road.

'It's easy,' he said and we believed him and we all learned how to ride Betty's bike at the same time, even though Vera and Philip were really dwarfed by it. Though she let us use her bike for practice, it soon became clear that having a bicycle of our own was the most desirable thing in our lives.

One boy who lived at Greetwell and who had just left school but not as one of the privileged seven, already wore long trousers, which I thought was impractical in the heat of that summer. He had an old racing bike that he pedaled for all he was worth up and down our road as if to show off. He also used to snatch a loaf from the baker's van while it was doing its deliveries and eat it in one go. In contrast, his considerably older brother used ride his bike very slowly in front of the petrol station in small casual circles. He never said anything, but he always wore a smile. The story was that he fell out of his pram onto his head when he was a baby and he never learnt to speak, even when grown up.

Though there were a few other children at Greetwell we tended to keep to ourselves, climbing trees and exploring the Common. Once while we were blazing Indian trails through the tall bracken, Michael happened to come upon and watch a half-naked courting couple. When he described the incident to us he said that it was fun to watch them, but when they saw him, the boy was very threatening and used foul language.

Sometimes on Saturdays Nadia would feel extra generous and give us enough money to take the bus to Brigg where we went to The

Grand cinema that showed films that attracted crowds of children from the area. A Saturday matinee at the cinema was known as 'The Three-penny Rush' with Johnny Weismuller's Tarzan films and a whole range of westerns among the favourites. Characters like Tom Mix and Roy Rogers were even well-known to Nadia and she called them 'cuhvboys', which made us laugh when she said it. Soon even the Grand began to show post-war westerns with new big names like Alan Ladd and Gary Cooper and the western film culture invaded the playgrounds at school. We shot each other with our index and middle fingers with the thumb bent to suggest the hammer of a Colt 45, and shouted, 'Pchh! You're dead!'

'No I'm not! I was quicker on the draw. I'm Roy Rogers, remember!'

And it wasn't long before the toy shops in Scunthorpe and Brigg did a roaring trade in toy Colt 45's, the more expensive ones having real leather holsters and revolving magazines and hammers that could take caps and make a sound like six-shooters. These were so desirable that every parent who had a son was under pressure to buy one but strangely enough the very presence of these weapons was the death of playing-cowboys and Indians or goodies and baddies. The arrival of realistic toy weapons changed the way we played and we were more fascinated by making an exploding sound with caps than chasing the opposing side with pretend weapons. We became more interested in whirling a shiny toy six-shooter in the hand and competing to be the fastest shooter in the West than pretending to be Gary Cooper or the villain. But this was just a novelty and the six-shooters gave way to other things.

The autumn term brought changes at Scawby School. The old horse chestnut tree was felled, leaving a broad stump almost level with the playground and the wall that had bulged out onto the pavement as the tree grew, had been rebuilt straight. The front play-ground was consequently much lighter, less leafy during the autumn, but sadly devoid of conkers.

Both Miss Everton and Mrs Gray had retired to be replaced respectively by Miss Rowlands and Miss Sells and as we all moved up a class, Philip and Vera had Miss Rowlands, Michael Miss Hazelwood and I was under the charge of Miss Bowles.

Since both the new young teachers had come straight from training college, they were only in their early twenties and looked very young compared to their predecessors. Not only that, but the new teachers themselves looked as different as chalk and cheese from each other. Whereas Miss Sells was pale, thin, slightly freckled and sandy haired, Miss Rowlands had thick dark brown hair, a good complexion and was endowed with a well-formed and generous bust, the contours of which were clearly displayed behind a white lace blouse.

'Cor,' said John Anderson as we leaned over the wall at playtime. 'With tits like that it wain't be long afore she's married!'

After that we knew her from across the road as Titty Rowlands and someone had proved John Anderson right by noticing that she was already wearing an engagement ring. That apart, Philip and Vera thought that she was a good teacher, better than Mrs Gray.

Once again my move to new a class came with mixed feelings but this time of a different kind. I was now the youngest to start with Miss Bowles. Though it felt good, almost a relief, not to be starting a class at the upper end of the age range, I felt that the class did not have the same superior status that it had to me when I was with Miss Hazelwood. The people that I admired like Tommy Smith and the others among the superior seven were now at superior schools and those who remained did not seem to have the same aura.

The physical signs of the top class however were still there. Not only was I in the largest room in the school, together with the oldest children, my desk that was also larger, had a porcelain inkwell fitted into its front part that also had a grove to hold pencils and pens. Miss Bowles produced a kind of black ink by mixing a black powder with water and kept it in a large bottle that she used to fill our inkwells. Soon I was scratching across the paper trying to write with a steel nib on a wooden handle, making dark sepia-coloured blobs in the process. It took time to get used to not dipping the nib too deeply into the inkwell and not pressing too hard to cause the nib to splay, trip and scratch or blot our new exercise books.

Apart from the half dozen or so that had gone up from Miss Hazelwood's class, a new boy had joined the top class. He introduced himself to me as Jim, but when Miss Bowles went through the register before we started class, she read his name out as James

Duncan. When she came to my name I was reminded that it was through Miss Bowles that my surname came to be pronounced 'Crews'.

Jim was a few months older than me but from the very start we got on together. He had dark fair hair and wore a brown blazer, grey cap and short grey trousers, a grey flannel shirt and narrow striped tie. These clothes would have combined to make him the neatest dressed boy in the school, were it not for their worn, somewhat second-hand appearance. At playtime he was not noisy and explosive like most of the boys. He was quiet in his way, using guile and subtlety to outmanoeuvre opponents in games such as cops and robbers. Though he was competent in most subjects his greatest talent was art, which was something I also enjoyed. Though I soon realised that his draughtsmanship was better than mine, our efforts were always pinned up as the best paintings in the class, whether it was pictures of galleons in the Spanish Armada or paintings of Father Christmas.

Being the top class we were given the doubtful privilege of learning the principles of gardening. It was taken for granted that while the boys would cultivate the vegetable garden, the girls would be busy with the flowers. But when Miss Bowles noticed that Jim and I did very little with our spades she decided that we were better suited to helping the girls weed the flowerbeds. This we did using trowels to dig tunnels under the plants in such a way that they were not immediately noticeable and we made it look like we were weeding by making sure that there were some weeds in a little heap beside us. Most of the time however, we were busy pushing small dinky cars through the tunnels that we had excavated and when we saw Miss Bowles approaching we quickly covered the entrance to the tunnel to resume our so-called weeding. We were sure that she knew that we were up to something but she must have decided that it was not worth going into the matter.

Jim was also clever at making small catapults out of wire and elastic and using them to fire small clods of clay at the girls when Miss Bowles was not looking. He was not only an expert at messing around without drawing the teacher's attention, he was good at avoiding any planned physical exercise, whether it was gardening or games. In the autumn and spring terms the boys were encouraged to play football in the nearby Scawby Park while the girls, under Miss Bowles' supervision, played shinty. Football was not for Jim and me: we just messed about climbing trees, organising twig boat races on the brook that ran through the park or just going for walks looking for interesting objects. Miss Bowles could not supervise both her girls and us at the same time.

At playtimes the noise that we children made could be heard from most parts of the village and the screams and shouts coming from both sides of the road combined to make a din that was totally incompatible with the silence that is associated with churchyards. Since the school was next to the churchyard, any person making a visit to pay respects to a dearly departed would have done well to avoid mid-mornings, midday and early afternoons when any prospect of silence would be impossible. Sometimes, however, a funeral at just those times was unavoidable.

The vicar and Miss Bowles must have reached an agreement to keep the children indoors when there was a funeral in progress and all the pupils received an order to stay indoors, which caused groans of disappointment when the weather happened to be fine. But Jim and I didn't object at all to being confined to class during playtime because for us it meant extra time to draw while the teachers did not have a real break. I only experienced this type of confinement twice, as the vast majority of funerals did not coincide with playtimes.

Scawby church was of the ordinary village gothic type built some time in the sixteenthth Century. It had a square embattled stone tower displaying a black clock with gilded numbers and hands on all four sides. One of the clocks did not work while two of them seemed to keep reasonable time. Though the school was next to the Scawby centre of Christianity, I felt that I had very little to do with the church, even though we sang Christian hymns and said prayers that might well have been said in that church. For me the church was nearly out of bounds for I knew that Vera and I were not officially Christian: Nadia told us that we had never been christened. On the other hand I knew that Michael and Philip had been christened when they were babies, making them officially Christians. So when Nadia said that as Lex would be christened that autumn and we might as well be christened at the same time, we were both keen to become official Christians. I felt that becoming a member of the Church of England would help my feeling of being English and meet my need to belong to my community.

The ceremony took place without incident, my little brother Lex being only slightly startled by the drops of holy water sprinkled over his face while the vicar repeated the words that made him a member of the Church of England. The ceremony reminded us that now he was officially called Alexander Harold Neale, while his new godparents, Harold's cousin Connie and his brother Cedric stood in solemn responsibility. He then made utterances to welcome Vera and me officially into the Church.

The Reverend Ure was a tall wiry man with thick, steel-grey hair and a pair of steel-framed glasses that sat on a face that was weathered from all the cycling that he did to visit his parishioners. His grey-blue eyes twinkled as he spoke. I wondered where the holy water came from as he dipped his hand into the bowl. Was it imported all the way from the Holy Land? His soft nasal voice repeated the words necessary to ensure that we were christened as Vera and Ivan Paul. He sprinkled a little holy water as he uttered the ceremonious words, though the ceremony itself was simplified because we had no godparents. I was christened at the age of nine and Vera at six.

Shortly after our christening Vera insisted that we go to Sunday school that her friend told her had started the Sunday before, but as Michael and I were not that keen, she and Philip caught the bus to Scawby after Sunday dinner leaving us feeling almost heathen. When they returned they showed their new attendance booklets to collect Sunday school attendance stamps, each stamp depicting a biblical scene in colour and as they had just started they were also the stamp for they previous week. They told us that a prize was rewarded for a book full of attendance stamps at Christmas and the attendance stamps were rather attractive.

We enjoyed the Sunday school bible stories but I still could not grasp the total meaning of the Lord's Prayer. I could get the gist of 'Our Father, which art in Heaven,' but the only meaning of 'art' that I really knew was to do with drawing and painting, so I guessed that it must have been a holy way of saying 'is'. Now I knew that our new father was called Harold. Was 'Hallowed' a holy version of it? That was a mystery that remained so for some time.

I had seen notices on the far side of the Common that said 'Trespassers will be Prosecuted' and which Michael told me meant a gamekeeper could catch us and maybe shoot us for being on private land. So as I understood it, the Lord's Prayer told people like game-keepers to forgive those that trespassed on private land. I left it at that as I was too shy to make a fool of myself by asking what these holy words really meant and it took a long time before I could grasp the meaning of the older forms of English and their biblical contexts.

Betty told Nadia that Mr Curtis needed potato pickers on his farm and any children over the age of eight would be welcome to earn themselves a little pocket money. When Michael and I decided to try it, Nadia warned us that as it would be cold we were to dress warmly and wear our Balaclavas. It was about a twenty-minute brisk walk to the farm, our breaths coming out in steaming plumes to meet the cold late autumn air. When we came to a field where a number of women and children were filling sacks with potatoes, we stopped and were shown to a woman who gave us a sack to fill.

'Yeh'll get three ha'pence a sack,' she said. Her nose protruded from her headscarfed head like a reddish purple potato as she spoke and handed us a sack each. We joined a group of older children and began to pick up cold clayey clods that we recognised as potatoes. The wind bit from the east. As I filled the bottom of my sack my hands began to get numb with cold and I found it increasingly difficult to control my fingers to pick up potatoes that were too small, or lift those that were too large. Michael, who was more adept than me and seemed to stand the cold better, managed to fill nearly half his sack, while I had done barely a third. I soon realised that it was a hopeless task, as the older children could drag their sacks with them as they went along, while we had to run to and from our sacks when they became too heavy to move and the running did little to warm us up.

'I'm giving up,' I said, 'It's too cold.'

'Me too,' said Michael, though I felt he could have continued. 'We won't get paid for just half a sack.'

'I know,' I said realising that we had given somebody a pennyworth of picking.

Feeling beaten and dejected, we left our sacks and walked back as quickly as we could to the warmth of our house. On the way I thought about Michael's mother and that it was easy to see why she died of pneumonia after being out in the cold picking potatoes. She was, it seemed, also a heavy smoker.

As nearly all adults, except Nadia and Harold smoked and the tobacco companies tried to attract even more customers, they restarted a marketing trick that was popular when Harold was a boy, cigarette cards. Companies like Wills and Players produced card series of usually fifty depicting a whole range of themes from military uniforms to famous film stars, footballers, flags, cars, battleships, wild flowers, birds and just about any theme that was collectable. It wasn't long before we joined in the collector's mania that was boosted by complete or nearly complete collections from Harold and Cedric, some in heaps and some neatly arranged in special albums. Michael collected cars and flags, while Philip had film stars, Vera flowers and I had birds and battleships. There was much swapping and bartering on the playground and under cover in class.

November, I found, was the time when the oldest pupils had to prepare for and take an important test that was to decide their whole futures. It was called 'The Intelligence Test'. Compared with the previous year, there were not as many in this group and they did not seem to have the same air of superiority. When I asked one boy called Leslie White what the test was like, he said, 'I dunno, but it wasn't easy.'

Leslie was a cheerful boy who laughed in a series of guffaws, his jaw dropping to make him look almost like an idiot, which made him, quite unjustly, an object of derision by boys who were no better than their image of him. The result however was that they teased him by chanting:

Leslie White

Had a fright

In the middle of the night

Wind blew. Shit flew. Leslie White never knew

That winter was hardly snowy at all and we did not have a white Christmas. Father Christmas did, however, keep us occupied nearly

215

the whole Christmas holidays by providing us with a no. 3 Meccano set and thanks to the newly installed central heating, we were able to construct things in comfort in the front room after Harold had shown us the basics. As we had all learnt to read, Nadia combined her shopping with visits to the Brigg library to borrow books that included a whole range of Enid Blytons. From that time on we joined the famous five in the Mountain, Castle, Island and other sites of adventure. She also selected books that she read to us in the evenings before bedtime and one of these was the story of a demoiselle crane that got shot in the wing on its way south from Siberia. When N Karazin wrote the book he must have had a good knowledge of the geography of eastern Russia as I was impressed by his description of the countryside as seen from the air by a flock of migrating cranes. It was, in fact, called Cranes Flying South.

The books that Miss Bowles read to us were also set in the countryside, the English countryside and the author who succeeded most in awaking a longing for nature signed himself as BB. His story of the three brothers who ran away from home to hide out in a large forest called Brendon Chase fired the imagination, making me wonder if there was a huge pine tree in our area where the honey buzzard nested. How wonderful it would be to live out in the wilds, to hunt rabbits and roe-deer and live off their meat, to catch sight of exotic butterflies like white admirals and purple emperors, to build one's own den and make friends with a charcoal burner called Smokoe Joe. When I talked about it at teatime, Harold said, 'We've got that book at home. You can read it when you like. It was one of my favourites when I was young.'

And both Michael and I read it with great enthusiasm, often talking about it and taking walks in our adjacent conifer wood with our imaginations burning and wondering if the sound of a wood pigeon crashing through a tree top might be caused by a honey buzzard. I desperately wanted to know more about birds, but there were no books on the subject at the library, at least for lending.

Once again it was spring. We sang Easter hymns and the songs of spring and summer to remind us that life outside home and school offered exciting opportunities out in the countryside. When a boy called Brian Brown who was in the same class as Michael, came to school with a small box containing birds' eggs wrapped in cotton wool, we wanted to go bird nesting. He showed us a linnet's nest in a hawthorn hedge and showed us how to tell if the egg was 'bubbed' (whether it had a developing embryo) by seeing if it floated on water, before piecing both ends with a pin and blowing out the contents. Though small and skinny, he was so expert at climbing trees and high bushes that he was known as Bunker Brown.

On the Common we found a yellow hammer's nest with dark squiggly markings on the buff-coloured eggs. Bunker said that the bird was called 'the scribe' because the markings on its eggs were like writing. Also on the ground we stumbled across nests of pheasants, grey and French partridge all of which had so many eggs that we did not feel guilty taking one. It wasn't just the fascination of how the eggs varied in size, colour and markings according to the species, it was the excitement of the hunt. Bunker Brown had found a corn bunting's nest in a field near the school, and he showed us its rather large heavily marked egg and told us that it was rare. Where did he, the son of a grocer, get all his knowledge from, we wondered? Michael and I formed a joint collection which we stored in a cotton wool lined shoe box and when Nadia found out she let us collect on the condition that we only took one egg from a nest and did not take extras to use as swaps.

Once again the playground was busy with boys and girls playing their separate games, but I did not try to play football again. Instead, Jim thought that it would be fun for the boys that didn't play football to chase girls, catch them and confine them to a cul-de-sac passage that was formed by a space between the side of the school and a high wall bounding the churchyard. The girls that were caught were made to kiss the boys, which caused a lot of screams and giggles. We called the game kiss catching and the game kept its name despite the fact that it changed to the girls being made to pull their knickers down on being caught, while we thought we were being fair by showing them our willies. Inevitably, one of the girls put an end to it all by telling Miss Bowles who darkened with anger when we were called in after playtime.

'If I catch any of you boys misbehaving with the girls in the back passage or anywhere else, you will be severely dealt with,' she said.

Three years after the war had ended the prisoner of war camp was finally evacuated. Otto and his friends had all gone back to Germany and as the camp seemed totally deserted we soon found a way in through the barbed wire to explore the huts and surroundings. It was so different from my concentration camps that a comparison hardly entered my head. As the huts were not locked we could enter and leave them as we pleased and found that the ex-prisoners had left nothing behind except a musty smell. To me the most interesting thing was that one of the water tanks was dismantled from its tower to lie on the ground and collect rainwater. By late summer it harboured great diving beetles and their monstrous larvae that gave a vicious bite when given a chance, as well as dragonfly larvae that looked like aliens from another planet. These we caught and put in jam jars for inspection.

But the camp was not empty for long. By late summer families that for untold reasons were homeless occupied those musty smelling huts. Harold said that they were squatters and that as it was possible that they might steal from houses in the neighbourhood, we were to be on the lookout.

With the squatters came their children, dirty-looking with tatty clothes, but they played together in the camp compound like any children and it wasn't long before they joined us in the bracken on the Common playing cowboys and Indians with home-made bows and arrows.

Lex had reached his first birthday. It was a sunny Saturday morning and Harold sang to him in his fine baritone voice, 'Oh what a beautiful morning! The corn is as high as an elephant's eye and it seems to be climbing right up to the sky '

Lex could talk a little, pronouncing my name as 'Van', Michael as 'Cagoo', Vera as 'Beya' and Philip simply as 'Pip'. He was beginning to be a little boy but he walked with his bottom, shuffling along using the cheeks of his backside like legs, which made us all laugh.

He had also been moved to Vera's room where he had a bed that had railings like a playpen. He soon learned to stand up and rock the bed by holding the railings and making the bed creep slowly towards Vera. Though she thought it very funny at first, she soon became tired of Lex's noisy attentions and begged to change places with one of the boys in the loft, so that she could have some peace in the mornings. Nadia decided that the best solution was for the oldest child to be with the youngest, which I did not mind, as I was an early riser by nature.

But I felt depressed with the thought that I was getting old. Two days after Lex reached the age of one, it was my tenth birthday: I had actually reached double figures and that depressed me. I didn't want to become an adult. I wanted to play all my life. But all depressive thoughts were dispelled when I opened a present; the brown paper wrapping obviously covered a book. It was a bird guide with coloured illustrations called 'Name this Bird'. Now I could see what the birds whose eggs we had taken looked like. How fantastic to get just what one wanted!

'Ivan,' said Nadia when ate breakfast that morning. 'Why don't we invite some of the squatter children and have a party?'

Nadia knew that as Harold was away at work he could not possibly object.

'What a good idea,' said Vera.

'Yes, I'd like that,' I said. So after breakfast we ran into the camp and invited a boy called Daniel whom we called Danny and one called Eric, and Vera invited a girl called Josephine.

Danny had washed his face, combed his blond hair and wore long grey trousers that did not have holes in the knees. Eric looked more or less the same, though he never looked very untidy and dirty any way, while Josephine came wearing a clean dress.

We all tucked into trifle, jellies, jam sandwiches and a small birthday cake that Nadia baked using eggs that Grandma gave her and decorated with icing and ten candles. Then we all got dirty and scruffy again out on the Common.

Apart from the arrival of the squatters there were other changes that summer. Harold and Nadia had found second-hand bicycles for Michael, Philip and Vera, and I was given the use of his old red bike that he had modified and adjusted for me to be able to ride. This was a relief for Betty, as she was no longer pestered by us for the loan of her bike to practise our skills. This opened up new horizons and gave us opportunities to explore our surroundings, one of the big challenges being to cycle all the way up Mottle-ash Hill on the main road between Scunthorpe and Brigg.

We wore and tore and grew out of our clothes, and despite all the mending and patching that Nadia did, they made holes in her budget. As the plus fours had done their bit and were worn beyond repair, they could not be handed down to Philip. As Harold's business was not all that lucrative, she had to buy most of our clothing on instalment, which was made possible thanks to the services of a pleasant and considerate sale representative who carried a range of items in his van. We sometimes came across Mr Dobbs talking to Nadia, his cockney accent contrasting with the North Lincolnshire dialect that we had become used to hearing around us. He was always dressed in a light grey double-breasted suit, his black shoes shone and his black hair was thick and sleeked back with ample Brylcreem.

'Down't warry Mrs Neale,' we heard him say. 'You c'n pahy next week. It wown't cost you nathink extra. Oi'll see to it.'

And so, thanks to Mr Dobbs Nadia could see to it that we were adequately clothed for the new term on his generous terms. Despite this, Nadia had to run the household on a very tight budget, which we were told to observe by making sure that we spread our butter, Bovril or jam as thinly as possible on our slices of bread.

As I complained that I had difficulty in seeing the writing on the blackboard Nadia took me to see the optician in Brigg, who said that I needed glasses as I was short-sighted, though not as severely as Vera. A week later I took the bus to collect a new pair of clinical glasses at no cost to anyone except the taxpayer. Like Vera, I did not think my new glasses improved my appearance, instead I felt that I looked more like Jan.

Harold was so preoccupied with trying to earn a living from his business and making the house comfortable for our large family that he had little time for his own leisure. But we knew that his life was more than just work and house improvements. Some of his possessions were kept in the garage instead of the house either because there was no room or because Nadia refused to have them. The garage, no longer filled by Grandad's old Ford now housed many items that were a part of Harold's past, the most recent being three Samurai swords, which we would draw out from their ornate scabbards to admire the long razor-sharp shiny steel blades.

The discovery in the garage of a pair of split cane fishing rods and a box of tackle that included two fine old wooden reels with brass fittings inevitably provoked questions about fishing and

'Couldn't you take us to go fishing, Daddy?'

I asked the question, the still vivid memories of fish and fishing when we visited the Nederlofs in Holland emerging like rays of sunshine piercing a cloud.

'One day, when I have time,' he said.

He made time one sunny summer Sunday when we walked along the Messingham Road about a mile from the crossroads and came to a pond by the roadside surrounded by reeds and sallow bushes. Nadia, Vera and Lex stayed at home.

We watched spellbound to see the red-tipped feather float bob with a bite. Harold jerked the rod to one side and we watched it bend and vibrate as he wound in a shiny small roach with a silver body and red fins. He carefully took the roach off the hook and gently released it back into the pond. 'You can't eat these,' he said and when he caught several more roach we began to show more interest in the surrounding heathland than Harold's fishing.

After half a dozen small roach he called us and said that one day he would take us to a place where there were big fish and that he would get us some tackle so that we could fish ourselves. But there was no more fishing that summer. Harold was too busy and we had so much else to do like biking, playing on the Common and playing with the squatter children in the camp.

18. Scholarship

Though that autumn term began with no changes in classes. Philip and Vera were in their last year at the infant school with Miss Rowlands, who had become Mrs Turner, while Michael was still with Miss Hazelwood, also at the back of the room because he smelt of garlic, but now joined by some of the squatter children. When Miss Hazelwood had taken the register Michael told us that he heard her sigh,

'First we have to put up with foreigners, now we have squatters!'

I somehow felt more important. I was now among the oldest pupils and I had started my last year at Scawby County Primary School. At the back of my mind I knew that the big hurdle of the scholarship was beginning to loom up before me. None of those who had just left had passed their scholarship, while the names of the superior seven from 1947 were already exalted in gold on one of two large black-boards. Both boards were about half as high as the wall, were lined with gilt and decorated at the top with the Nelthorpe coat of arms flanked by 'SCAWBY SCHOOLS' while the sub-heading was 'The Nelthorpe Trust SCHOLARSHIP ROLL OF HONOUR,' all written in gilt letters. I wondered what 'The Scawby Schools' implied: were there several schools in Scawby, or did it mean that the infant and junior schools were regarded as separate? The older of the two boards went back as far as the beginning of the century. Each name, year and name of future school was more spaced out and took up a whole line, which showed that it was clearly more of an event for someone to pass his scholarship in our parents' generation. The more recent board that started with the name of a person, who had passed his scholarship in 1922, suggested that either there were more pupils or they were cleverer or the scholarship standard had been lowered. Whatever the reason, the names, years and next schools on the more recent board were arranged in two columns with the name of the superior seven starting nearly at the top of the second column. By scrutinising the boards I could see that never before had seven persons passed their scholarship in the same year. But just as Miss Bowles was proud of them, she was disappointed in the most recent results when not a single pupil had passed his scholarship.

Every time I stared at those boards, I was reminded of the importance of passing my scholarship, not only just because my mother told me how important it was, but because I wanted it myself. But I hardly dared to imagine that my name would be written in gilt letters on the Roll of Honour.

The result was that I became more intent on making progress in the three R's and seemed to get on reasonably well in arithmetic, could hold my own in reading aloud, but was poor at writing, not only at writing neatly but also at spelling. This was in sharp contrast to Carol Clarke, a short girl with wavy light blonde hair and large blue eyes, who moved up with me from Miss Hazelwood. She had not only managed to get through nearly all the range of colours of arithmetic exercise books, and had started the most advanced, her handwriting was neat and even without spelling mistakes. If I could be as clever as she was, I would have no worries about passing my scholarship!

Even gardening became a more serious pastime and Jim and I did not fool around as much. When we were about to go out, the September heavens opened up and one boy said,

'It's silin' wi ree-en!'

'It's pouring with rain,' said Miss Bowles correcting his Lincolnshire dialect, 'but we can go out in a few minutes when it stops.'

We helped to dig up the potatoes in wet soil that would have been wet clay, had it not been for generations of school gardeners who cultivated it and fertilised it with trenches of manure. The products of the school garden vegetable harvest were displayed for the harvest festival when we sung: 'We plough the fields and scatter the good seed on the land. But it is fed and watered by God's almighty hand.'

In October, about a month before the intelligence test Miss Bowles let us familiarise ourselves with the type of problems by giving those of us who were in our final year examples of tests from previous years. When I brought the booklet of tests home, everyone felt stimulated to tackle the problems, including Harold who was asked to solve the most difficult ones that no-one else could do, those that came at the end. When he came up with the answers we sometimes could not understand his reasoning.

'Never mind,' said Harold. 'You'll do well if you can answer most of them and concentrate on doing the ones that you can do correctly.'

I had to go to school using the public bus service on that early November Saturday morning, the morning of our intelligence test. Miss Bowles spoke to us kindly, told us where to sit, our places being spaced out by at least one desk between. With a little mounting tension we sat equipped with several sharpened pencils and a rubber, waiting for Miss Bowles to give us our papers. From the given moment, I more or less followed Harold's advice which was also given to us by Miss Bowles and skipped over those problems that seemed difficult, coming back to them when I had made sure that I was satisfied with the ones that I could answer.

Afterwards, Jim and I thought it wasn't as difficult as we had expected and that opinion seemed to be echoed by most, including Carol.

Miss Bowles took up another book written by 'BB' called The Little Grey Men. It was about the last gnomes in England who lived in an old oak and how their lives changed when they found a large clockwork model motorboat stranded by the stream that flowed near their home. They managed to salvage the boat called The Jeanie Deans and wind the motor to start an adventure that had us spellbound and longing to hear each episode. Their ability to talk to the animals and birds during their adventures deepened my interest in wildlife and nature.

However, I was not that interested in everything that Miss Bowles read. She sometimes resorted to reading poetry, which I found so boring that once I quietly took out a copy of Dandy that I happened to have with me and became totally absorbed in it. Suddenly, I found the comic gliding away from me on the top of my desk and looking up I saw that Miss Bowles was holding it and waving her forefinger from side to side in a forbidding manner, though she never said a word. I was so absorbed in the comic that I didn't even notice that she had crept up to me while still reading the poetry. I felt ashamed of my behaviour, which Miss Bowles must have known for she didn't punish me.

When one of us was at home ill with a cold or flu we could not avoid hearing the radio which Nadia listened to while doing the housework. There were programmes such as Music While You Work in the morning and in the afternoon she had become an addict to Mrs Dale's Diary which she followed every day after having Lex on her knee during Listen with Mother. I laughed as I watched Nadia following and acting out the nursery rhymes together with Lex. We would also listen, especially when the presenter said, 'Are you sitting comfortably? Then we'll begin. Once upon a time...' The story usually made Lex sleepy, which allowed Nadia to listen to Woman's Hour in peace.

When at the end of the school day Miss Bowles finished reading an episode out of a BB book there was always something to follow at home, since the BBC also made sure that both children and adults had something to follow on the radio. Around teatime we followed Dick Barton - Special Agent, which gave way to Paul Temple and Journey into Space, not to mention schoolboy series such as Just William and Jennings and Derbyshire. Our general knowledge was improved by another radio favourite that featured mixed-age secondary school teams competing in a programme called Top of the Form.

While Nadia was quite taken by the lives of Dr and Mrs Dale and their family, it was spies, the pranks of naughty schoolboys, and the weird fantasy of radio sci-fi that set our imaginations alight. Whatever the theme, thanks to the BBC we really became immersed in the middle class British way of life and it was Nadia that pointed out that the best people speak like they do on the BBC.

We noticed that BBC middle class children addressed their parents as 'mummy' and 'daddy', but in the Scawby School environment that sounded both sissy and toffee-nosed. The local 'mam' and 'dad', however, had the working class feeling that we knew Nadia would not accept, so at home we continued to address Harold and Nadia as 'Daddy' and 'Mammy' until one day Vera came up with a practical solution:

'Look, Mammy,' she said 'why can't we call you "Mum"' and Daddy "Dad"', like you call Grandad. I think it sounds much better. Don't you think so, Mike?'

'Yes, much better.'

She looked at Vera, a little surprised by the common sense that came from her seven-year-old daughter.

'All right, call me "Mum", she said, pronouncing the word in a flat way that suggested uncertainty. 'But you'd better ask Daddy himself whether you can call him "Dad".'

Of course it was fine to call him 'Dad'. In any case, with his head full of business worries, Harold had no strong opinions on the matter.

The business was, in fact, a cause of tiredness, frustration and worry and began to cause tension between Mum and Dad that sometimes broke out into rows in our presence. One cause of the problem was that the business partner, Mr Cook, did not pull his weight. He often did not come to the building site when he was needed and drew out more than his share of the small profits that they had. This had caused Harold to dissolve the partnership and Mr Cook took with him his motorbike and sidecar, which pressed Harold into acquiring a new vehicle.

That October, while we were under the tree grubbing around for chestnuts, we heard an irregular chugging sound. On looking up we saw a tall black van shaking and swaying its way up the drive and we could clearly see that it had two giant British bangers painted on its side. We ran towards it and when it stopped Harold climbed out with a broad grin on his face.

'What do you think of that?'

'Are you going to start selling sausages?' I asked.

'Don't be silly! This is going to be our new car! It's a 1932 Ford in pretty good condition.'

I looked at the registration number. It was MV 1366. I found it easy to remember because for some reason I made it stand for My Van 1366, the year 1366 having no significance to my knowledge, except that it sounded important, like 1066, a date already made familiar to us by Miss Bowles.

Soon Harold had stripped the back of the sausage van down to the bare chassis and it wasn't long before he had converted it into a shooting brake using deal for the framing and aluminium sheeting for the panels and floor. He then streaked the woodwork with brown and buff tones using a special roller to produce the effect of wooden panelling. We thought it was a fantastic result, but as Nadia didn't like anything pretending to be what it wasn't, she rather turned her nose up at it. As far as she was concerned it was still a sausage van.

Harold used the Ford mainly for travelling to and from a building site, as well as for carrying necessary items and tools. We could see that one day he might take the family out on a tour, as he had already made a long back seat that could easily be fitted in to take us 'boys' while Lex could sit on Nadia's knee at the front.

A few days before Christmas, we all helped with the decorations, painting pinecones red, silver and gold to hang up on the Christmas tree and making coloured paper chains to suspend up on the ceiling. There was no longer any shouting up the chimney in the front room, as we knew that Father Christmas was just for small children. Vera and Philip knew the truth earlier in their lives because Michael and I could not keep our mouths shut and Lex was still too young to know about the mysterious white bearded benefactor in red.

On Christmas Eve we took the bus to Brigg to do our shopping with pocket money that we had saved. As our assets limited our imaginations, Christmas shopping was a matter of finding notebooks and pencils, rubbers and pencil sharpeners. Nadia had already hinted that she'd love to have a bath with Elizabeth Arden bath salts and lavender soap, but as Vera and Philip had already bought those items I went into Timothy White's and Taylor's and resorted to buying her a comb. Harold was to be showered with combs, handkerchiefs, shaving soap and packets of razor blades, both for his birthday and Christmas five days later.

Once again we were overwhelmed by the Christmas with which our parents managed to regale us. A new fountain pen for me, an extra Meccano set for Michael and me, new second-hand bikes for Vera and Philip, stockings filled with small useful things, fruit, nuts and chocolates all contributed to making us happy together, as a family.

The winter proved to be quite mild with very little snow, which made January a bore. February was a time of feverish activity both at school and at home. Using old scholarship papers that Miss Bowles had given me, we practised reading comprehension. We discussed various essay topics and tried to work out how long it would take to fill a bath, empty tanks of water, at what point two trains should pass each other when travelling at different speeds and how many men were required to dig a hole at a certain depth when one man dug a hole a third the size in a certain time. Harold was always needed and he was keen to lend us his logical mind.

My head buzzed and on the day gave in to a streaming cold, causing me to sniff and blow my nose through the writing and calculating. I knew that I had done badly, both in the arithmetic and the English. I felt resigned to failure. Realising that perhaps I could have done better, Nadia made an appointment to see Miss Bowles on the following Monday after school, while we took the school bus home as usual.

When she returned she said that Miss Bowles was very sympathetic and praised me for being an intelligent and conscientious pupil, which my school reports clearly showed. She admitted that though my cold might have been a factor, more significant was the fact that I had only two and a half years to learn English and attend school, apart from having spent a third of my life in a Japanese concentration camp. She said that though she couldn't promise anything, she would mention my background as mitigating circumstances and if they would take that into account there might be some hope.

Hope came during the Easter holidays in the form of a typed letter signed by the headmaster of Brigg Grammar School. The letter asked me to attend an interview at the school at the beginning of May. An interview! I had little idea what that meant. Would it mean more tests? Would it mean that I would have to answer a lot of difficult questions put by the headmaster and other important people in the school? No-one, not even Nadia could tell me exactly what an interview consisted of, or exactly what it implied, except that it meant that there was hope. It certainly meant that at least I had to look as presentable as possible, which involved buying new shoes and socks, a new shirt and tie and washing my jumper.

'Presentable' meant being almost wholly dressed in grey except for polished black shoes and a dark blue tie. Mr Dobbs saw to it that I had a new pair of short grey trousers, grey socks to just below the knee and a grey flannel shirt. My grey jumper was only slightly worn and the stains were easily washed away.

Back at school I was relieved that both Jim and Bill had also been called to interviews, but on different dates from mine.

It was the first Wednesday in May. As Nadia and I stood at Greetwell Corner waiting to travel to Brigg, I paced nervously around looking at the gravel and soil that had been exposed by thousands of expectant bus users. Though I saw the fresh, varied greenery of the hedges and trees, the vigour of late spring, I gave the onset of summer hardly any thought since my mind was totally occupied by the interview that was to come.

An asphalt drive, shaded by trees on the right and bounded by what must have been the old school building on the left, sloped slightly up to lead us round the corner past some more modern buildings and into the heart of the school. There was no sign of any boys, but when we entered the corridor sounds of voices that came from behind walls and frosted glass suggested that school was in progress.

We followed the corridor as it turned and led to a wider lobby occupied on one side by the bottom of a flight of grey stairs on one side of which was a wall of dark wooden lockers. The dark brown doors and lockers, the glazed brown tiles of the wall and the cream-coloured ceiling dimmed the effect of the light that came from a large window above the stairs and a solitary ceiling lamp. The whole effect was gloom. Several boys of about my age sat on chairs placed in a semi-circle in front of the lockers and as we stood to take in the scene, a slim smiling woman whose hair was compressed by means of a tight bun greeted us:

'Good morning! You must have come for an interview,' she said looking at me. 'What is your name?'

'Ivan Kruys,' I said in what must have been a low voice.

'Oh good! Then of course you must be Mrs Kruys,' Ivan's mother, she said beaming at my mother.'How do you do?'

'How do you do? Yes, I am Ivan's mother, but my name is Mrs Neale.'

'Oh! How do you do,' Mrs Neale. 'Do take a seat. The headmaster won't be long.'

I sat down on the nearest chair opposite to a large somewhat corpulent boy who still had his cap on. He looked as nervous as I felt.

'You should take your cap off before the headmaster comes,' said my mother.

'Yessah,' said the boy with a terrified look on his face. He tore his cap off his head to draw a lock of hair over his eyes as he did so. He then stuck his hands into his pockets.

'And you should take your hands out of your pockets when you see the headmaster.'

'Yessah.'

I began to feel so ashamed of my mother that I wanted to disappear.

'What's your name?'

'Bernard Nelson, sah.'

'You shouldn't call me "sir", only the headmaster.' said Nadia.

I was ashamed of my mother for not minding her own business, for being the only parent to accompany her son and for her Russian accent, but was comforted by the fact that Bernard appeared at least as nervous as I was.

'Yessah.' said Bernard, even more nervous than before.

A door opened to reveal an enormous man in a double-breasted grey suit.

'Ivan Kruys.' said the man in a way that seemed to sound as if he said it with his mouth closed.

As I stood up I felt Nadia pat my back.

The man withdrew into a small, well-lit room to sit behind a light-coloured wooden table.

'Sit down,' he said making a half-hearted gesture towards a chair that was placed opposite his.

'Thank you, sir.'

'Well now, Kruys, why do you think you want to come to this school?'

His mouth expressed a faint smile but the rest of his large red face was cold, his deep close-set eyes glowing under bushy eyebrows, boring into me like daggers.

'So that I could have a good career, perhaps go to university, sir,' I said, going over what Nadia and I had rehearsed at home.

'I see. And what would you like to be when you are grown up?'

'I think perhaps an architect, sir.'

'Why?'

'Because I'm quite good at drawing, sir.'

'But you have to be good at mathematics and English as well and your scholarship paper showed that you are not very good at those subjects.'

The lower half of his face broadened into a one-sided smile while his eyes remained deep and anything but smiling. It was almost as if he pointed out my inadequacies with a note of triumph.

'I will try to be better, sir.'

'All right Kruys. You may go now.'

'Thank you, sir. Goodbye, sir.'

I left the room with my heart pounding and closed the door behind me to be faced by the smiling woman with the tight bun.

'Now you can come with me to the master's common room,' she said in a kind voice.

I followed her along the darkest part of the corridor, wondering what the next ordeal was to be. She knocked on a door to cause a resonant 'Come in' that sounded almost as if it were sung.

The door opened to leave me confronted by several middle-aged men who were spaced around an enormous table that nearly seemed to fill the room and the room itself had a stuffy atmosphere caused by a mixture of the smell of books, tobacco, old sweat and dust. Apart from two windows and the door, books and piles of exercise books lined the whole room. A rather thin man with a shiny bald head fringed with white hair spoke first:

'So you're Ivan Kruys!'

Before I could say anything he continued, 'You can sit there.'

'Thank, you sir.'

I found myself sitting in a polished wooden chair with a round back.

'I understand that you live at Greetwell and go to Scawby Primary School. Is that right?' Though his face was expressionless, his tone was gentle and he spoke with a fine base voice that seemed to resonate even in that crowded room.

231

'Yes, sir.'

'Though you didn't do very well in your scholarship paper, especially the English, you did very well in your intelligence test. This means that we think you have the ability to do better. You have after all, as we understand it, only lived in England for less than three years.'

'Yes, sir.'

'What do you like doing best either when you are at home or at school?'

'I like reading and drawing, sir.'

'Very good.'

He paused and looked round towards his colleagues as if to invite them to ask me something, but they just seemed to nod their heads.

'That will be all, Ivan. You'll hear from the school in due course.'

I liked the way he called me 'Ivan' instead of the way the headmaster called me by my surname, even though he did pronounce it like Miss Bowles did.

When I told Nadia all about the ordeal she thought that it sounded like they were going to accept me to the school.

We were left in doubt for most of the term until Nadia gave me a type-written letter addressed to me, but which she had already opened while we were at school. That letter, with its official paper headed 'Brigg Grammar School' and signed by the headmaster said that the school was pleased to accept me as a pupil at the start of the autumn term of 1949! An indescribable surge of elation flowed through me lifting me up above the world around me and numbing me to such an extent that I could barely feel my mother's hugs and kisses.

It was true that I was to go to Brigg Grammar School, on a par with the Superior Seven two years before, but my own doubts began to tarnish my silver crown. Was I really that clever, or was it thanks to words put in by Miss Bowles? After all, the only successful part of my examinations seemed to be my intelligence test. Would that suffice to allow me to survive the environment of a grammar school?

But since those questions could not be answered I had to concentrate on my future and the fact that I really had been accepted.

My last days at Scawby School went by like a dream highlighted by a small envelope that Nadia handed to me after school. She hadn't opened it. It was addressed to me in type, but the last part of the address written 'Scawby, Brigg' was crossed out in ink and replaced by 'KIRTON LINDSEY, GAINSBORO', also written in blue ink.

She gave me a knife to open the envelope to reveal a letter that had its own address, SCAWBY, BRIGG, LINCOLNSHIRE, printed on it, dated in type the 23rd July 1949.

It read, 'Dear Ivan', written in ink by a pen whose nib splayed out as the writer pressed out the letters. The rest was typed as follows:

'The managers of this Scawby School learnt with much pleasure at their meeting last week of your success in winning a County Scholarship in the recent examinations.

They asked me, as their chairman, to write to you on their behalf to congratulate you and also to send you this cheque for five pounds from the Nelthorpe School Charity in recognition of your good work.

That Charity was set up 250 years ago to reward, help and encourage children of our Scawby School who during their time there have shown readiness to profit by their oppotunities and ability to put them to good use as you have done.

The names of many children of this village who started their career by passing on to the Brigg Grammar School or to the Hogh School are inscribed on the Roll of Honour to commemorate their good work. Your name will now be inscribed on that Roll.

The managers and I wish you success in your future career on which you have already made such a fine start.

Yours sincerely,

It was signed 'O. S. Nelthorpe' in the same flowing style made so rich by a nib that splayed a little under pressure. I wondered what kind of pen he used. Was it a fountain pen or a really old-fashioned quill? After reading the letter again I noticed the typing errors and showed them to Nadia who said that his secretary was either very old or careless.

For me there was no doubt that the five pounds was to be spent on a new bike.

Miss Bowles announced that as Jim, Bill and I had passed our scholarships we were to go to Brigg Grammar School, Carol to the Girls' High School and Allan, a quiet boy who had asthma, had passed his scholarship but he was to go to Scunthorpe Grammar School.

19. Dutch Roots

The summer holidays took on a new dimension, one of the reasons being my new bike. Harold took the van into Scunthorpe and returned with a brand new Dayton Roadster cycle. It had a black frame that was trimmed with a fine green line and shiny chrome handlebars and wheels.

Nadia wrote to Jan to tell him that as his son had passed his scholarship to allow him to go to a better school, she needed a contribution from him towards a compulsory new school uniform. This unleashed a bitter exchange of letters in which Jan thought the whole idea of school uniforms was an outmoded British extravagance. But he had to give in, as he could hardly suggest that I went to an ordinary secondary school instead. Nadia took the opportunity to suggest that it would also be a good idea for Jan to see his children after an absence of more than three years. As he could hardly refuse that either, Harold and Nadia took Vera and me to Hull to board a small cargo boat that took passengers to Rotterdam. Nadia had persuaded Jan to cover the cost of our passage. The voyage was a little rough but with the *Tabinta* experience still relatively fresh in our memories we took it in our stride and arrived in Rotterdam thirty-six hours later to be met by Jan.

It felt strange to see my father again, though he looked more or less the same as I remembered him, a man who was my father practically in name only. Vera and I felt it easier to regard Harold as our parent and though we called him 'Dad', we knew that he was not our biological father.

As Jan spoke to us, his English sounded quite good but had a different kind of accent to that of Nadia. He spoke to us by referring to himself in the third person.

'Pappy does not like your mother's attitude. She says that Pappy does not care about you. Did you know that Pappy pays her a lot of money every month for your upkeep? Your Pappy is a poor man.'

We did not say anything and as we were far from anxious to hear his side of the arguments between him and Nadia, we let him ramble on until he had got it out of his system and by the time our train had reached The Hague he seemed a little more pleasant. We took a cab to 78 Hugo de Groot Straat and arrived at a house very similar to the one we had in Amsterdam before we came to England. The dark green door opened a few seconds after Jan pressed the doorbell but instead of being greeted by a person we were confronted by a steep narrow staircase that was dimly lit at the top. I noticed that a thin rope, parallel to the rail, lead from the top down to the door latch, which meant that someone had pulled it to let us in. As soon as I realised that, the door at the top opened to reveal a woman standing at the entrance of a well-lit room.

Auntie Hanny, as she was introduced to us, was Jan's landlady, but it was soon clear that she was more than that. She had grey hair done into a loose bun and wore light-coloured glasses that softened the effect of her rather heavy grey eyebrows and grey eyes. She might have created an impression of grey stringency, were it not for the fact that her eyes, as well as her mouth, smiled.

Her large room told the story of her life. Early twentieth-century paintings hung on the cream-coloured walls: some abstract, others with a discernible motif that took the form of a Dutch landscape, a still life or a boldly painted nude. Thick oriental carpets covered both the floor and a large table at the far end of the room, while a large alcove at the street end of the room accommodated a black baby grand. Below the pictures, low bookshelves ran along much of the wall and their tops were decorated with numerous ornaments that included model aeroplanes, small wooden sculptures from the former Dutch East Indies, as well as family photographs. Both Vera and I could sense that this new woman in Jan's life was someone to be respected, a woman with taste and education.

She spoke to us warmly with a kind of English that was hesitant only because she seemed to search for precisely the right words, which when she uttered them, were well pronounced. Yet her aura of culture and warmth had a tone of sadness. It turned out that her husband was a pilot in the Dutch Navy, which explained why most of the model aeroplanes were scaled-down replicas of the sea planes that her husband flew before he was shot down by the Germans early in the war. The photo-portraits of him that stood beside the models showed that he was good looking, the archetypal war hero who died for his country to leave a sad widow.

And this sad widow had now found a lodger in the form of Jan, who was anything but a hero, anything but cultured. And yet it seemed that Jan was more than just a lodger in Hanny's house. Vera and I discussed the possibility that they might get married, but Vera thought that Hanny could easily find a better man. However, their marriage seemed even more plausible after I went to the toilet one night and caught Jan slinking into Hanny's room with his pillow in his hand.

What would Hanny find in him? Was there a serious relationship between them? Vera and I discussed the situation in our room up in this large narrow Dutch town house that Hanny owned. Jan had his own bedroom and was also given a room that he made into a carpenter's shop, neatly arranged to house his tools. That was something he appeared to have in common with Harold, though since we saw only one of his creations, a little stool, it seemed that his main occupation was to keep the room perfectly tidy and dust-free. Otherwise he would cycle home from work, the KLM's insurance offices that lay somewhere on the outskirts of The Hague, pick up the newspaper and read before the evening meal and listen to the news on the radio afterwards. If he spoke to us it was only to gather more information in order to express his bitterness towards Nadia. He seemed to have very little interest in our welfare and did not seem at all impressed by the fact that I had passed my scholarship, probably because it could imply a greater financial burden on him.

For her part, Hanny made us feel welcome. She took us to parks, museums and art galleries. She took us to visit her nephews and nieces, most of whom were about our ages and when we played, we even picked up a little Dutch again. Though most of the people of Holland cycled, a popular alternative for children in towns was a large scooter with thick, soft, white rubber wheels. They could be made to go fast on the pavements and the ride was soft and smooth. Vera, who developed a close relationship with Hanny, told her that she would love to have such a scooter at home and Hanny said that she would mention it to Jan.

Jan took a few days off from work and they took us on the back of their bikes with pillows strapped on the carriers to visit Scheeweningen. Thousands of people milled on the beach and sheltered from the cold winds by sitting in wickerwork seats with high backs while we played in the sand. The North Sea water was too cold for bathing.

Hanny took us to the zoo at Wassenaar, a well-treed suburb of The Hague. Then while Hanny and Vera stayed in town, Jan took me fishing along a stretch of canal that was rented by the KLM angling club. His suggestion to go fishing reminded me of that fantastic visit to the Nederlofs over three years previously and the fact that Jan liked fishing gave me a sense of kinship with the man who, after all, was my biological father. At last, I felt I had something in common with him, something that could be the basis for a better relationship.

When we arrived, after about an hour's cycling, my bottom was sore from the jolting ride along the path to the canal and there was a strong breeze that made the water rough and opaque. Jan untied his rod from the cycle frame and tied a thin line to the tip, for there was no reel like Harold had when he took us fishing. The rest of the tackle, the float, the lead weights and hook were similar except that he used a maggot instead of a worm for bait. He let me hold the rod. We waited for signs of a bite, but for half an hour the float only moved up and down with the waves along the canal without showing any exciting jerks caused by fish.

Finally, Jan said that as it was too windy for fishing, we should give up and head for home and it was going to be hard cycling back into a head wind. I was disappointed and thought he gave up too easily, but I said nothing and watched in silence as he packed the tackle and tied it to the bike.

When we arrived we were both hungry and the smell of cooking dispelled all my thoughts of our fishing failure. As Jan and I ate in ecstasy, revelling in the delight of Hanny's fluffy potatoes and cooked endives, the steamed cod and exquisite white sauce, I noticed that my real father and I could enjoy at least one thing together. Vera had clearly enjoyed her tour of the town with Hanny and while we ate she had much more to say about her day than I had about our fishing trip.

On the next day Jan had arranged a visit to Uncle Wim, who had survived a concentration camp, returned to Holland, got married and become the father of Pieter, a little boy about a year older than Lex. Though I recognised him, I could not decide whether it was thanks to what I remembered of him in Java before camps or whether it was because of photographs that I had seen since. He was darker skinned than Jan, almost as if he were partly Javanese, in contrast to his new wife Hetty who had an almost white complexion. Though they spoke in English to me with the standard questions like, 'How do you like it in England?', they both seemed quite reticent and gentle, which I found appealing.

After meeting Wim and Hetty, Jan took Vera and me on the train eastwards to see Klosters, the house that belonged to the Kruys family, the house where I was born. We passed through the towns of Utrecht, Apeldoorn and Deventer to finally arrive in the village of Diepenveen. As we walked up the pebble drive I noticed that Klosters looked like I imagined it from the photo that Nadia showed me, but because the photo was not coloured, I took it for granted that the walls of the house were grey instead of brick red. The roof and the little tower were, however, slate grey and topped by a wrought iron fence-like decoration to give the house an almost palatial quality. When the owner let us take a brief look inside I was surprised to see a large polar bear skin stretched in front of the fireplace. Jan said that skin once belonged to my grandfather and must have been bought by the new owner along with the house. We didn't spend much time at the house. Though he said very little about his time there, I got the impression that Jan felt sad to see it again. For our part, neither Vera nor I felt any emotional attachment for the place.

My eleventh birthday was spent in Holland. Jan gave me a fine new wristwatch, which I was told to look after because it cost him a lot of money, and Hanny gave me a beautiful yellow propelling pencil made by Kohinoor. Vera bought me a discreet tie-clip, which she chose with Hanny's help while we were on the fishing trip. But the biggest surprise was a present from Uncle Wim and Auntie Hetty, given to me when they came round for coffee. It was a book: Winnie-the-Pooh by A. A. Milne, English, in its original language. Wim explained that it was very good and had become a classic and that I would enjoy reading it.

Though, thanks to Hanny, we were given the opportunity to mix with children, her nephews and nieces, we were obliged to communicate in broken Dutch. This seemed to oppose all my efforts to be British and made me feel that I had no nationality and did not belong to any country. Nevertheless, since the thought of living in Holland and with Jan was absolutely out of the question, I reasoned that whatever my background, my roots had taken hold in England and British I would be. Besides, I was about to start at a really good British school. With that in mind and the knowledge that Jan had great difficulty in showing any interest in us, especially in Vera, we longed to return to Greetwell.

On the voyage home the sea was calm and the morning sun shone through our cabin porthole while I heard a member of the crew singing 'Lavender Blue' as he worked. I read and thoroughly enjoyed Winnie-the-Pooh and hoped that I would see Uncle Wim again sometime.

Harold had neither the time nor money for a proper holiday, but he did take us on day trips after we had returned from Holland. He took us to Thornton Abbey and Lincoln to see the cathedral and castle. He also took us to a weir on the upper reaches of the river Ancholme called Brown's Bridge. We waded out into the muddy water where there were open patches that were not choked by water lilies and splashed at each other in sheer joy. When Michael said that he had succeeded in swimming a couple of strokes of a kind of dog-paddle without his feet touching the bottom, we all had to try, and we all tried to convince each other that we had begun to be swimmers.

Harold then went off to do a spot of fishing while we dried ourselves and gorged ourselves with Nadia's sandwiches to satisfy the kind of hunger that cold muddy water can achieve. He returned for his share of the picnic with an empty line dangling from his rod to tell us that he had lost his tackle on an enormous bream. He actually saw it and said it must have weighed at least five pounds.

That summer, spiced by my new bike, the day outings, the fantastic playground consisting of the old camp and the Common, as well as the better aspects of the trip to Holland, came to an end with preparations for Brigg Grammar School.

Once again the household economy had to be stretched to provide me with the school uniform and other necessary items. The school had sent a carbon copied typed list that demanded the purchase of a pair of sandals as well as the full uniform. As the list also included full football kit, Nadia was also forced to associate the game with grammar school.

When Nadia shopped around in Brigg she came to the conclusion that it was cheaper to buy an ordinary navy blue blazer and school badge separately instead of buying the ready-made school blazer. So she took me to Brigg where she bought me a blazer with so much room for growth that the sleeves came down to cover the palms of my hands. It also sloped slightly at the shoulders. She stitched the school badge that she bought at Elwood's on the breast pocket so neatly that it looked like it really was a part of the blazer and I felt very proud when I put it on. With the new school cap and light and navy blue striped tie, a new pale-coloured leather satchel, also from Elwood's, I regarded the image that presented itself in the mirror: a grammar school boy! Mr Dobbs provided the shirt, underwear and short grey trousers on credit with easy terms, as usual.

The next thing that Nadia considered needed to be renewed was my English. Not only did she want to be sure that my language matched the intellectual standards that she thought were required by the grammar school, but she also wanted to be sure that my English was not tainted by the Lincolnshire dialect.

After seeing an advertisement in the *Lincolnshire Times,* she took both Vera and me on the bus to Brigg to see a lady who taught elocution. I wore my new grammar school blazer, torn between being proud to wear it and aware that I hadn't actually started the school yet. Though I could just about understand the reason for my taking elocution lessons, I found it hard to grasp why Vera should also need to improve her speech, since her speech was both clearer and more effective than mine. She was a natural talker and with a few sharp words she could hold her own against anyone, regardless of age. Nevertheless, as she was as foreign in origin as I was, Harold must have agreed that we both needed elocution lessons.

We alighted from the bus on the market place and walked over the bridge to arrive at a small shop window of what appeared to be a perfume shop. The window displayed fancy shaped bottles containing liquids that might have been coloured water. Pastel-shaded fine fabrics were arranged around the bottles to make them look special. A cream-coloured sign over the window had 'Florence Worthington' written in large black copperplate writing. As it appeared to be a shop we opened the door, without knocking, to cause a bell to jingle. I was struck by the heavy scent of perfume that pervaded a room that looked more like a bedroom without bed. A woman who looked a little older than Nadia met us with a smile.

'Good morning, can I help you?' The smile mode of her eyes was fixed.

'Good morning. I'm Mrs Neale. You must be Mrs Worthington. I telephoned you about elocution lessons for my children.'

'Oh yes!' she said, giving both Vera and me a glance each. 'It's Miss, by the way.'

'Oh, I'm sorry. I didn't realise.'

'That's all right. You see we three sisters who own both this and the wine shop next door, have never had time to get married.' She giggled a little. 'Now, let me see if we can arrange an appointment.'

She went over to a piece of furniture that looked more like a bedroom dressing table, pulled open a drawer and took out a diary.

'When I telephoned I thought that you could start with them today.'

'Oh no, I'm afraid that would be impossible! I have this shop open for customers on a Saturday morning and I really can't give elocution lessons at the same time. This means that I only give lessons on Wednesday afternoons when it's half-day closing. How about half past two this Wednesday?'

'Yes, that would be all right,' said Nadia with a muted tone.

'Good! Now, may I have their names?'

'Ivan and Vera Kruys.'

Here we go again, I thought, and I had to go through the ordeal of first Nadia spelling out our Dutch surname and then explaining that it was Dutch and that we had only lived in England for three years and that we needed to improve our speech. Fortunately, however, my fears were unfounded on that occasion as only the spelling of our surname was necessary.

'Yes, I understand,' said Miss Worthington. 'We can make a start if Ivan and Vera can memorise these simple verses so that we can use them for the first session on Wednesday.'

She handed Nadia a few small typewritten pieces of paper that Nadia put in her handbag.

'See you both on Wednesday at half past two,' she said and we said goodbye while we opened and closed the door to make the bell jingle again.

At home we looked at the typewritten pieces of paper and we read them aloud together.

'Jonathan Joe had a mouth like an 'o'. Oh, no John, no John, no John, no.'

There were other similar verses.

'She sells seashells on the seashore.'

'The rain in Spain falls mainly on the plain.'

Then Vera expressed what I was thinking, her speech centre being sharper than mine:

'This is boring! Do we really have to do this and repeat these stupid verses?'

'Never mind if they are boring,' said Nadia. 'You must practise them to improve your speech.'

I didn't know whether my speech was going to improve, but after a couple of visits to elocution lessons Vera refused point blank to continue and I learnt to pronounce my O's with my lips pouted when I did it in front of Miss Worthington. She must have considered that I was making progress, as the pieces of typed paper were getting larger with short poems instead of lines. Tennyson and Wordsworth came into the repertoire but I felt a bit of a pansy saying 'I wandered lonely as a cloud."

20. A Third-Former

Term was to start on Monday the 11th of September, a week after term started at Scawby. While Vera and the boys were at school, I had to keep myself occupied with Lex and prepare for my new life at the grammar school. As Vera had become tired of being woken up by him, we changed beds so that I had Lex as my new roommate. I invented stories for him and we acted out some of them based on two made-up characters, Mr Brown and Mr Green, who lived in their own houses but went out together on all kinds of adventures. This amused Lex greatly and formed the basis of as close a relationship that can develop between two brothers with nine years' difference in age. Lex was made to feel as mature as a two-year-old could get and I became about six years old. We also listened to the radio and I joined him when it was time for him to Listen with Mother with Nadia after lunch.

The week passed quickly and it wasn't long before I was standing at the crossroads waiting for my first trip to the grammar school as a pupil. Waiting at the bus stop was a boy that I recognised from Scawby School. His name was Henry Shaw and he wore the Brigg Grammar School uniform. He was of the same age group as the Superior Seven but as I knew that he had not passed his scholarship and was not one of them, I wondered how he came to be at the grammar school.

'At Scawby I'd passed the intelligence test but was ill for the scholarship. After my first year at the Scunthorpe Modern they told me I was too good. So they sent me to the grammar school last year an' they put me in the 'B' stream. I came top of the class an' now I think they're putting me in the 'A' stream.'

'So really there were eight of you that passed the scholarship!'

'Yes, yeh could say that, but I'm a year behind at the grammar school.'

'And there's an 'A' stream and a 'B' stream, but they're not in the same class?' I said, trying to work out the system at the school.

'That's right. It's a daft system really. Yeh start at 3. There's no class one and when yeh start it's eether 3A or 3B.'

'And A's where all the clever kids go?' I said, as if to conclude that he was bright.

'Yeh could say that,' he said, looking at the ground.

Just then the sound of a diesel motor and the squealing of brakes made us look up to see a red bus that was more streamlined than the old green bus that took us to Scawby School. At the same time a girl of about fifteen came puffing towards us as the bus squeaked to a halt. She was uniformed in navy blue and wore a small green hat that seemed to be a cross between a beret and a boy's school cap without the peak. I knew that she lived down the road from us and that she was called Margaret and that she had two older brothers that were either in their late teens or early twenties. She puffed out 'hello' to me as she climbed on her bus that drew away before I could reply. At the same time, another bus appeared behind it.

'That's ours,' said Henry

Before the bus throbbed to a standstill, I saw boys that looked almost like men sitting at the back with their school caps perched jauntily towards the backs of their heads. In sharp contrast to the green bus, the ear-splitting noise of unrestricted junior vocal cords was lacking: instead there was the sort of background talking sounds that one might hear on ordinary public transport. As we embarked, the talking ceased momentarily, to resume as we took an empty seat near the front. Younger boys occupied most of the seats near the front.

Henry and I did not exchange many words on the journey to Brigg and we went past our old school while keeping our thoughts to ourselves. I looked out of the windows but saw little, as my mind was almost completely occupied by wondering what was to come. Would I end up in the 'B' stream? How would I know? What were the teachers like? Would each class have its own teacher? I was burning to pose these questions, but knew that I would know in the fullness of time without having to ask anyone.

The bus stopped outside the red-brick building that was vaguely familiar from the time of the interview and I found myself walking up the drive feeling lonely among the mass of boys that came from other buses as well as my own. As I went by the old building, I noticed that one of its bricks had the inscription 'T. Brooks 1820' neatly incised into it. Everyone wore uniform, with only the smallest boys wearing short grey trousers like my own. Everyone wore school caps with a small version of the school badge at the front, each cap perched at varying angles. I followed the crowd of uniformed boys into an open space almost enclosed by school buildings. The area was nearly totally occupied by boys, some standing in groups, some kicking a ball, others laughing and generally mucking around while others stood alone silent in the hubbub of puerile noise and activity.

Henry told me to follow him to the changing rooms where I had to change to the sandals that I had in my satchel and he showed me the third-form area of shoe lockers. He then left me to change while he went to chat with some of his classmates. After leaving the darkness of the cloakroom, I stood to survey the scene with a sense of bewilderment in the quadrangle, until I saw Jim and Bill standing together and leaning against a wall of the school building. They looked as bewildered as I felt, but we managed to exchange hellos and continued to stare out into the crowd.

Suddenly, as if by magic, the noise and activities stopped with shushing sounds and we could see that the cause was the appearance of the large red-faced man in a grey suit who I recognised as the headmaster. Standing about him were several men who wore black gowns over their jackets and who I assumed were the teachers. I remembered seeing teachers portrayed in comics with such black gowns and wondered if they wore mortarboards as well. After absolutely all the noise had died down the headmaster spoke:

'The following boys are in form 3A and are to join Mr Jones.'

Compared to the headmaster Mr Jones was short, very short. He held a sheet of paper up high to be noticed. The list was read in alphabetical order using surnames only but followed by initials when two boys had the same surname. I then knew that I was graded as second rate and to be put in 3B, for my name was not among them, but I noticed that both Jim and Bill were to be in 3A and they walked away to join Mr Jones.

'The following boys are in form 3B and are to join Mr Tabrams,' boomed the large man and my heart pounded in anticipation of my

246

surname. Then I heard him pronounce it 'crews' just as Miss Bowles did.

Mr Tabrams was an elderly man of about sixty who held his hand up casually to collect his form. It seemed that we were divided into 'forms' instead of 'classes'.

'Come on boys,' he said in a fine baritone voice as he led the way into the main building after our list had been read out. Though not as short as Mr Jones, he was not tall, but stocky with a good-sized paunch that could be seen protruding beyond his gown. He walked with a straight back and head held high in military fashion. He led us through the same corridor that I remembered from the day of the interview and showed us into a room that was opposite to the lockers at the base of the large staircase.

He made us take our places at random and I found myself standing behind a worn wooden desk somewhere in the middle of the room, which though it smelt of furniture polish, felt stuffy. Mr Tabrams took a long pole with an attachment at the end to open the top windows on one side of the room.

'There's nothing like fresh air,' he said. 'Welcome to Brigg Grammar School and welcome to form 3B, a fine form in one of the finest schools in Lincolnshire. I'm your form master and my name's Tabrams but you must never address me as Mr Tabrams. Always call me 'sir'. Always call any master at this school 'sir'. I know that most of the masters here have nicknames and you will soon find out, if you don't know already, that the boys usually refer to me as Tabby Tabrams, but remember that you are to call me 'sir' when talking to me. I shall be taking you for art and English.'

His grey eyes shone a little under his bushy eyebrows and his fleshy jowls trembled as he twitched his finely trimmed grey moustache.

'Soon we are to go to assembly and you will need these hymn books, taken from 'Ancient and Modern'.' Two piles of small green books lay on the table in front of him. - 'I'm going to go through the register and the boy whose name I read out will leave his place and collect a hymn book. As these hymn books are irreplaceable you must write your name in yours and look after it until you leave school.'

He went through the register, each boy being called out by his surname and I fetched my new little green book when 'crews' was read out. It had the Celtic cross embossed on its cover and I felt its contours before writing my name on the inside with my fountain pen. While he was going through the register I shot glances at the others in the room and noticed that the boy called Bernard who called my mother 'sir' was also in the same form. He then went through the register to find out which boys were going to have school meals so that he could collect dinner money.

When every boy had collected his hymn book and mentioned his dinner status, Mr Tabrams went on to talk about how privileged we were to be at the school, that we had to work hard and that we must be loyal both to the school and to our houses. He explained that we belonged to a 'house' and he pointed to a row of painted cardboard shields that were hanging high above the long blackboard to show that each house had a coat of arms. I could see the name of each house under the appropriate coat of arms. As the house that we belonged to depended on where we lived, he went through the register again and when he mentioned our names we were to say what our nearest village was. Since mine was Scawby, my house was Nelthorpe, those living in Brigg belonged to Ancholme (after the name of the river), those from Scunthorpe, Sheffield, those living east of Wrawby, Yarborough and those who boarded in the school were simply in School House. Mr Tabrams explained that every house had a house master and that he was Ancholme's and that mine was Mr Lewis and that every house had a motto, Nelthorpe's being 'Fortitudine', strength, the same as the school's.

A bell rang to call the forms to assembly and we found ourselves next to a dais at the front of large form room with a high ceiling. A grand piano was placed beyond the dais and behind it there was a floor-to-ceiling concertina partition made up of wood and frosted glass that when drawn out, would separate the assembly hall into two form rooms. It was the oldest part of the school, the original building that was erected 280 years previously when the school was founded. Somehow those two united form rooms managed to contain the whole school, including the masters all of whom took their places within a few minutes.

A man with silvery white hair sleeked on his head and wearing a gown that had once been black but had faded to a dark greyish green took his place behind the piano. At the same time the impressive form of the headmaster mounted the dais. After welcoming the third-formers to the school and the whole school to a new academic year he asked the school to sing the school song:

'Twas in the days of Charles, The second of the name. In his domain at Scawby, A man of fairer fame. There dwelt the good Sir John. A Nelthorpe true was he. His motto ours shall be: Fortitudine! Unselfish in his riches, And mindful of God's poor, Our founder gave broad acres To open up the door...'

The school song continued while I surveyed the assembly hall and its crowded occupants and felt very small and insignificant. The headmaster boomed out a prayer and we sang a hymn that made our singing efforts at Scawby sound like a whimper by comparison.

As the school emptied itself out of the assembly hall the master at the piano stood up and said in a voice that sounded like rubbing two matchboxes together:

'I want you, you, you, you', he said, pointing to me and continuing to point at various others in the third forms, 'to come to this room at break.'

Another schoolmaster with a blacker gown over his light grey suit was standing by the piano. He had light wavy hair and was grinning to such an extent that his eyes were nearly slits.

When we entered our form room, which happened to be adjacent, Mr Tabrams was already standing behind his table waiting for us to take our places. Several piles of new exercise books reminded me that we were about to start the serious business of being educated.

'I'm going to give you an English grammar and essay exercise book each,' said Mr Tabrams. 'Keep your books clean and avoid dog-ears! You can write your names and titles neatly on the front. Now you shall also have a general book each for rough notes and the like. You can call them rough books or general books, it doesn't matter but look after them!'

He then went round to hand us thicker exercise books with light blue papery covers. After that he proceeded to write our timetable on the blackboard. He wrote the names of the subjects in large copperplate writing.

'Copy this in your general books,' he said. 'I would like you to be able to write like this and not scratch about with your pens and write like a fly that had escaped from an inkwell.' I noticed that the timetable confirmed what Henry told me on the bus: that we had Wednesday afternoons off and came to school on Saturday mornings.

'For your homework you are to write an essay about what you would like to be. Your essay can be about a job but it can also be about anything else: if you would like to be a cat then describe what it is you like about the cat and why you would like to be a cat. If, on the other hand, you would like to be someone famous like Napoleon or Jesus Christ, your essay has to tell the reader why. Now this is how an essay should be written.'

'Please, sir,' said a boy with his hand up.

'Yes, Sutton, isn't it?'

'Yes, sir. When do we hand our essays in?'

'Next week. That's the usual. Most masters give you a week for prep.'

It was not only the first time I had homework but also the first time I heard it being referred to as 'prep'.

He went on to tell us about writing an essay, about introductions, motivations and endings, while I only half listened and thought that it would be nice to write about being a bird.

The English lesson came to an end with the sound of the bell ringing. I soon learnt that the bell marked the beginning and end of nearly every happening in the school. On the timetable it said 'maths' for the next lesson.

Each subject had its own coloured exercise book and what was called 'sums' by us and arithmetic by Miss Bowles had become arithmetic, geometry and algebra with Mr Cheeseworth our new mathematics master. As it was also his first year at the school, Mr Cheeseworth said that he felt a special bond with us and admitted to us, almost in confidence, that he was straight from Oxford and was only twenty-three years old. He went quickly through some long divisions and multiplications to put us all on a common level, presumably before going on to new areas to feed into our partially receptive brains.

When the break bell rang I felt a lump in my throat at the thought of having to report to the two masters by the piano. Another boy from my form joined me in our fight to get to the right door in the dark corridor filled with boys rushing towards the exit. I opened the door with hesitation, wondering whether I ought to knock.

'Come in, come in,' said the same grating voice as the one that called us at assembly.

'Now then,' rasped the silver-haired master as he went back to the piano, 'What's your name, Willie?'

'Prescott, sir,' said the boy whom he addressed.

'Right, Willie. Sing this verse.'

Prescott sang the first verse of a hymn after being told the hymn number and given a start on the piano. He sang in tune and quite well, I thought.

'That will do, Willie.'

'Prescott has a very pleasant voice,' said the wavy-haired master, his eyes disappearing completely as his smile broadened.

'You're in the school choir,' rasped the silver-haired master.'

'When you go to assembly tomorrow, you stand with the choir over there,' he said, pointing to a space next to the door and opposite the dais.

When it came to my turn I felt nervous but by that time more prepared and sang the verse as close to the tune as I could.

'That's nice,' said the smiling master, 'You're in the school choir.'

In this way I too became a member of the school choir, though not all the boys told to stay behind were selected. I was surprised that Bill Harley wasn't even asked to have an audition even though he was regarded as the best singer at Scawby. On my way out to join the rest of the school at break I also wondered how boys to be auditioned were selected. If Bill Harley was anyone to go by, it clearly wasn't because of a boy's reputation as a singer: it was probably just random selection, or did the masters observe how people sung during assembly?

By the time I had followed the dark corridor, then empty, out to the open space known as 'the quad' I noticed that there was a crate that still had some full bottles of milk and that nearby an older boy was standing by a large tray on a trestle. With a mixture of reticence and curiosity, I approached him to see why he was standing there. As the tray was at about the level of my chest I had to go quite near in order to see what was in it. Currant buns! The sight of a few currant buns lying on the tray made me feel quite hungry, and despite my shyness, could not resist the temptation to ask if I could have one.

'They cost a ha'penny each,' boomed the boy in his man's voice.

I handed him a halfpenny from my pocket money and took a brown bun and sunk my teeth into its cinnamon-flavoured softness, a little moist and still warm. I then washed the bun down with cold milk sucked up through a straw, just like at Scawby.

Just as I had finished, the bell also sounded the end of break-time. I found myself being swept along back into the corridor by the crowd of boys while we were inspected by a senior boy to make sure that we were wearing sandals and not black-soled outdoor shoes that might mark the corridor floors. I hadn't even had time to change into my outdoor shoes.

Somehow knowledge about the workings of the school, its routines and quirks, seemed to be acquired almost subconsciously, without question, a bit like a Kipling Just So story. Someone seemed to know that we had to change our sandals back to shoes in order to have lunch at the refectory across the playing fields and someone seemed to know the way to the refectory. And those of us who didn't know at first just followed the drift and became part of the school machinery. It seemed that as the 'B' forms were to have dinner in the first session, we were to make our way without delay.

Like the canteen at Scawby, the refectory building did not look as though it had been purpose-built. It looked as if it had been built sometime during the latter half of the nineteenth century, possibly as a dwelling house, that of the headmaster or of some teacher or someone else who had something to do with the school. A ragged queue of younger boys had already formed and as we joined it, the refectory door opened to exchange the familiar smells of canteen food for the entrance of hungry pupils. A young man in a light grey suit walked passed us to stop and reprimand a boy in front of me for not changing his sandals. He seemed to be too young to be a school master and too old to be a schoolboy and he wore a tie that was like the one that I wore but with additional red stripes.

'That's a prefect!' said a boy behind me in an urgent whisper.

'Prefect' sounded to me almost like 'perfect', which was what one presumably became at the end of one's time in grammar school. He certainly seemed a good deal superior to the ordinary boys and his status seemed to be that of an adult, since he was able to jump the queue to have his dinner.

Once inside, we collected our cutlery, and served through a hatch were plates already filled with food. Though the prefects had their own table the rest of us could sit where we liked, which meant in practice that we sat in our own peer groups. The meals resembled those at Scawby, the vegetables being overcooked and thick brown gravy poured over the meat and potatoes and dessert was the familiar combination of a pudding and custard. As we ate we began to get to know each other the way boys do, by telling jokes, talking about the teachers and trying to be tough by minimising the importance of the lessons.

It was also a time when knowledge about the school was pooled and this resulted in my learning that lessons were called 'periods', that the silver-haired teacher was called Willie Black because, as I had already noticed, he called everyone 'Willie'. The other teacher was called Teddy Davies because his initials were T for Thomas, E for Elwyn and D for his surname. I also found out that the next year's forms were Lower Fourth, followed by Upper Fourth, then Lower Fifth, Upper Fifth, Lower Sixth and finally Upper Sixth. The latter was the form of the prefects and the boys that sold buns at morning break were from the Lower Sixth, as were those that checked footwear after breaks and dinner. It seemed that the sixth formers had the power to inflict punishment on unruly boys, usually in the form of what were called 'lines', the exact meaning of which was still a mystery to me.

On leaving the refectory I saw Jim standing in a queue of 'A'-formers that had already begun to line up outside the door. All the third-formers looked new in their uniforms, except Jim whose blazer seemed worn despite the new school badge, and his cap had a duller appearance than those of the other boys. We exchanged our experiences of the morning. He told me that form 3A, his form, was in a wooden hut, which sounded very primitive for a grammar school. He laughed when I told him that I was chosen to be in the choir, since he had no interest whatsoever in music and I knew that he was a groaner if he tried to sing.

In an effort to try to reduce my sense of bewilderment and come to terms with my new environment, I spent the rest of the dinner break exploring the layout of the school.

Facing the playing field was a large late-Victorian brick building that was the boarding house. A row of beech trees lined one side of the playing field to give way to a row of large wooden huts that housed what appeared to be more form rooms. I imagined that Jim's form was one of those. The main school building bound the quad on two sides. The cloakrooms bound the third side and then a long cycle shed that gave way to a toilet block that had a row of sophisticated urinals, of the public convenience type, at each end. It was much more sophisticated than the smelly trough at Scawby. I heard titters coming from one of the closed toilet doors and thought I could smell cigarette smoke as I walked by. I went from the toilet block to the cloakroom to change back to my sandals in readiness for the bell to beckon us back to class. When it started ringing I was one of the first to enter the school while it was still being rung, which allowed me to see both where it was located and that it was operated by a sixth former who made it ring by pulling a rope.

My first day at school seemed to be both my longest and shortest day at the same time, with new impressions, new masters, new subjects and information coming in all the time, and I went to catch the school bus home with this newness buzzing in my head. As we waited outside the school I saw Henry who told me that he was moved up into the 'A' stream, which put him in Lower 4A. And that meant, he told me, he was to have Latin, which only A-formers could take.

Nadia was as keen as mustard to hear about my first day at Brigg Grammar School and I told her as much as I could about all that I had gathered about the school, including my meeting Henry and that only A-formers could take Latin. Nadia said that though it was quite all right starting in the 'B' stream, she felt that it would be good if I could manage to get into the 'A' stream to take Latin.

When I told Nadia what I intended my English essay to be about, she became quite emotional, almost angry.

'Don't you understand that by being given such a subject to write about, your English master doesn't only want to improve your English, he also wants to see to it that you have the right attitude to life, the right ambitions, the will to improve yourself. If you write that you would like to be a blue tit, what sort of a person is he going to think you are?'

'I don't know. I like the look of them and I thought I might describe what it might be like to fly and to nest in a hole in a tree.'

'You eediot! Why don't you write about being Winston Churchill, one of the greatest men of our time? Or even Shakespeare? Or why not a famous painter like Rembrandt, but a blue tit?

I felt quite empty. I supposed my mother was right and that being good at school was mostly about doing your best in the boring subjects.

'All right, I'll write about Winston Churchill, but you must tell me more about him.'

And Nadia proceeded to tell me that despite the fact that he was a poor pupil at school he learnt about leadership during the Boer War. He then became a politician and was finally asked to lead Britain to victory during the Second World War and that it was a pity that he was not leading Britain instead of Mr Attlee.

I plodded out an essay on Mr Churchill that took up almost a page of my scrawly writing and explained in a few short sentences why I would like to be like him. The marks that I got a week later were in keeping with the enthusiasm I had for the essay.

But Nadia was very keen to help me to do my prep in the best possible way. When Tabby gave us a book about Robin Hood our task was to answer questions at the end of each chapter and she would test me on vocabulary which we had to learn by heart, with words like 'prelate' and 'wench'. I couldn't understand why one had to learn words that clearly no one used but tried to learn them on the assumption that it was all part of the privilege of going to grammar school. I was left to do other subjects on my own, however, Nadia's only concern being that I had completed my prep.

But as the first weeks went by I felt myself getting out of my depth. Much of the language used in various subjects was more advanced than I could cope with. In chemistry and physics it took some time for me to understand what the headings 'Object of the Experiment', 'Method', 'Observations', as well as 'Conclusion' meant and in my ignorance I misspelled them when we had to write up the experiments neatly after jotting them down in our rough books. What made the matter worse was that my handwriting was terrible. I just wasn't able to write neatly and my spelling was atrocious. Obviously these defects didn't help to produce neat and legible presentations of history and geography and I was worse than mediocre in mathematics. Gymnastics wasn't that bad: we just aped the movements that Mr Jones carried out.

Together with form 3A we changed for games into our football gear one day after lunch and because I had never played a game of football in my life, I was told to join a group of boys that had a similar status. This meant either being a linesman or just watching those who were deemed good enough to play. Our useless group, which also included Jim, was referred to as the 'scrags' but as we were officially regarded as reserves we always had to turn up changed ready in our kit.

Very soon my hopes of becoming a capable pupil at a grammar school had started to crumble. My preps were often returned with marks as low as three or four out of ten and the odd occasions when I managed a five or six were very much an exception.

Being in the choir, which stood in front of the prefects, helped me to feel a little special but the only subject I felt good at was art. Tabby often gave me an eight or nine and he would often put up one of my efforts on the form room wall. But my success in art was not enough to boost my morale and my confidence in coping with the other subjects reached low ebb. I decided that rather than do prep and get low marks, I might just as well go out and play at home and simply do the minimum necessary to show that I had made some attempt when the prep was too difficult. And when Nadia asked me why I had so little homework I simply lied that I had already done it at school.

During the whole of October, music periods were taken up by rehearsing parts of Handel's 'Messiah' and Willie Black made sure that we could sing the treble part of 'Their sound is gone out into all lands'. We then rehearsed with the Lower Fourth who sung alto and finally with the rest of the voices in the school. The rehearsals were often carried out at the expense of certain periods, which also meant that there was a little less prep.

The actual concert was open to parents and was held at The Grand cinema on the Friday before half term. Even to me, one of those who took part, the singing was so impressive, so professional, that once again I was proud to be at the school. Nadia, who came in a new hat that she made using a pair of pheasant feathers as decoration, was so proud that the choir music brought tears to her eyes. The concert also included a piece played by the school orchestra and there was prize-giving to those who had come top of the form and to those who had won scholarships to universities. Henry came onto the stage to receive a book token for coming top of 3B the previous year. The whole afternoon had the effect of dragging me out of the feeling of hopelessness and made me feel that I must try to do better in the future, for I knew that I was among the worst in the form.

But the new injection of pride in my new school and its status was short-lived. With the reality of my situation at school my desire to do better withered like a weed in winter. As it was such a change in standard compared with primary school I could not suddenly produce the required standard in the key subjects. My prep was still well below standard and as often as not incomplete. Furthermore, if the subject was either uninteresting or difficult I would daydream my time away during school periods. Mr Lewis, my housemaster even came to Redgates to discuss my obvious difficulties at school with Nadia, but to no avail. It was Mr Lewis who led my interview in the masters' room and he must have been instrumental in persuading the headmaster to accept me. When the headmaster read out our positions in form, his close-set eyes peered at me over his glasses and he said:

'You'll have to pull your socks up, Kruys!'

I found myself bottom of the class, of the whole school.

21. Latin

I was a disappointment to myself, my mother and Mr Lewis and my morale was where my name was: at rock bottom. I might have felt some boost in my personal esteem when I was chosen to sing the Page part in 'Good King Wenceslas' with Mr Cheeseworth singing the king, were it not that my voice was almost completely stifled by an intense stuffy cold. Once again I not only showed how incompetent I was, but in front of the whole school and a lot of parents.

Though the Christmas holidays allowed me to get away from the realities of school and my inadequacies, I was not happy to return in January, back to the drudgery, back to being the bottom of 3B, the lowest of the low.

How was I going to improve? Nadia perked up the start of the year a little by buying us a new boys' magazine called 'Eagle' and we were given the first issue to read and see what we thought of it. We all, including Vera, liked it for being exciting, informative and amusing all in one with Dan Dare and his adventures in space as far in the future as the 1990s, when we would be old, to stimulate our fancies. Dandy and Beano paled in comparison. Would there really be spaceships then? Would cars be jet-propelled and one-wheeled? Would green aliens like the Mekon invade us? We wanted Nadia to subscribe to Eagle and of course we wanted to be members of the Eagle club and wear the discreet gold Eagle badges. The Eagle was like a ray of sunshine in the dark sky of school.

I did not relish the thought of telling Henry at the bus stop that I was bottom of 3B.

'You'll be all right once you settle in,' he said to me.

It was Tabby Tabrams who saved me, unawares. Instead of painting the usual watercolour based on some topic, he decided to show us how we could print neatly with rounded letters that could be described as being calligraphic if one used a suitable pen. It looked quite pleasing when I tried it and I became so impressed by my own efforts that transformed my writing from an illegible scrawl

258

Latin

to neat printing. I used the same style in the periods that followed.

The first period was history when Mr Thorpe made us copy his text and drawing of a Saxon item from the blackboard. The effect pleased me and the new style made me both aware of the appearance of the words, their spelling and meaning. I used the new approach in all subjects and the effect was nearly too good to be true. The marks I received went up to seven or more and this was the case in all subjects, except mathematics and English essay, but even then I improved because of both better morale and a better concentration in what I was doing. I was beginning to enjoy school and felt more at ease both during periods and with the others in my form.

The change to my newly acquired brightness happened at the same time as, and was rather similar to, that of the gloom of winter giving way to the spring of 1950. Even our physical activities changed character so that one frosty morning in February Mr Jones took us for a run up to Wrawby and back instead of the usual PT sessions. He told us that we were to train for the big cross-country run at the end of term. It felt good to jog down the drive, down past The Grand, the police station and the Girls' High School out into the country where the frost, untouched by pedestrians, glistened on the pavement. But by then I no longer chatted with my neighbour. I began to find it hard to keep up and every cloud of steaming breath felt as if it were the product of a greater effort than the breathing of the rest of the boys, who began to draw away ahead of me. Only Chatty Brown, a large, unathletic type and Butch Nelson were behind me. Even Tarzan Wilson, the smallest and weediest boy in the form could keep up with the mainstream and I realised that cross-country running was not for me. Nadia said that perhaps my three years in concentration camp might have contributed to my poor stamina.

But unless we had a doctor's certificate we were forced to run, at first during PT periods and then during games when I joined Jim with the stragglers. We paused to look for frogspawn at the quarry pool in Wrawby and continued to jog slowly before the games master came back to look for us. We were useless at games, among the scrags at football and the stragglers in cross-country, and by the time we arrived back at school we hadn't much time to change before the

259

school bus home was due to leave.

Earlier in the term all the third-formers were given running numbers that were more or less alphabetical in order. We were told what size they were to be and their colour depended on what house we belonged to. Fortunately for me, third-formers were not compelled to run cross-country and with that information I was relieved to look forward to being a spectator on the day.

The end of the spring term came with the reading of our term positions. Though I knew I had improved I felt even tenser as the headmaster started to read out the names. The top boy was the same, a quiet bespectacled boy with fair hair called Paul North who did well in most things, including football. As I thought about him I heard my name being read out as fifth and that came as so much of a shock that he had gone through the whole list before I realised that the headmaster was addressing me to say that I had done much better.

That was what I needed - encouragement. Prep felt easier, I became less of a daydreamer in form and at the start of the summer term even games was more fun, especially as we were doing athletics. I was in both the 100- and 220-yard semi-finals, but not good enough to reach the finals on sports day. After sports day, however, we had cricket and once again I joined the familiar non-sporty boys idling about in the scrags.

Nevertheless, my undeveloped ball sense did not discourage me in other aspects of school life and I continued to put academic work to the fore.

Instead of PT we had swimming. The pool was a rectangle of pale milky blue water measuring fifteen yards by five with a depth that ranged from three feet to six. As only a few boys, mainly those from Scunthorpe and Brigg, could really swim they were allowed to use the deep end as they wished. Despite my experience at Brown's Bridge the previous summer I was still a non-swimmer and was made to jump in the shallow end with the majority of my form. At fifty degrees Fahrenheit the water felt so cold that it was hard to move at all, but we were made to lunge for the opposite side and grab the iron rail that skirted the whole pool. The cold made my body feel so stiff that it could only sink and the last thing it could do was float to the other side.

But in July, towards the end of the term, the temperature of the water crept to over sixty. This made it easier to relax in the water and I finally did manage to float across the pool and do a few strokes, first of dog-paddle, then a form of primitive crawl. And the next step was to do that from the deep end to the shallow and finally to achieve a length and this I did one Wednesday afternoon when Mr Lewis gathered the Nelthorpe house beginners for that purpose.

My achievement in swimming was matched by coming third at the end of term and when I told Nadia the news she said that it was clear that I must go up to the 'A' stream. To this end, she wrote the head-master a letter requesting that as she considered Latin to be important for my education she would be grateful if he would put me into the 'A' stream after the summer holidays. I delivered that letter to the secretary to hand to him and Nadia received a reply a few days after the end of term saying that he would do as she requested but it was against his better judgement. He explained that only the top boys are moved up, but as it was the first time in his experience for anyone to request a transfer in order to take Latin, he would grant the transfer.

The summer of 1950 was rather cold and wet. As the tap water at Greetwell was nearly like liquid chalk, clogging up the pipes and gobbling up the soap, Harold had rigged up a large corrugated iron tank to gather the rain water from the roof so that Nadia could wash her hair in the copious soft rainwater provided by the wet summer.

That summer the squatters left the camp to move to council houses in Scunthorpe and their huts were demolished and the whole camp cleared to leave only the concrete foundations as remnants to show that there was once a prisoner of war camp there at all.

There was a change of neighbours. The Hudsons moved to be replaced by the Lawsons, a couple with a son of Michael's age called Terry who had a young brother about a couple of years older than Lex.

Terry came over to us to play and he showed us a game called 'tintinalorum' when one person stood by an old tin can while the others went to hide. After counting to 100 he would shout, 'ready!' and look for the others. His job was to find the hiders, if possible without the hiders knowing that he had found them. He would then rush back to the tin and kick it while shouting 'tintinalorum Philip!', if it were Philip he found and Philip would then join him to look for the others. If, however, Philip kicked the tin before him, he was allowed to hide again and try to be the last to be kicked out and win the game. It was the best outdoor game we played and we had Terry to thank for it.

Terry's father, who worked at the steelworks, was a keen swimmer and took us all in his black Wolseley car with leather seats, to the Scunthorpe baths. Though smelling heavily of chlorine, the water was warm and clear instead of cold and cloudy like at the grammar school. We admired Terry's stylish crawl and Mr Lawson's ability to swim two lengths under the clear chlorinated water without coming up for breath. Even Terry's little brother could swim. As beginners we could only improve.

Then we joined forces to take a trip to Brown's Bridge to churn the muddy water by actually swimming but we did not dare to dive into the deep water behind the lock gates like Terry and his father.

'See, I told yeh you'd be all right,' said Henry in a breaking voice, after I told him that I was to start in Lower 4A. The school bus arrived with a few brand new uniformed smaller boys at the front. Henry and I sat a few rows behind and we talked about the holidays, the masters and what might be in store for the next term. He told me that he was fifth in his form, which made me wonder whether the jump to A stream would be so great.

When we waited in the quad for our names to be read out I was relieved to hear that mine was actually on the Lower Four A list together with Paul North who went up to the 'A' stream with me. Our form room was next to the music room and our form master was Teddy Davies, who taught music, English and Latin. He smiled amiably as he talked, his wavy fair hair combed as immaculately as the pronunciation of his words, telling us that we were privileged to be able to learn Latin.

Latin came to us in the form of a worn textbook called 'Latin for Today', but whose title had been altered on the cover by nibs of the past to 'Eatin' for Today'. Underneath the title it said 'First Course', which made the schoolboy alteration even more suitable. The first sentence of the textbook was designed to lure the student into

believing that Latin was both easy and interesting: 'Discipuli
picturam spectate'. In fact, at first the language proved to be so easy
that at the first end of term test everyone had over 98 per cent and
I was disappointed to get only 99.

I continued to attend elocution classes, perhaps a little more spo-
radically. Miss Worthington had so many pupils that she decided to
put up a show that would be held at the Corn Exchange. Though she
gave me a small role in a one-act play I had to attend rehearsals the
whole time, which occupied most Wednesday afternoons in the
autumn term. There were two girls of my age in the play, one was
the coal merchant's daughter, while the other was the daughter of
one of the local butchers. I was far too shy to talk to them and they
seemed to be aware of my shyness. While we were waiting behind the
scenes for our cues, they stood and giggled while they pointed at
their budding breasts under their short-sleeved vests at the same
time as they stared mockingly at me. I felt myself blush, not knowing
whether I should continue to look at them. One of them had already
quite well developed breasts that stuck out like two light bulbs underneath her vest, despite the fact that she was only twelve and while I
stared up at the ceiling, I wondered what they really looked like.

The play itself seemed to go on without a hitch and Nadia was
there to watch it and realised that she would only waste money and
my time if she continued to send me elocution lessons. She also knew
that my pronunciation and diction would not get any better at that
stage.

I seemed to settle down into my new form without feeling the need
for the extra exertions that I feared were necessary to keep up in an
'A' stream. I was once again in the same form as Jim, my old friend
from Scawby, which meant that my new form was not entirely
strange. On the other hand, Bill, who seemed to be like a fish out of
water at the grammar school, did so badly that he was relegated to
the 'B' stream. He was silent and withdrawn and did not seem to
have any friends and it wasn't long before he left to attend a
secondary modern in Scunthorpe where his education would suffice
for him to take up a trade.

My own progress at the end of the first term in the 'A' stream was
not as good as I had hoped. As he read out the end of term positions,

I heard that I was twenty third and the headmaster looked sternly over the top of his glasses, his close-set eyes piercing me with a look of triumph.

'You'll have to do better than that, Kruys!'

He must have implied that my position was well below the level that warranted a move up to the 'A' stream and I knew that I had to show him that I was worth both the move and Nadia's efforts to initiate it.

Meanwhile, at Scawby School, Michael, Philip and Vera were all in Miss Bowles' class and said how they enjoyed listening to her reading The Little Grey Men. Michael had taken his intelligence test and was preparing for his scholarship, which he found rather daunting.

We continued to enjoy the Eagle paper, which was such a success that the publishers produced a girl's equivalent, known simply as 'Girl'. Though Nadia subscribed to it on Vera's behalf we all read it nearly as eagerly as we read the Eagle. We had also discovered that Woolworth's were selling a new type of pen that did not need fluid ink. It was a ballpoint pen known as a Biro. However, though ballpoint pens were cheap, we were not allowed to use them at school, except in our rough books.

At Christmas, three-year-old Lex was the only one who believed in Father Christmas but for his sake we all had to go through the motions of shouting up the chimney and hanging up our stockings. Following our example he stuck his head so far into the open Rayburn that we were worried that his long dark blond locks would catch fire and Nadia had to shout, 'Not so far in, Lex, Father Christmas can easily hear you!'

Nadia even had a very large woollen stocking for me to tell Lex that I had borrowed it so that I would get more presents. This made Lex also want a giant stocking but Nadia told him that as Father Christmas does not reward greedy boys, he would be wiser to use his own small stockings. The result was, of course, that I was to show Lex that all I got in my large stocking was an orange, while he had both his stockings bursting with toys and sweets.

We had one of the geese for a somewhat greasy, but very tasty Christmas dinner. Afterwards, as we listened to the King giving his Christmas speech on the radio, we all noticed that apart from his speech impediment, he sounded as if he were ill. His breath wheezed as he talked, which made it sound that every word was an effort.

The Lawsons had acquired a new wonder known as a television. We were invited over to them on Saturday afternoons to watch a new series called 'Black Ace', a kind of cops and robbers biplane series of episodes with a Biggles-type hero. The apparatus was housed in a fine veneered cabinet and had a small light grey screen. We watched in fascination as it warmed up to produce black and white linear patterns, followed by frames of pictures that rolled up or down out of the screen to finally stabilise into a blurred image that was much inferior to what we saw at The Grand. But we were enthralled both by the series and by the thought of having a kind of cinema at home, while we knew that a television of our own was out of the question. Television at the Lawsons' on Saturday afternoons became a regular event, sometimes in the evenings as well when they invited all the Neale family to see some variety show.

After the start of the spring term I joined the grammar school troop of boy scouts and was recruited as a tenderfoot in the Peewit Patrol that was rivalled by the Seagulls, Owls and Curlews. I was inspired to join by an active member in our form by the name of Tom Derringer after he told me what fun they had at summer camp and all the other activities. I persuaded Nadia to dig into the household purse to cover the cost of a uniform. Though I enjoyed the indoor games, the patrol rivalries, learning the different knots, I was less enthusiastic about inspections and standing to attention; perhaps I had subconscious associations with my past. Furthermore, after the novelty wore off it was not so much fun staying on at school to do my homework and eat sandwiches before the start of the scout evening and to have to catch an evening bus home.

While my position stabilised at the grammar school it was Michael's turn to go through the process that decided his future, the goal being to join me at the school and I looked forward to showing him the ropes and for his company on the bus. However, he seemed to struggle at least as much as I had and when we realised he wasn't called for an interview we were all sad with the knowledge that he didn't pass his scholarship. We knew that he wasn't brilliant, but we also knew that he had the potential to make something of himself.

The thought struck me that if he were given the mitigating circumstances that I had, perhaps he would have got through. But he had the comfort of knowing that he would have a second chance at thirteen and there were a few at the school, who like Henry, started after the age of eleven. On the other hand there were so many at the grammar school who wasted their potential by leaving at fifteen to become labourers or apprentices in some trade whose requirements were nothing more than an ordinary secondary school education. What use had they of Latin or algebra or physics? Why couldn't Michael have been given their chance? These points were all raised when we discussed Michael's situation after school.

Cross-country day was on Saturday morning. I was all in white, except for my number 162 that Nadia had stitched in large neat blue numbers across my running vest and I stood in a long line of juniors that stretched across the playing field. Though I felt the tension of the start of the race I had no illusions of gaining any points for Nelthorpe House by running within the standard time of twenty-nine minutes. My aim was to get round the course without accident and if I could do so by running without pause then so much the better.

An elderly master with a shock of wiry grey hair fired the starting pistol and I found myself running with the crowd of 120 white-clad Third- and Lower Fourth-formers faster than I intended. After about half a mile my lungs burned and I slowed down as the mass continued past me out into the countryside. As I jogged, I tried to see to it that I was not the last. However, when after about two miles I came to Brickyard Lane strewn with water-filled holes and ridges of mud, my running style automatically changed to a series of hops and side-steps to avoid the puddles and mud, while others splashed through regardless. I didn't know why I did that. Perhaps I was afraid of falling face down into a puddle or perhaps it was just a dislike of getting dirty, but I kept on hopping and avoiding the dirt until I reached the gravel road that led to town and school. The very thought that I was approaching the school seemed to spur me on and as I entered the drive I saw Nadia waving among the spectators and I ran on to pass a tall heavily built boy from my form to come in as ninety-ninth.

Nadia told me afterwards that she felt increasingly more anxious as she saw mud-splattered boys passing by with no sign of me until at last in the distance she could make out a clean white runner approaching that she knew could only have been her son. She said that I stood out as the only boy to arrive totally unsplashed by mud and she said that if I hadn't bothered about getting dirty I might have done better. She had, after all, a washing machine that took the drudgery out of washing clothes, she said. I doubted whether it would have made much difference.

Instead I looked forward to athletics after Easter. Being one of the youngest in my year I, together with half a dozen others whose birthdays were after 1st of June, were told to join the third form when they had athletics. We were not sorry to miss Teddy's Latin: we could always catch up. We joined a queue of white-clad third-formers that fluttered about like handkerchiefs on a clothesline.

The tallest in my form, indeed of anyone under fifteen in the school, was a boy in my form called John Timson. Nobody called him either John or Timson: he was simply known as Lanky Timson because he was, at not yet thirteen, nearly six foot tall. When queuing for dinner he would often have to put up with jokes like, 'What's it like oop there, Lanky? Is it cowd?' Though he was very tall, he wasn't thin and had to carry a fairly heavily built body that could sprint, long and triple jump better than anyone else. But his large body couldn't cope with long distance running: he was the one that came hundreth behind me in the cross-country race. Lanky was good at nearly everything, but he didn't boast and was quietly spoken, neat in appearance, intelligent and as mature as his height would suggest. In fact it was hard to believe that he was only a few weeks older than I was.

When it came to his turn Lanky thundered down the track like a cross between a greyhound and a bull. He hit the board with a thud and whizzed over the sandpit easily a yard further than anyone else did, to break the junior record for long jump. I wondered what it must feel like to be top at everything, to write as neatly as he did, to have a rough book without making it dog-eared, to be respected not only because you were large. Still, in the midst of these thoughts it came to my turn. I knew that the idea was to run as fast as possible and to hit the board without overstepping it and I ran with those two factors in my mind, perhaps also slightly aware that we second-years had to show those first-formers a thing or two.

I hit the board and sailed over the sand faster and easier than I could ever have imagined and much better than a year previously when athletics was new to me. I heard several gasps of amazement when I landed and then I was confounded to find that not only had I jumped further than the standard of ten feet, but had actually landed a foot or so behind Lanky at over thirteen feet, and in doing so, was second. That meant points for my house, as well as being selected to represent the school during the inter-schools championships. The triple jump, or hop, step and jump as it was known, was less successful owing to a series of no-jumps. Needless to say, Lanky excelled in that as well as in the sprints.

I represented Brigg Grammar School juniors as a long jump reserve, while Lanky actually ran and jumped for the school to win and give the school many points. Nevertheless my passive role gave me a certain amount of pride and contributed to that important need for me to belong. It was also an antidote to the humiliation of being a scrag in the ball sports.

The only merit that my swimming had was that it was better than those who still couldn't swim. There was one boy, Ted Rendle, known in the form as Rinso Rendle, who learnt to swim early in his life as a treatment for polio. His walk had a slight drag to it, but he swam like a fish and won all the junior races. When Jim entered the backstroke on the day of the school swimming gala, the spectators gave out a series of titters and whispers and I wondered what the joke was until I heard someone saying,

'Look at him! He's wearing his sister's knickers for swimming trunks!'

Poor old Jim always seemed to look tatty, but his mother making him wear his older sister's knickers instead of swimming trunks was the last straw. His father worked at the sugar factory, which meant that his family income must have been at least as much as ours and they must have been able to afford reasonable clothing. However, on the next swimming lesson he wore new navy blue trunks.

Academically I began to justify my move up into the 'A' stream, having reached thirteenth position at the end of the spring term and eighth by the end of the school year, with no comments from the headmaster on either occasion.

22. Half an Acre of Nettles

Harold's building business was not going well. As his standards were high he and his men took too much time to carry out the different stages of a building job, which in affecting both the contract and the cost of labour, cut down drastically on the profits. Furthermore, the daily need to commute from Redgates to at least as far as Scunthorpe or Brigg, both for visiting sites and builders' merchants, did not make life easier. It was also clear that eventually we were all going to attend secondary schools in Brigg. So when a Victorian red-brick house came up for auction in Brigg our parents snapped at the chance.

We knew nothing about it until it was a fait accompli. That early summer of 1951 Nadia beamed with the news that we were going to move to Brigg to an old but larger house with a large garden. As the house had been empty for some time and was in need of renovation, there was very little bidding at the auction and they got it at the knockdown price of £1,600. They were quite confident that Redgates would fetch at least that price. By coincidence the house was previously owned by the Worthington sisters.

That Sunday we piled into MV1366 to drive to Brigg and inspect our future home. Between the two bridges we turned down a small street that was lined by old Victorian terraced houses on one side and wooden fencing on the other. We came to a halt where the little street ended to be confronted by a pair of high closed wooden gates that were spiked at the top and that were flaking with old bluish paint. The gates were supported by pillars, each capped by a pitched stone with 'WESTFIELD HOUSE' carved into the one on the right. Harold opened the gates with a grating sound while we held our breath with anticipation. Both the gates and a high brick wall enclosed a small yard in front of the buildings, which made the whole property seem private and secluded, as if it were well away from its nineteenth-century terraced-house neighbours.

The house was more like a Victorian relic than a future home, the dim lighting in the hall revealing a floor with coloured patterned tiles. A large round-topped window that was decorated with coloured glass at the edges and looked like it belonged to a nonconformist chapel lit the wooden staircase. The air had the stuffiness of disuse and decay. Surprisingly, there were switches and old brown cables that suggested that once the house was modern enough to have had electricity and one of the original carbon filament light bulbs was still hanging in an outhouse room. It was certainly large, almost double the size of Redgates, a fact that made us all realise that there would be more room for individual bedrooms as well as the family in general.

If the garden at Redgates could be considered large, what Westfield House had would be more suitably termed by an estate agent as 'grounds'. Harold said that the total area of land was nearly an acre. Along the front of the house, which faced away from the entrance gates, there was a patch of long grass and weeds that must have once been a lawn. As we waded through the long vegetation, we found a plaster statue of Napoleon, the paintwork of which was still quite well preserved. The people who owned the house at one time must have been quite well off. Beyond the lawn and separated from it by an overgrown privet hedge, there was an orchard with tall mature apple and pear trees. Next to the orchard and running along the length of the property to occupy more than half of it was a large sea of tall nettles that Harold said was a paddock. A group of tall Lombardy poplars grew at its centre. For us it was like being on a jungle adventure.

When we waded through the long undergrowth of the orchard we could see a wooden hut surrounded by a half-rotten wooden fence nearly immersed in nettles that were almost as tall as we were. What a fine den that would make! The thought made us ignore the effects of the nettles as we crashed through them to reach what must once have been a pigsty, but closer inspection and the smell of rotting timber told us that its only future in the long term would have to be demolition. We found several pigs' lower jaws that perhaps showed that some of their feed came from the remains of their own kind. The whole paddock, about half an acre in size, seemed to have been used for keeping pigs that grubbed up and fertilised the soil to give way to the profusion of nettles after they were gone. The burning rash on our arms and legs from our explorations lasted for some time, but the jungle also provided a remedy in the form of large dock leaves that seemed to ease the worst affected areas when crumpled and rubbed into the rashes.

Afterwards, when Nadia asked us what we thought of the place, we were not very enthusiastic at first. For one thing we did not want to leave Greetwell Common, but when Nadia described what was planned, we began to enthuse a little. She said that Vera would have her own bedroom while we boys would be only two to a room. It also meant that there would be no need for the long wait on Sundays and that as we would all eventually go to school in Brigg, there would be no school buses.

Redgates sold easily at the asking price and Harold and Cedric worked the rest of that summer to modernise Westfield House and had done enough to enable us to move just before the start of school. Cedric helped with the removal. Our grey goose and a white gander, which we had left at Redgates and which we called Darky and Whitey joined the move. We took over a house that was liveable in but needed much more work on it before it could be pronounced as comfortable, but as far as we children were concerned the timing was good. Lex was nearly five and ready for school. Michael, having failed his scholarship was about to start at Glebe Road Secondary School in Brigg, while Philip and Vera had only one year left at Scawby and would take the double-decker service bus.

That autumn Harold worked hard in his spare time to make the house more comfortable while we all had to put up with avoiding both setting cement and treading on piles of old plaster and wood. He replaced the old wooden sash kitchen window with a long steel-framed window that took up the whole length of the outer kitchen wall. He tiled the floor with greenish marble chip tiles and made counters and a long kitchen table that was supported by just two legs made of thick metal piping that was screwed into the floor. The counters and tabletop were surfaced with black Formica and the effect was to make the kitchen almost ultra-modern. A coke-fired Rayburn cooking stove supplied the hot water and he fitted the whole house up with central heating that had its own boiler housed in what was previously a large pantry and what became a boiler room, toilet and cloakroom. He made a huge sitting-cum-living room, subsequently known as the 'big room', by joining two rooms and their part of the hall with the removal of the hall walls and replacing the front door with the former kitchen window. A large French window was fitted on the paddock side to give extra light. He inserted a large open fireplace at one end by casting cement and concrete into a mould to form a hearth and mantelpiece.

Harold's skills seemed to be boundless. He concreted the floor and tiled it with the latest woodchip tiles. The major changes to the four bedrooms upstairs were central heating and the blocking of the old fireplaces. He really tried to give Nadia the type of home that she expected when she was first confronted by Redgates five years previously, but it meant more expense and the inconveniences of having to live with things half done for some time to come.

Michael and I helped a little by spending hours scraping old brown varnish from the banisters and stairs and painting them with a pink undercoat. Harold finished them off with white gloss.

With Harold's help we learnt how to manage the heavy ladder to pick the keeper apples and wrap them in newspapers for storage on trays that were stacked in a small storeroom in the large multipurpose outhouse. We enjoyed the fruits of our orchard with Cox's and Worcester's providing an extra bite at school breaks.

Such a large house meant not only much more space for the family, but much more space to clean, a task that was too much for Nadia to cope with on her own. Soon after the house became habitable and we were sitting round Harold's new kitchen table after school, Nadia made a declaration:

'Look, boys,' she said, 'I have slaved in concentration camps and have worked till I collapsed with exhaustion, but looking after you and running the house is almost worse. If I go on like this you won't have anyone to look after you because I'll be dead. We can't afford to have a home help like Betty so I suggest that you help me instead. I'm not asking for much, but this is what I want you to do: I want Vera to help me clean the kitchen. This means on a Saturday morning you, Vera, can clean the stove, wipe the counters and sweep and wash the kitchen floor.'

'I don't mind at all, Mum, as long as the boys do their share,' said Vera.

'They will. Now you, Michael, are in charge of the big room, which you dust and vacuum and then you polish the floor.' Michael nodded in silence.

'Ivan, you and Philip are in charge of the bedrooms. You make the beds and when Michael has finished with the Hoover you can hoover the bedrooms. You will change the bottom sheet and pillow cases every week and put the top sheet on the bottom. During the week you all make your own beds.' She paused.

'That's all I have to say. Do you think it's fair?'

We all made noises of agreement, then one thing occurred to me.

'But I'm at school on Saturday mornings,' I said, knowing that I would not get out of doing my duties, but wondering what Nadia's solution would be.

'Then you can do the rooms either on Saturday afternoons or as soon as you come home from school.'

We fell into a cleaning routine on Saturdays and Nadia praised us saying that she could not possibly have done it without us. She also added that Vera and Michael were the best workers and that Philip and I were a little careless with the hoovering and that we must be sure to remove all the fluff under the beds. When using both the Hoover and the polisher Michael would hum tunes to the back-ground noises of the machines, which was something that Nadia noticed first and we could confirm when we had the opportunity to listen. He gave the impression that he actually liked cleaning the big room and polishing the floor.

It wasn't as if we dirtied the room much or marked the floor, for the big room was practically out of bounds to us except near the double doors that Harold made; that was where we could tinkle on the old upright piano that they acquired for next to nothing. If we had any friends over, the kitchen became the social centre of the house, which sometimes evoked the crowding reminiscent of Redgates. In fact the kitchen was where we lived. That was where we ate, talked and often did our prep. The kitchen was not only the social centre, but also the nerve centre of the house.

Apart from the West Terrace row of houses opposite, Westfield

House had two neighbours. On the one side was the Salvation Army building that did not seem to be in use. On the other side was Timms's bakery that together with our house formed the actual cul-de-sac of West Terrace. In contrast to the Salvation Army building, the bakery was a hive of activity, baking bread early in the morning and the large electric dough mixer at work later in the day to prepare dough for the baking early the following morning. As soon as we had moved, Nadia introduced herself to old Mr Timms as his new neighbour and customer and when she sent us over to get a loaf of bread he would give us a bag of cake cut-offs that remained after trimming Battenberg cakes and Swiss rolls. We may as well have them, he said, otherwise they would just end up in the bin. For us the bits of marzipan and cake were a tasty addition to our cups of tea after school. We also became acquainted with a half-grown black and white cat that Mr Timms acquired to keep down the mice. We never did find out what the bakery called her, but because she affectionately insisted on licking us whenever we met her, we called her Licka.

It wasn't long before the baker's apprentice showed us Licka's first litter of kittens on a piece of sacking at the back of the bakery. When we rushed into the house to ask Nadia if we could have one of Licka's kittens before they were to be drowned, she consented on the condition that we fed it and looked after it. She must have said that with her tongue in her cheek and we knew that she knew that we would not buy food for it. Nevertheless, we were the owners of a black cat with white paws and a white nose with a tip that was so dark pink that it was almost red. We called him Rudolf. The baker's boy didn't drown all the remaining kittens: he left Licka to look after one that had a white face but for a black streak that covered his left eye. We called him Hitler. He was wild and we rarely saw him.

We had to be content with our official and unofficial cats. The geese provided a little extra money when Nadia could sell their fertile eggs, but as Whitey became increasingly aggressive, Nadia put an advert in the paper and sold them.

At school, we continued with the same subjects in the third year, form Upper 4A. Teddy began to show us Latin in its true colours: words with endings that kept changing according to a tangle of cases, declensions and conjugations, which must have given rise to the poem known at countless schools:

'Latin is a language as dead could be. Once it killed the Romans, now it's killing me'. As a light relief, Teddy also quoted the old jumble of Latin words that only made some sense in English:

'Caesar adsum jam forte. Brutus adarat. Caesar cortan omnibus. Brutus sic in at.'

Teddy Davies was a keen teacher, anxious to make sure that we knew his subject and keen to be liked by the boys. Almost too keen. Once when a fair-haired boy called Fison, who might have been described as 'pretty', expressed a problem concerning the declension of some verb, Teddy said, 'Don't worry, Fison, come and sit on my knee at your desk and I'll show you how.'

Despite Fison's protests, Teddy did as he promised.

On other occasions, if he were annoyed by someone in the form, he would say, 'Consider your bottom smacked, boy!'

In the early 1950s sexual matters were rarely discussed at home, in public or at school and even in biology the word 'sex' was mentioned only in the context of gender and reproduction being described as 'sexual' or 'asexual'. So that when a rather sophisticated boy in my form referred to Teddy's behaviour in our form as being homosexual, I hardly understood the meaning, but pretended that I knew what homosexuals were until it gradually dawned on me. I gathered that Fison knew, when he remarked afterwards in our between-period waits for the next master to arrive, as a boarder that there was at least one 'homo' in the boarding house. We concluded that Teddy would have loved to be a master in charge of the boarders, but he had a house and wife in the town. For his part Teddy must have sensed that he was being quietly ridiculed for he no longer asked pupils to sit on his knee. However, he continued to tell boys to 'consider their bottoms smacked' when they misbehaved.

I continued to keep my head up at school by finding myself between eighth and fourth positions in form and though regarded as a hopeless case in ball games I held my own in athletics, a redeeming factor on the sport side.

As time went on, it became clear that Brigg Grammar School was no ordinary grammar school; its three hundred years of tradition helped to give it the feel of a British public school. I began to feel not only a worthy pupil at the school but decidedly British in all but name. Almost subconsciously I wanted to eradicate all that had to do with my foreign past and I never mentioned it at school. It was as if I started life in England and concentration camps and my Dutch and Russian roots never existed. I felt that I was as English as anyone else was and tried to ignore reminders of my foreign past.

While walking back from school I happened to see my mother in the distance. What if she saw me and started talking to me out there on the pavement and what if someone heard that strong Russian accent of hers and saw me to be her son? No, I could not stand that. It would mean displaying my foreignness for all to see. I had to avoid her. I quickly crossed the road and dodged into a shop doorway, hoping that she had not noticed me.

I waited until the coast was clear and continued my walk home as if nothing had happened.

I sat at the kitchen table to do some of my prep before she came home to give me my lunch. As it was Wednesday afternoon, she must have gone out to do some last-minute shopping before the shops closed. She came in about twenty minutes after I did.

'Why did you try to avoid me in town?'

'When? I didn't see you,' I lied.

'Are you ashamed of me, or something? You should never be ashamed of your mother. What have I done to deserve it?'

'I'm not ashamed of you and I didn't see you,' I said with a double lie.

'I know you saw me and now I know that you are ashamed of me, but remember, I am the only mother you have.'

I said nothing but knew that she was right. But I also knew that she didn't keep to the background like other mothers, English mothers. In my presence, she had the annoying tendency of reminding others of my foreignness. Her foreignness cut both ways. Sometimes she had the initiative to interfere with positive results, like talking to Miss Bowles and persuading the headmaster to put me in the 'A' stream, but at other times she caused me deep embarrassment, not just because of her accent, but by not knowing when to say nothing.

Vera had too strong a personality to be ashamed of her and Michael and Philip took her as she was. I was the odd one, but I couldn't help myself.

Both Vera and Philip had passed their scholarship, Vera to gain entrance into the Brigg Girls' High School and Philip to secure a place in the grammar school. But by the autumn of 1952 I was already fourteen years old and in the Lower Fifth when third-formers were hardly noticeable, except that they were as small as Lower Fifth formers were huge to me when I was third-former. Besides, by then Philip had heard so much about the grammar school that nothing was quite as new to him as to me when I started three years previously.

As far as the masters were concerned, Tabby had retired to be replaced by a new art master whose appearance suggested that we were to have lessons in modern art. His wiry hair stood up almost as if he had had an electric shock, which inspired Jim to call him Tarbrush, but as his surname was Crosby he was soon to be called Bing. His art lessons in fact proved to be inspiring, with an emphasis on graphics, the theory of proportion and perspectives, how to do lettering and posters and still life. Rather than abstract art, Bing's art lessons dealt with the depiction of modern life, which for several others and me were inspirations, a breath of fresh air.

The timing of his arrival was significant to me. Bing came to the school just at the same time as I began to feel a surge of several interests waking up within me.

Though at Westfield House we had to spend time picking apples and scything nettles as well as doing our share of the housework, it was where we felt a part of our town and community as a family. For me, it was also where I developed my interests. As Michael and Philip weren't interested, I often went fishing on my own either by the river or at the pond at the bottom of Mill Lane. Though my catches were nothing to shout about, unlike those of the busloads of anglers that came from Sheffield to fill their keep nets with enormous bream, I enjoyed the tranquillity and if a fish came my way it was just part of the fun.

That summer, Jan and Hanny were on a tour of eastern England. They had already seen Cambridge and decided to travel north to Lincoln where they would be staying and where they had decided they would like to meet all of us. Michael, Philip, Vera and I took the bus from Brigg to meet them at the bus station. They were much the same, Hanny being warm and welcoming while Jan seemed to stay a little in the background. But he seemed to have taken a liking to Philip whom he called 'Fillup', and he laughed at his smallness and his perky ways. We went to see the usual sights, the cathedral and the castle, and they took us to have tea and cakes at a tearoom.

To give my father his due, he was very good at remembering our birthdays. While we still lived at Redgates he sent Vera, at what must have been some expense, one of those thick-wheeled scooters that she so admired. And while at Lincoln he took the opportunity to allow me to choose what I wanted for my birthday. When I ventured to suggest a pair of binoculars, he agreed, provided that they would not be too expensive. He bought me a pair of eight-by-thirty's that came with a leather case and when I tried them I could see the detailed architecture of the cathedral that was not visible with the naked eye. I was pleased with them. We all enjoyed the meeting, including Vera who had no time for Jan. On the bus home Vera said Jan would never have taken the initiative to come over if it hadn't been for Hanny.

Brigg was where, with the aid of the new binoculars, I went bird-watching and learnt to recognise redshanks, greenshanks and sand-pipers that fed on the settling ponds by the sugar factory. Philip and I once took a bike ride to an area of marsh and heathland known as Manton Common to hear the bubbling call of the curlew, the drumming of snipe in downward flight and the anxious requests of the lapwing wanting us to keep away from its nest. By then, egg collecting belonged to the past and instead we collected the memories of what we saw and heard. We stumbled across the nests of each of these species and admired the camouflage of the eggs and how they were always arranged with their points inwards so that each clutch looked like a large four-leafed clover. One pair of lapwings had made their nest on a dried cow-pat.

That summer Harold cleaned the old MV1366 of bits of wood and cement dust and he took us to Reighton Gap, a caravan site that was located just south of Filey on the Yorkshire coast. As the vehicle could manage no more than thirty miles an hour and we were getting large, it was a long and uncomfortable journey.

We were given the use of his cousin Connie's old five-berth caravan placed in the middle of a hundred others. Somehow two adults and their five children had room to sleep and crowd around a fold-up table at meal times. The beach consisted of a stretch of light sand broken by rounded chunks of white chalk, some of them weighing more than a ton and many pieces of chalk were shaped by the sea to look like giant white eggs. Though the North Sea water was too cold for swimming, we spent most of our time on the beach. Nearer the headland, the cliffs were sheer and white and had piles of white boulders at their bases to make it look like the beach was at the edge of a glacier. We caught shrimps in the pools between the white boulders, or watched the small flocks of sanderlings running on the beach to keep up with the edges of the waves in search of food, while the kittiwakes screamed around the cliffs.

One warm night the crowded caravan became almost unbearably hot, so that most of us had difficulty in sleeping. Michael, however, was snoring and then paused to say in his sleep:

'I am ever so hhot. I am sweating-gg.'

Michael showed us that Nadia's constant nagging about our pronunciation was reaping some benefit, at least it had reached the depths of his subconscious. We all laughed when Nadia told him about his elocution on the following morning.

After that holiday Harold realised that the old sausage van was no longer fit to be a family vehicle. He removed his shooting brake creation and converted it into a small truck that would serve him better for his building business.

The business itself was not going well. Harold came home worn out and irritable and the more Nadia nagged him with her suggestions the worse the atmosphere in the house became. Most of these conflicts came at teatime when we were all assembled round the long table in the nerve centre of the house, which made it more like a nervous centre. Nadia was very thrifty and made sure that we spread our jam or peanut butter as thinly as possible on the slices of bread that was bought cheaply from the adjacent bakery because it was surplus that had not yet become stale. We had to be careful with our school uniforms to make them last, but they only lasted a short time anyway because we grew out of them.

280

I was growing so quickly that I outgrew not only my clothes but also my cycle, whose saddle and handlebars were adjusted as high as possible. I was aware that if I were to continue to use my own bike I would need another, new or second-hand, and that required money. That meant some kind of a job.

As luck would have it, an older boy called Bob, who once took us on the river for a row in his boat, came round to ask me whether I could take over his paper round when he left school. He was to start an apprenticeship at the steel works. He said that if I could meet him at WH Smith's at six on Monday morning he would show me how to sort the papers as well as the extent of the round.

It turned out to be a short and easy round that included the whole of Bridge Street and the few side streets of terrace houses. I took over a large brown canvas bag that held the daily papers and periodicals and soon learnt to sort them out according to the list of customers on the round and write their surnames on the top of the paper and, when necessary, the address. I noticed that Paul North also had a paper round which he had already had for a year and judging by the fullness of his bag his round was twice the size of mine. Strange that he never mentioned it at school, but then he was rather a reticent type. Nevertheless, it was a coincidence that the two boys that went up from 3B to the A-stream should be the only ones in lower 5A to have a paper round.

It was interesting to note which of the daily papers were the most popular, and who took what. *The Daily Mirror* was by far the most common, followed by an assortment of papers that included the *Daily Mail*, the *Daily Herald* and the *News Chronicle*. Then there were the oddities: only two households, one of which included the Worthington sisters, took *The Times*, while two households took the *Daily Worker*, one the *Manchester Guardian* and one the *Daily Telegraph*. I discovered with a certain amount of annoyance that often those that took the thickest papers had the smallest letterboxes. When I familiarised myself with it, the whole round took twenty minutes on foot and I soon learnt to put up with having to get up forty minutes earlier in the pouring rain or biting cold because the reward was seven-and-six a week. I had already set my sights on a new Raleigh cycle with racing handlebars and a metallic green frame for sale at

Curry's the hire purchase terms of twenty-five shillings a month. After I had saved for the deposit of three pounds it would only take fourteen months to pay for it.

I proudly wheeled my new cycle up the drive, feeling like a young man owning a new car, rather than a boy with a new toy.

I was fourteen, going on fifteen, and aware that there was life beyond school, fishing and bird watching, but what? We talked about girls and some even had girlfriends, but for most of us girls existed on the other side of the fence that divided the grammar school from the high school. That fence could only be reached by walking three hundred yards across the large playing field and even then there was a fence beyond it on the girls' side. Though a few older boys did manage to communicate with their girlfriends across the fences, getting in touch with the girls in that way was impractical. We were socially isolated and there were no opportunities for the mixing of the sexes at our age at all.

However, this situation had prospects of changing when one day the police inspector's son in my form said that his parents had joined the newly formed old-time dancing club at the Corn Exchange and they wanted younger people to join.

There were several boys in my form who wanted to join, including my friends Jim and Ken, but we could hardly go in our school uniform and I had nothing else that I could wear. Ken had a sports jacket that he wore for chapel on Sundays and Nadia told me that she would try to find a jacket for me at a jumble sale, where she might also find a suitable shirt and tie.

Instead of a jumble sale, she found a stall selling second-hand clothes at the market on that Thursday and came home with a fine two-button modern-looking jacket. When I tried it on it was a little too large, the shoulder pads drooping a bit and the sleeves slightly too long, but it felt like a good start to my social life.

The Corn Exchange hall was vibrant with the strains of old classics that came out of a record player. While the middle-aged and elderly practised their old-time dancing skills, we stood in the background, too shy to ask girls of our own age to dance. But it wasn't long before the old ladies whisked us off to learn the steps to the waltz, the quickstep, the military two-step, the gay Gordons and the square tango. The girls seemed to learn more naturally. We then plucked up courage to dance with them, we concentrated on getting the steps right because our conversation skills were virtually non-existent.

Despite the rigidity of the uniform, subtle changes in fashions were creeping in at school. Rock and roll had became popular and some boys had started wearing drainpipe trousers and thick crepe-soled suede shoes and the school ties were done up in wide double Windsor knots. Though they maintained that all the indoor sandals had crepe soles, the headmaster reprimanded them. But in their teenage defiance, they kept up their Elvis image until they left at fifteen to take up a trade.

23. A Place in Society

It was 1953. We came home from school one late October afternoon to find Nadia in tears.

'I have to tell you,' she said, 'that Dad has gone bankrupt. This means that we no longer have an income and that until he finds another way of earning money, we cannot pay our mortgage and our debts and we are entirely dependent on family allowance. I don't want any of you to tell anyone about this.'

Fortunately we could still live at Westfield House.

Harold and Nadia persuaded the council to give them a mortgage to tide them over. This meant that in practice the local council owned our house. We laughed at the thought that we lived in a council house that was not on the council housing estate.

Somehow, we managed to get by. Nadia bought the cheapest bare essentials to keep us going, but just before Christmas we were surprised to see four dead ducks lying on the kitchen counter when we came home.

'I still can't get over it,' she said. I went to the market yesterday evening to see if there was anything going cheap when I saw the auctioneer and asked him how much the ducks were. He said, 'Mrs Neale, they are to be sold by auction and it may be to your advantage if you come back first thing tomorrow morning. I'll see what I can do'.

'When he saw me this morning he quickly started the auction before anyone else came and he actually knocked them down at the first bid - to me! I got them for four shillings the lot!'

Knowing the situation, we had no special wishes for Christmas, but as Lex had a burning desire for a Dinky toy articulated lorry, Nadia paid Mr Green a visit at his toy shop to ask him if he could possibly consider letting her have the lorry on credit.

'Of course, Mrs Neale! You can take it now and pay when you can.'

'I think I can pay you the week after Christmas'.

'Mrs Neale, I know I can trust you and your family. You can pay when it is convenient.'

Despite the fact that we did not mention the bankruptcy to anyone, the whole town seemed to know that Harold had gone bankrupt and clearly instead of that situation putting us in disgrace we received a lot of sympathy and credit from various shopkeepers. I began to realise that far from being treated as a foreigner, Nadia was very much accepted and liked by the inhabitants of Brigg. Otherwise we would not have had an amazing Christmas dinner and Lex had his prized articulated lorry.

But the sympathy of the town did little to solve my problem. I still had the desperate need to be the same as all the others and the only aspects of my personality that I wanted to show were those that seemed British in character.

I still could not cope with the imitations that some of the livelier members of my form gave of Nadia when she visited the school together with other parents on occasions such as sports days. Though they could copy her Russian accent almost exactly, I found it hard to laugh at their performances.

I was not proud of my behaviour and I still could not understand why I was also ashamed of being different, of being a foreigner. I no longer felt ashamed of my mother, only ashamed of myself.

Fortunately the family depression caused by the bankruptcy did not last that long. In reply to an advert in the paper, Harold landed a job at an American airbase near Lincoln. He was put in charge of the erection of all the buildings the Americans required to set up airbases in central and south Lincolnshire, which meant that they would employ him for several years to come.

As the bases were some distance away, he stayed with the Americans during the week and came home for the weekends.

He was a changed man. Harold became more like the Uncle Harry who met us with a sunny smile in Java. From being uncommunicative and grumpy he came home at weekends full of stories about the Yanks and their slaphappy ways. But despite their easygoing attitudes, they told him that they appreciated his high standards and common sense. Furthermore, the security of an income that was far better than he had had from his own business altered the whole atmosphere of the household. Apart from enjoying a better standard of living, Harold and Nadia could begin to pay off their debts to the council. His new job also gave him perks like a cheap ex-army car and a worn rotary mower that he renovated to relieve us from incessant scything of the paddock.

It was the spring of 1954 and the time had come either to take school even more seriously or leave and take up a trade. I knew that I must aim for a place in university but I was not clear about what I wanted to read: all I knew was that my interest in biology and natural history had grown.

In preparation for the GCE at 'O' level, I began to try harder in each subject, especially those that I felt were more important for my future area of interest. However, as we were limited to eight subjects the actual subject of biology had to wait until the sixth form when we were allowed to do re-takes and other subjects.

As it was a fine sunny day in May, I decided to walk to school after lunch at home. I walked along at a leisurely pace as I had twenty minutes before the next period started. On the main street lined by pubs and shops and bustling with the usual lunchtime activity, a tall blonde girl suddenly took my attention. She turned into Woolworth's some thirty yards ahead of me. As I seemed to be drawn to her, I followed her under the pretext of buying some fudge, an irresistible favourite sweet. While buying my four ounces, I stole a glance at her while she was buying something at the haberdashery counter and felt even more drawn to her, but I was far too inhibited to approach her. I wandered about pretending to look at the various counters until she completed her purchase and then followed her out at a discreet distance. She did not seem to have noticed me. I couldn't get her out of my mind; her wavy blonde hair, her large blue eyes, her slender tallness all dominated my mind at the expense of all else and I ate my fudge without really savouring it.

Not long afterwards there was a photograph of her in the *Lincolnshire Times*, one of the prize-winners from the High School. Her name, Elizabeth Beck, was in the paper and it turned out that she was in the fifth form, the same year as me. In secret I cut out the picture after the paper was thrown away onto a pile in the

outhouse. I then copied her picture in soft pencil on a small piece
of drawing paper and plucked up courage to show it to her younger
brother who was at the grammar school. I asked him if he recognised the miniature portrayal.

'Why, that's my sister,' he said. 'It's a good likeness.'

'Thanks,' I said. He then gave me a knowing look.

I could not get her out of my mind. I left my bike at school and
walked at lunchtimes, in case I should catch a glimpse of her. I
wanted to see her, almost content to admire her at a distance,
because I hadn't the courage to talk to her. I worshipped her at a
distance. I even sung the latest pop songs with her image dominating them. I tried to make myself look smart, combed my hair with
care, placed my school cap at the right angle, all to somehow draw
her attention, at the same time as being too shy and inhibited to
receive it.

That impossible situation destroyed my concentration both at
school and at home. Though Nadia insisted on everyone being
quiet at home while I was supposed to be revising, I just sat like
Ferdinand the Bull under his cork oak and dreamed away my
revision time for the 'O' levels.

While sitting the actual 'O' levels, I already knew that I was not up
to scratch and that made me nervous in anticipation of a disaster, so
that by the time the chemistry practical came, I told Nadia that I was
too nervous to cope. She took me to the doctor, who prescribed a
new drug called Oblivon. 'That'll make you feel relaxed,' the doctor
said.

After taking the tablet, which looked like a transparent miniature
blue submarine, I was certainly at ease on the morning of the
chemistry practical exam. I felt so carefree that I simply mixed
whatever test-tubes came to hand, wrote down fictitious results and
thought the world was my oyster.

When the effects of the Oblivon wore off I knew that I must have
failed the practical and did not use the drug again.

After the end of term I tried to get over my infatuation and went
on bike rides with my best friend Ken, who was one of those who
came top or second in the form without the slightest effort. But I
couldn't resist persuading him to join me on a cycle tour that went

past Liz Beck's house in a small village set in the Lincolnshire Wolds. He just laughed and said that the exercise would do us good.

The 'O' level results, which came out after my sixteenth birthday, were as bad as I expected.

Despite the Oblivon, I had passed chemistry, together with physics, English language and had the highest grade in French. I failed in the subjects that required revision, English literature, Latin and geography, and I only just failed maths. However, four subjects was enough to allow me into the sixth form to take physics, chemistry and biology at 'A' level. Lanky and Ken had top grades in all eight subjects and I found that Liz had passed six.

Being a sixth-former had a few privileges, including the inspection of footwear of the lower forms of school life at break, selling currant buns and ringing the bell to mark the end of every period, break and dinner. As far as the headmaster was concerned, to be a sixth-former one had also to come up in social status, which Paul and I realised when he called us to see him at his study.

He sat behind his study table in his customary grey suit, his face as red as usual, his penetrating eyes shaded as always by his thick eyebrows, only he had put on a wider smile.

'I understand that you both have a paper round in town.'

We both said, 'Yes, sir.'

'Well, as doing that sort of job to earn a little extra money is not fitting for a sixth-former at this school, I want you both to cease and devote your time and energy to your 'A' levels instead. Do you really have to do your paper rounds?'

'Yes, sir.'

'Then I suppose there is nothing I can do about it, but I'm letting you know that I'm against it. You can go now.'

'Thank you, sir.'

When we were out of earshot from the headmaster's study, we both said that we would continue to do our paper rounds, despite what the big slob said. Besides, what other jobs were there to supplement our parents' pocket money?

I had learnt to control my continuing infatuation for Liz without having to talk to her and was able to revise for my 'O' level retakes that Christmas. Teddy had chosen to take on Holmes, a handsome chap who had passed six subjects but failed Latin, for extra coaching, while telling me that if I wanted to retake Latin I would be on my own. In my determination to show Teddy that I was quite capable, I did half an hour's revision every morning in bed before getting up for my paper round, learning by heart the Julius Caesar and Virgil translations.

I was relieved to pass all the retakes with reasonable grades, much to the surprise of the headmaster. Teddy came to congratulate me with apologies that he did not take me on, for Holmes had failed again, despite his tuition. For my part, I suspected that if he had have taken me on, I wouldn't have tried so hard to pass.

That summer, as well as adding biology and geography to my 'O' level collection, I became a British citizen. As we were still officially Dutch minors, Nadia had applied on the behalf of Vera and me under the Minor Citizens' Nationality Act.

Also that summer, Harold decided to build a tennis court at one end of the paddock and we boys helped him to dig out and lay a rubble foundation for a hard court. We then helped him to lay the asphalt and grit. Though the netting was too close to the baselines, we all became reasonable tennis players and developed an eye for a ball. It was also an excellent way of entertaining friends, both for our parents and us, which led to a more developed social life.

The start of the Upper Sixth was the beginning of the culmination of seven years of grammar school education, though half of the sixth-formers stay on to do a third year in the sixth form. It was the headmaster's practice to make all the third-form sixths school prefects. From the second year he chose one or two of his favourites, or those he considered were worthy of respect, such as high achievers academically or in sports. As I knew that I didn't fit into any of those categories, I was right not to expect to be made a prefect. And those of us from the second year that he did select, like Lanky and Holmes, deserved their new status. He did not, however, choose Ken, who was considered the most intelligent in our year. Though Jim started in the sixth form, he left to do his national service in the RAF when he had turned eighteen and we lost contact with him.

It was a year of both hard work and decision. Though I passed all three subjects, I was unable to pursue a career in biology, the study of living things, that awakened as an interest early in my life in Java. During a parent interview the headmaster told Nadia that as he considered that my academic abilities did not match up to achieving a degree in biology, he would not try to help me get a university place if I chose to read that subject. He might, however, consider helping me if I chose something less academic. As he seemed to have the right contacts at his old university, Cambridge, he was able to give the school a good name by helping to enable the brightest to enter Oxbridge. At the same time I knew that he had little time for the non-elite that constituted most of the sixth form. After discussing the situation at home I decided to opt for dentistry. That was what my mother started reading in Harbin so why not me? It was after all a respectable profession and I was good with my hands.

I was offered a place in the diploma course at Sheffield, but as I was determined to achieve a degree, I decided to stay on at school for another year to improve my grades and take biology at scholarship level.

Ken left to read physics at Birmingham, but before that we celebrated my attaining the permissible age to drink alcohol. I got thoroughly drunk while attempting to drink half a pint of ale at each of the fourteen pubs in Brigg. I don't think I got beyond the twelfth and Ken, who was still on his feet, had to drag me home totally inebriated and vomiting like a gushing sewer.

At the start of my final year at Brigg Grammar School, my self-confidence received a blow. Contrary to my expectations, the headmaster did not make me a prefect and when I was not called to his study together with the others of my year who stayed on, I felt bitter and degraded. It wasn't that being a prefect itself was so desirable, it was more that in not being chosen to be a prefect, I was regarded as being inferior to my peers. I never liked the man, but on that day I hated him. I knew it hadn't to do with my paper round because Paul was made a prefect despite his.

What I still felt deep inside me came to the surface. It was my foreignness. I didn't fit in. The headmaster must have rejected me because I was not really British.

At break Mr Thorpe, my housemaster who was also deputy headmaster, came to the sixth form and indicated that he wanted to talk to me. To my surprise, he asked me whether I would like to be captain of Ancholme House.

'But I'm not a prefect,' I said, my lips quivering with emotion.

'That doesn't matter. I think you'll make a good house captain.'

'Thank you very much, sir.'

I thought that he meant what he said and felt that my morale had been restored.

On the next day we had a house meeting at break and Mr Thorpe announced that I was house captain, while two bright sparks from the year below me who were already made prefects, grinned at me. After years of attending house meetings I knew what the procedure was and set about organising the sports events of the term by delegating.

Later that day I was called in to see the headmaster. Tom Beck, Liz's younger brother who was in the year below me was also in his study.

'Ah, Kruys,' he said. This time his face was both redder and the smile on its lower half broader than usual. 'I see you've been made house captain. As that is something beyond my jurisdiction, I shall have to make you a prefect. One can't be captain of a house without being a prefect! Here's your tie, and this is your tie, Beck. I would like you to join Kruys, so that we can balance the numbers.'

I knew that bit about the numbers was a weak cover-up on his part to make it less obvious that, thanks to Mr Thorpe, he was forced to make me prefect.

On the following morning at assembly he simply announced that he had decided to appoint two new prefects, Beck and me.

From then on, I enjoyed the best year ever at the grammar school. I sensed that in order to fire enthusiasm I must take part in as many events as possible. Though I was still poor at football, I found that my newly acquired ball sense improved my cricket enormously, playing unconventional strokes to gain runs for my house. In the end, under my leadership the house did better than usual in sports, to come second after School House, which was something that Ancholme House had not achieved in years.

I improved my grades enough to gain a senior county scholarship and a degree place at the dental school and I felt that, despite a headmaster who helped only those that he favoured, I had achieved a degree place at a university. It didn't matter that I was not going to pursue a career that I wanted most, for the need to be like everyone else had disappeared.